❝❝Hilarious, courageous, provocativ
the light for seekers of all paths, remind
transformation begins exactly where we
had a gutsy, wise, funny little sister who
be *Post-Traumatic Church Syndrome.*"

— Elizabeth Gilbert, author of *Eat, Pray, Love*

❝❝*Post-Traumatic Church Syndrome* is a brilliant, emotional, and
audacious rampage through religious sensibility, an exploration I
recommend without hesitation. Enjoy!"

— William Paul Young, author of *The Shack*

❝❝Reba Riley is a natural-born storyteller and writer who I expect to
be reading for many years to come."

— Brian D. McLaren, author/speaker (brianmclaren.net)

❝❝Whatever your beliefs or lack thereof, whether you pay heed to a
savior or a spirit animal, you should read this moving, funny, thoughtful
book. Reba Riley has traveled the unlikely mystic's path and come back
with an enormously entertaining, immensely hopeful report. "

— A.J. Jacobs, author of *The Year of Living Biblically*

❝❝*Post-Traumatic Church Syndrome* is real. Been there done that.
If you have been there too, this book is going to let you know you
are not alone. Prepare to be encouraged to leave outright abuse of
spiritual power and dogma of the kind that kills the soul. Prepare to
survive. Courageous and wonderful Reba Riley to the rescue!"

— Frank Schaeffer author of *Why I Am
an Atheist Who Believes in God*

66 *Post Traumatic Church Syndrome* is a literary and philosophical triumph. Reba Riley reveals the strength of spirit through the vulnerability of flesh with tears, laughter, and soul-stirring moments of profound revelation. Her first book—certainly not her last—is so much more than a memoir about faith; it's a celebration of all that defines the human condition."

—Christian Piatt, author of *postChristian: What's left? Can we fix it? Do we care?*

66 This is such a good book. Written like a novel, it's a firsthand account of the author's yearlong bid to overcome the legacy of crushing religious experiences. Setting herself the challenge of encountering thirty religions by the age of thirty could have been a rather shallow exercise in spiritual tourism—but it isn't. What results is gloriously irreverent and profound in equal measure, full of humanity, compassion, and insight. The book is very much a Christian journey, but nonetheless it has a lotto say about spiritual experience as a whole....In willing to be vulnerable, flawed, and confused, Reba Riley shares something powerful, essential, and incredibly real."

—Nimue Brown, author of *When A Pagan Prays*

66 Reba Riley's spiritual journey has become an invaluable resource for countless people who are shedding religion for a more open and authentic spirituality. By identifying and describing the dynamics of *Post-Traumatic Church Syndrome,* she has paved the way of freedom for many who are suffering from religious pathology. Despite her brilliance, Reba has a down-to-earth, compassionate, and humorous way about her. She has a gift for storytelling, which makes her writing both enlightening and entertaining. If you're up for an adventure in exploring new possibilities of expanding and deepening your relationship to yourself, God, others, and the world, read Reba Riley."

—Jim Palmer, author of *Divine Nobodies* and *Notes from (Over) the Edge*

"Riley's book is so compelling: beautifully written, exceedingly funny, and refreshingly honest. As she described her journey of spiritual and physical healing, I rooted for her with every page. Riley's story is also compelling because it is our story, our journey. We can identify with her spiritual pain, her questions, her prejudices, her fears. Her experience proves that if we are willing to open ourselves up and listen, we too can find God everywhere and know the Love that is for us all. It is a book of profound hope."

—Kristen E. Vincent, author of *A Bead and a Prayer: A Beginner's Guide to Protestant Prayer Beads*

"If your soul has ever doubted, if your feet have ever lost their way, if your halo's always just a little askew, or if your heart has been wounded by a faith community, Reba Riley's humorous, honest memoir about exploring the 'Godiverse' is just the thing for you."

—Sarah Thebarge, author of *The Invisible Girls: A Memoir*

"Written with beckoning eloquence and humor, Reba Riley describes an amazing interfaith journey through the depth of her broken humanity in a quest for healing and the face of God. *Post-Traumatic Church Syndrome* is a most valuable and inspirational guide to those on a path toward enlightenment, and especially to those seeking healing from spiritual abuse. It should be on the shelves of every counseling center and divinity school."

—Franklyn Schaefer, author of *Defrocked*

"Moments of laughing and tears. It provided much needed closure for me in many ways. I love Reba Riley and her heart and work. I'm honored to be her teacher and also, through her book, her student. (Deep bow of respect.) Namaste."

—Bushi Yamato Damashii, Roshi/Zen monk at Daishin Buddhist Temple & Mindfulness Center, and former Baptist minister

Post-Traumatic Church Syndrome

A MEMOIR OF HUMOR AND HEALING IN 30 RELIGIONS

Reba Riley

CHALICE
PRESS
ST. LOUIS, MISSOURI

Cover art: iStock Photo
Cover design: Brigid Pearson
Interior photos: Photos on pages 1, 53, 97, 143, 235, 244, and the back cover are by Kelly St. James Photography with creative director Erin Mickley. Photo on page 169 by Marquelle Garcia Photography. All rights reserved.

This book is sold with the understanding that neither the author nor the publisher is engaged in rendering psychological, medical, financial, legal, or other professional services. If expert assistance or counseling is needed, the services of a competent professional should be sought.

www.ChalicePress.com

Paperback: 9780827231207   Hardcover: 9780827231337
EPUB: 9780827231214   EPDF: 9780827231221

Library of Congress Cataloging-in-Publication Data

Riley, Reba.
Post-traumatic church syndrome : a memoir of humor and healing in 30 religions / Reba Riley. — First [edition].
    pages cm
Summary: "A woman about to turn 30 and dealing with health challenges finds that she wants to reconnect with faith, just not with the religion she was raised in. She decides to visit 30 different faith traditions before she turns 30, and finds that her journey encompasses more than just visiting different houses of worship"— Provided by publisher.
ISBN 978-0-8272-3120-7 (pbk.)
1. Religions. 2. Riley, Reba—Religion. 3. Riley, Reba—Health. 4. Celiac disease—Patients—United States—Biography. I. Title.
BL80.3.R55 2015
200.973—dc23   2014042959

For my Mom and Dad, who helped me find my path,
and
For my husband, who enabled me to walk it.

Contents

Post-Traumatic Church Syndrome
[n. pohst-tr*uh*-**mat**-ik church **sin**-drohm]

1. A condition of spiritual injury that occurs as a result of religion, faith, and/or the leaving, losing, or breaking thereof.
2. The vile, noxious, icky, and otherwise foul *aftermath* of said spiritual injury.
3. A serious term intended to aid serious spiritual healing—without taking itself too seriously in the process.

See Also: *Post-Traumatic Religion Syndrome.*

Abbr.: *PTCS, PTRS, #PTCS, #PTRS.*

Not to be confused with: *A mental disorder or medical diagnosis. This author is not a doctor, nor does she play one on the written page.*

Origin: *Back of a bar napkin,* 2002.*

---

* *May or may not have been transcribed in blue eyeliner.*

Part 1
Summer

1
Falling

"What's a girl like you doing stuck in a place like this?" the bartender asked, muscles straining against his hotel uniform as he threw down a cocktail napkin in front of me.

I looked around: three barstools, four dusty fake palm trees, fluorescent lighting. This was the kind of joint that offered vending machines in lieu of room service.

"It was a bad day, Josh," I replied, reading his nametag. "You have any Pinot Grigio back there?"

"Of course, honey!" Josh moved his toffee-colored hands to pour me a glass. "Why was it a bad day?"

Rocking a Vin Diesel–style bald head over a broad grin and big brown eyes, Josh the bartender seemed like the perfect person to spill my story to. (It helped that he was a captive audience and I his only customer.)

I twisted into a bar stool, unloaded my laptop bag, and sighed. "Okay… so this morning I left my house in Columbus to drive to a rural Kentucky lumberyard for a sales presentation—I sell nails and power tools—" Josh arched one brow in surprise. "I know, I know. I don't seem like the kind of woman who would hang around in lumberyards. But remember the job market in 2009?"

"Why do you think I'm behind *this* bar?" Josh laughed, gesturing dramatically to our surroundings

I dropped my head and groaned. "'Our nails penetrate 33 percent faster due to superior lubrication.' I regularly have to say those exact words to the kind of men who drink beer for breakfast and have girlie calendars in their work trucks."

Josh pursed his lips in a sour look that read: *I may like men, but not that kind.* "Lubricated nails?"

I hid my face in mock shame. "Oh, *honey*," he said, patting my shoulder. "It's okay. We do what we have to do."

"So true." I raised my glass in a faux toast. "Anyway—today, after four hours in the car, I arrived in the parking lot of a strip club. I checked the address and called the lumberyard. The owner said, 'Ma'am, you're at the right address in the wrong state.'"

Josh put a hand on his hip. "You should have just gone right on in. Strippers need lubricated nails, too."

Mid-sip, I nearly snorted wine up my nose. "Josh, you're exactly who I needed to talk to today."

He gave a little bow. "I'm here all night, princess."

"Just wait. It gets worse." I took a long swig. "An hour later I hit a huge pothole, blew out two tires, and broke both axels. The tow truck guy who showed up was this little redheaded dude in green overalls who spoke in a thick Irish accent. He took one look at my car and said, 'Lady, did you forget to have a beer on St. Patrick's Day?'"

"Your knight in shining armor was a leprechaun?" Josh lowered his chin in disbelief.

"A leprechaun who *chain-smoked* the entire way back to Cincinnati." I sniffed my hair. "Marlboros, ick! He dropped me off here while my car gets twelve hundred dollars' worth of repairs."

Josh clucked with concern.

I rubbed my face. "Today is only the latest in a string of bad car luck. In the past two months I've had four *other* tire blow-outs, one dead battery, one stopped starter, and two car break-ins. I'm on a first-name basis with the AAA dispatcher, and my mechanic gave me his cell phone number with great seriousness, like he was a surgeon on call."

"Probably because you're putting his kids through college. That's like the reverse of finding a pot of gold at the end of the rainbow," Josh sympathized. "I think you need another drink. This one's on me."

"Thanks," I said, sitting back on my stool and considering my absurd day. "You know what the leprechaun tow truck driver reminded me of? The Smurfs. I wasn't allowed to watch the Smurfs growing up because my parents thought they were demonic."

I was surprised to hear these words leave my mouth; this was not a Fun Life Fact to be casually shared like cocktail peanuts with a bartender.

Josh's posture changed from easy-listening bartender to Marine at attention. "No effing way! Me too! A teacher at my school said Papa Smurf was a symbol for the anti-Christ, just because he wore a red hat and all the other Smurfs wore white hats."

I tilted my head sideways and said slowly, "Where did you go to school? It couldn't have been…" Josh beat me to the punch line by breaking out into our small Christian elementary school's fight song. I joined in melodically as we burst out laughing.

"Shut the hell up," exclaimed Josh, his jaw slack. "You seem so normal and not Christian-y."

"Thank you? The 'normal' part is up for debate." I thought of the portion of my bad day I hadn't told Josh about, the part where I slumped over my steering wheel, sleeping at a rest stop because chronic illness made me too tired to drive three hours at a stretch. "But I definitely haven't been Christian-y in almost a decade."

Josh peered at me in belated recognition. "Wait. Are you the music teacher's daughter? Rebecca?"

I nodded. My mom had taught at Bridgeville Christian all the years my younger sisters and I attended.

"It's Reba now," I smiled, "That's Rebecca without the –ecc."

"Reba. Girl. This is *crazy*." Josh threw his towel over one shoulder and leaned back. "Remember the dress code? Bible classes? Scripture memorization? Never-ending altar calls? Oh, and the offense system— five offenses equaled a paddling? The principal once paddled me after I got caught making fun of the art teacher. I used to roll under the pews to escape chapel services, and then go smoke pot in the woods." Josh laughed, but the sound was laced with something I knew too well: grief.

To understand our evangelical school, simply take everything normal and stir in a measure of God. Learning to read? Start with *My First Bible* and a recording of "Bible Stories for Little Ears." Note the Proverbs-themed wallpaper in the reading group corner. Starting the school day? Pledge allegiance to the American flag, the Christian flag, and the Bible. Doing math? Enjoy lessons from *Beyond Math: Arithmetic from a Biblical Worldview*. (Even numbers weren't neutral.) Truly, there was not any aspect of life that could not be improved by invoking Christ. Even bathroom breaks could be accomplished to the glory of God, if one flushed the toilet with a joyful spirit.

"Wow. I was way too spiritual and serious back then to even think about rebelling, let alone doing drugs. All I ever worried about was whether Jesus was proud of me. God was my *everything*." I paused and looked into my glass. "Would you believe I was in ministry training? I wanted to be a Christian counselor. I even went through years of Christian college and studied at the Focus on the Family Institute."

Josh winced at the mention of Focus on the Family, an organization known for encouraging people like him to "pray the gay away". I exhaled a weary breath that far exceeded my rough day on the road. We both fell silent for a minute.

"God was my everything too." Josh took a deep breath. "Until I came out. I mean, that's the simple version. Losing faith happens by degrees."

"You don't have to tell me. I lived it. Not the coming out part—unless you count coming out as a nonbeliever. The losing-faith-by-degrees part."

Josh and I stared at each other in silent understanding. We hadn't left our religion; our religion had left us.

We didn't need to explain to each other what it means to lose your entire identity, or how it feels to lie to yourself—*faith doesn't matter, I don't need God, I can get along just fine on my own*—even when you know the lies will never be true.

I lifted my glass in an attempt to brighten the mood. "To God," I toasted, "the heaviest word in the English language, the word most likely to make me feel like I've been punched in the stomach!"

The joke fell flat. Even in jest, "God" was far too intertwined with a gray-haired father in the sky who doled out eternal punishment to anyone who didn't pray to his shiny son, Jesus Christ.

I tried again. "To the Godiverse?"

"The what-iverse?" Josh looked puzzled.

"Godiverse," I explained. "That's God plus the Universe—the only word I could come up with that's scandalous enough to be far away from the Trinity we grew up with, but closer than the great beyond."

"To the Godiverse," Josh agreed.

We clinked glasses, but our heaviness didn't lift.

"Man. This Post-Traumatic Church Syndrome stuff *sucks*," I exclaimed, slamming my glass down in emphasis. Josh cracked a smile at my phrase, so I continued. "C'mon…I *know* you know the PTCS symptoms: Prayer is out of the question; the Bible is something you use to mop up spilled coffee; you can't darken the door of a place of worship without sweaty palms, vertigo, chest pains, nausea, and vomiting." In an effort to keep things fun, I didn't mention the more destructive side effects of spiritual injury: anger, grief, despair, depression, failure to believe in anything, moral confusion, loss of gravity, and emptiness. "You may also experience hives, dry mouth, and a general tendency to avoid church like an escaped convict avoids cops."

Josh laughed. "Wow. I definitely had one major case of Post-Traumatic Church Syndrome."

"*Had?* I must have missed something. It seems like you're still suffering."

He looked away, thinking. "I get upset when I think about all the years I lost because I let other people decide how I could find God. But a few years ago I started going back to the Nazarene church I grew up in…and I've made my peace with it."

I choked on my wine. Nazarenes weren't exactly gay-friendly, and Josh wasn't entirely subtle. "How does *that* work?"

"I realized my past didn't have to shackle me." The pain fell away from his features, replaced by peace. "I decided to believe what I believe, practice what I practice, and not let anyone or anything get in the way of how I choose to find God. I don't let other people think for me."

I tried very hard to be happy for Josh, but the best I could manage was a fake smile.

"Good for you," I managed to stutter, my thoughts turned upside-down. Peace…what a beautiful, unattainable state. Or was it? If Josh could find peace, could I? And what would it mean if I did?

I yawned and threw down some cash. "It's been a really long day. I'm going to turn in. It's been great talking to you." Promising to keep in touch, we exchanged information and hugs.

"Reba," Josh called as I walked away, "Rejecting someone else's version of reality isn't the same as creating your own."

It's a nice idea, I thought later, crawling into my hotel bed, *but I'm way too tired to think about dealing with my spiritual issues.*

When I fell asleep, I dreamed that a large, unmarked van parked on the street in front of my house. God, shaggy-haired and lanky, hung out in the van's back cab smoking a cigarette. (Come to think of it, God looked a lot like Ashton Kutcher.) A black-and-white closed circuit television blinked on with a live feed of my life. God watched the screen for a minute before he blew out a slow smoke circle and turned to his divine camera crew: Kermit the Frog, Miss Piggy, and the entire cast of *Full House.* "You guys ready?" God asked. The crew nodded, serious as church. "Okay," God put on his headphones and cracked his knuckles. "Ready. Set. Action…"

"Baby, you have to get up. Everyone is going to be here soon," Trent whispered from the edge of the bed.

"Cancel," I croaked from beneath the pillow.

"But it's your party," my husband insisted, nuzzling my neck.

I attempted to move my limbs. As usual for a lost day—a day I lost to chronic illness—my body felt full of lead. I lifted the pillow and looked into my husband's clear blue eyes. "Is it really too late to cancel?"

"It's 5 p.m. People are already on their way." He flashed an encouraging Superman grin. "And I brought you espresso."

Untangling my body from the sheets, I gritted my teeth and searched inside myself for birthday cheer. Nothing.

"I'll be ready in an hour," I promised, dragging my drink to the shower in hopes that the combination of steam and caffeine would loosen the Sickness's painful grip on my body.

Wrapped in a towel twenty minutes later, I stepped from the shower and wiped steam from the mirror. My dripping reflection looked exhausted, so I forced a plastic smile and pantomimed a silent laugh until the mirror reflected the image I made sure everyone saw: a happy woman with green eyes and long, dark hair who had it all—great husband, successful career, new puppy, high credit score. A carefree woman who didn't suffer from a painful, chronic mystery Sickness that forced her to sleep her days away.

A woman who feels a hollow void where her faith used to live, came an unbidden thought.

"Whoa. Where did *that* come from?" I looked around my tiny bathroom, suspecting my shower curtain of spiritual harassment. It looked guilty of nothing more than being a little too red.

Shrugging off the intrusion, I returned to my smiling exercise until I felt the Sickness ripple through my joints. I braced against the pain with one hand on the sink and one on the mirror, taking deep breaths. When the pain lessened, I looked at my ashen reflection and saw the woman I really was: the one who had been crying in doctor's offices for years, asking why she couldn't be well.

A woman whose spirit is even sicker than her body.

I looked around accusingly again, this time at my throw rug, whose only failure was being not quite red enough.

The Sickness gripped my joints again. But somehow, beyond the muscle spasms and cramping, I felt the prick of a much deeper pain, one that had been steadily building ever since I'd run into Josh several weeks before.

I need to believe again.

I scanned myself for other signs of craziness: foaming of the mouth, perhaps?

I wondered if maybe I was still asleep. Yes, that had to be it. But I felt the steam on my shoulders, the bristling of the towel on my skin, the cool linoleum beneath my feet.

I need Josh's peace.

No, no, no… I tried to resist but it was no use because chronic illness doesn't fight fair: it weakens us and exposes our deepest pains and betrayals just when our body is in pain and betraying us. The dam of denial I'd carefully constructed around my Post-Traumatic Church Syndrome—the one I'd *had* to create in order to rebuild my life without God—the Sickness had been slowly but steadily dismantling it, and I hadn't noticed until it was too late.

Angry tears filled my eyes. Wasn't it bad enough that I couldn't fix my body? That I'd spent tens of thousands of dollars on doctors, specialists, chiropractors, naturalists, counselors, herbalists, massage therapists, medications, exercises, special diets, and magic vitamins? That I'd donated so much blood to testing that I was surprised I had any left? That I'd had everything from MRIs to chakras read and reread? All that money and no diagnosis that fit. All those treatments and nothing that helped. My body was getting steadily, heartbreakingly worse. And I was powerless to do anything about it.

And now this *spiritual* crap, too?

It was too much.Knees turned to jelly, I made it only three paces to the walk-in closet before collapsing to the worn, tan carpet beneath a rack of old coats. Tears spilled from my eyes, mixing with the water droplets from my hair to form small rivers on my skin.

I cried because I was too tired to fight, and I cried because the Sickness had worn me down, making me fragile where I used to be strong. Then, following the Universal Law of Meltdowns, I cried about embarrassingly trivial things: the stacks of undone To-Do lists, the overflowing, stinky laundry basket next to me in the closet. I even cried because I was going to have to wear ugly panties to my birthday party, damn it, because I'd been too sick to do laundry for ages. (For the record, these panties were very unfortunate-looking—the kind of full-rise, back-of-the-drawer paisley number that stretch from belly button to thigh.) It didn't matter that no one was going to see them; it was the principle. I cried because this seemed a sad metaphor for my life—how everything awful was just barely hidden under a sparkly dress.

But most of all, I cried because I *wanted* to fix my spirit but I didn't know how. It's not like I could return to the faith of my childhood: the speaking-in-tongues, falling-on-the floor, believe-it-all-or-believe-it-none gospel with a fiery hell for everyone who didn't buy into Christ. Though, at the moment, running backwards felt almost tempting. I knew I could simply curl up in a pew, clutch a Bible, and rest. But to do that, I'd have to repent with words I couldn't spit out, admit to sins I hadn't committed.

No. I could not go back there. I would not believe in a God who did not believe in me.

Post-Traumatic Church Syndrome is a bitch.

But I need to believe again, my heart disagreed, beating louder than my objections. *I don't want to be broken anymore.* Too weak and vulnerable to resist the thoughts, I put my head on my knees and allowed myself to wonder if there might be something bigger than the narrow religion I'd crashed into every time I considered faith. Something big enough to consider believing in.

I issued a strangled sob in the direction of the Godiverse: "Help me believe," I said from the floor of my closet, naked and shivering and crying. "Heal me."

I'd like to take credit for what happened next; I'd like to think I had some hand in creating the project that would overtake my life for the next year. But I didn't. The idea came fully formed, slipped under the door of my consciousness, a birthday card from the Godiverse:

Experience thirty religions before your thirtieth birthday.

Surprised, I blinked and sniffed. My tears abruptly stopped. The crazy idea fit me approximately as well as a prison jumpsuit. Considering the state I was currently in thanks to the mysterious Sickness, my twenty-ninth year was not a good time for taking on a spiritual quest. My twenty-ninth year was not a good time for taking anything but a nap. I didn't even want to go to my own birthday party, for Pete's sake, let alone work through my spiritual issues.

And what would it mean to "experience thirty religions" anyway? How would I choose them? The idea was full of problems: #1: I was sick. #2: I was too sick to travel. #3: I was barely hanging onto my life and my job as it was. I assumed it was only a matter of time before the people in my life found out I was faking everything from my daily schedule to Grandma's Special Recipe homemade macaroni. (Transfer Sara Lee to baking dish. Sprinkle crumpled potato chips on top. Heat and serve.)

If I added one more thing, I feared my life would end up a sad country song: I would lose my job, house, car, husband, and dog, then end up sleeping under a bench because I would be too tired to sit on it.

But the rebellious part of me that needed Josh's peace, the part that had asked to believe again, answered right back: *You could do it. You wouldn't have to travel very far.* And it started making a mental list: Hindu. Buddhist. Scientology. Amish. Native American. Mormon. Orthodox. Muslim… And then added the most seductive idea of all:

You are powerless over your body, but you can fix your spirit.

My head snapped up. This was nuts: fixing my PTCS seemed as impossible as healing my body. No, I said as firmly as I could. *Absolutely NOT.* And I promptly ran the other way.

Okay, I didn't actually run—I was still a very sick girl, and my closet was much too small to run anywhere. (Plus, I was naked and I think we can all agree that running naked, even away from the Godiverse in your very own house, is a bad idea.) But the idea of thirty religions forced me to my personal equivalent of running: I stood up, got dressed, put on my best fake beauty queen smile, and walked out the front door to my party.

My friends gathered just beyond the porch. Still distracted by what had just happened in the closet, I waved hello as I approached the steps. My high-heeled shoe caught on a nail, and I heard the small crowd heave a collective, horrified gasp as my feet flew out from under me.

If this had been a cartoon, I would have levitated horizontally for a moment before I bumped down the steps with a *Thud-Thud-Thud-Thud.*

I landed with hard *Thwack* on the concrete, my skirt upside down like an umbrella in a hurricane, flashing my husband, friends, two bums on the sidewalk, and the entire Baptist church across the street. "Hey baby," I heard one of the bums call, "I'd have paid for that show."

Well. If I'd known *I was going to flash God and everybody, I'd have worn cuter panties.*

Trent ran to my aid. "Are you hurt? Did you break anything?"

I tested my lower half. Though everything still worked, moving was painful. "I think 'broken' is a relative term," I muttered.

Trent offered his hand. I considered not getting up, but recognized the pain of staying down was worse than the pain of attempting to stand.

"This year can only go up from here," I said as my husband steadied me on my feet.

I couldn't have been more wrong.

2

Bruises

Contorting over my shoulder, I viewed the massive purple-blue-black-green bruise that stretched over my rear from back to calf. "Two weeks later, this bruise is still fantastic. Or should I say fan-ass-tic? From this angle it appears I got paddled by Zeus himself."

Trent raised his head from his law books. "It looks like someone tie-dyed your backside."

I kissed him. "I'm going to my first church this morning," I announced. *Yuck.* The words tasted like fiberglass insulation.

"Are you *sure* you want to do that?" Trent asked, his tone doubtful.

My husband's theology revolved around the Eagle Scout Oath, morning workouts, the Dean's List, Ohio State Football, and the Ten Commandments—in that order. His main memory of church was playing a shepherd in the First Lutheran Christmas pageant. He carried zero spiritual baggage, which was a good thing since I had enough to sink the *Queen Mary 2.*

From spousal telepathy, I knew Trent was thinking about a similar churchy announcement I'd made five years prior, back when we were still dating. After *that* church visit, he'd found me passed out on my couch, covered in Post-Traumatic Church Syndrome–induced hives, mumbling Benadryl-induced incoherencies about hating praise bands and preachers.

The Pentecostals of my childhood would have called my reaction to church demonic possession. I called it being allergic to God.

"'Want' isn't the right word," I sighed, walking into the closet to get ready.

I actively *didn't want* to go. Ever since the Breaking—the years in my early twenties when my faith and life had simultaneously shattered (unavoidable since faith *was* my life)—going to church reminded me of everything that had been broken: my calling to ministry, worldview, identity. Family. Friends. The meaning of life. The person who had been so sure of herself, so connected with God was gone—as surely as if I had lowered her into the ground myself. And when I went to church, all I felt was loss.

"Okay," Trent prompted from the bedroom, "If you don't *want* to go, why are you going?"

A valid question from a pragmatic man. "Be back in a sec," I said, giving myself time to think.

How to explain something I hardly understood myself?

The flip answer was that the Sickness had shown me how spiritually broken I was, and the project seemed as good an idea as any to root out the PTCS—like a sort of exposure therapy. I pictured the thirty religions as rungs on a ladder, something tangible to hold on to. This seemed like a way to take back some power where I felt totally powerless. (And, bonus: I suspected I might gather some great stories to tell at cocktail parties!)

But the much tougher, much *realer* answer, the one I was still wrestling with as I looked for a church-appropriate dress, was that whatever had spoken to me in the closet (the Something Bigger compelling me to believe again), it was still there, whispering: *You can be whole again. Healing is within reach.*

Armed with two outfit choices, I came out and flopped on the bed. "I think this is something I have to do to get over Post-Traumatic Church Syndrome," I said. "Kind of like how when you have a badly broken arm it has to be rebroken to heal properly."

"Sounds…painful?" Trent answered with an eyebrow raise.

"Tell me about it. But it's not like they have AA to recover from PTCS."

"Hi, I'm Reba, and I'm a church-a-holic," Trent quipped.

I rolled my eyes. "Hardly. But I did make this…" I reached to the nightstand and grabbed a torn notebook page scrawled with every religion I could think of and some I found online. I'd made the list a few days after my party, overcoming my own objections by telling myself I could quit the potential thirty religions project anytime. (It wasn't like I was going to turn into Indiana Jones, raiding my way to the lost ark or something.)

He looked my list over. "So you're going to find a new religion?"

"Ugh, no. I've already been there, done that, and burned the church t-shirts. I'm not going to find a new religion. I'm going to find myself. You know, like when people backpack Europe or quest across India?" With a courage I did not feel, I added, "And today I'm starting with Word Alive, the church I grew up in."

I'd decided on this plan reasoning that sometimes to move forward, you have to find yourself backwards. But it wasn't feeling like such a hot idea anymore.

Trent sensed my discomfort. "Do you want me to go with you?"

I smiled. I'd already considered inviting Trent. I knew he would come if I asked, but where I needed answers, he didn't even have questions.

Not to be outdone by Trent's offer, Oxley bounded into the room, a blur of black and tan puppy fur. "I volunteer as tribute!" he barked.

"You boys are sweet," I answered, rubbing my puppy's ears. "But I have to do this on my own."

In protest, or maybe to punctuate my point, Oxley swiftly peed on my church shoes.

I stopped at a traffic light on the hill overlooking Word Alive. The car behind me honked. I glanced in the rearview and saw the honker in his minivan. For a moment it seemed like my dad, motioning that I needed to hurry up, my mom in the passenger seat applying lipstick, me and my two younger sisters in the back seats poking each other's curls and patent shoes.

I took a deep breath, realizing this was decision time: I could drive forward and face my past or pull a U-turn and forfeit my spiritual future. The minivan honked again and I lurched straight ahead, pulled by an unseen string.

Circling the parking lot, I was puzzled to find it almost empty. It used to be so full that elders had to double as parking attendants, wearing reflective vests over their suits and ties and waving in people to park on the grass. It was a megachurch before being a megachurch was a thing.

Now the few cars present were a study in bumper stickers. After seeing, "Marriage = 1 Man + 1 Woman (No Exceptions)" and "Pro-Choice = Murder," I decided I didn't care for this parking lot's math. Pulling in next to: "Don't know Jesus? You're going to hell!" the PTCS symptoms started in earnest: blurred vision, sweaty palms, upset stomach.

Approaching Word Alive's doors, my panic level rose. A greeter grasped my hand firmly. "Welcome! We sure are glad you're here." I smiled through gritted teeth. "I hope you enjoy services here at The Palms."

I did a double take. "The Palms?" *Like Vegas?* "I thought this was Word Alive."

"It used to be," the greeter rocked back on his heels. "Pastor Tom changed it a few years back. Said we needed a new name for a new era of revival!"

The gray-carpeted lobby smelled exactly the same: ink toner and paint crossed with old lady perfume. Directly in front of me was a table covered with books for sale, the same table where I once begged my mom to purchase a t-shirt featuring cartoons of Jesus beating up Satan. The shirt was an extra-large size and far too mature for a nine-year-old, yet I bargained away six weeks of my allowance to make it mine. "What kind of child bargains her allowance for a Christian t-shirt with bad graphics?" a reasonable reader might wonder, if they were not acquainted with a child who believed Jesus was coming back very soon, possibly tomorrow at lunchtime. While we're on the subject, I was also the child who:

A. Listed "church" under the "hobbies" section of her Student-of-the-Week poster,
B. Made her Barbies speak in tongues,
C. Convinced friends that it was more fun to pray than play at recess, and
D. Informed her first-grade class that Santa, rearranged, was Satan.

At Word Alive Church, and at home, God was *Everything*. Anyone who thinks I'm exaggerating did not have the pleasure of growing up alongside inspirational paper products. To fully grasp the origin of my Post-Traumatic Church Syndrome, you need to understand my family's collection of "I will bless the Lord at all times" paper napkins, which helped even our humble trashcan hum God's praises on Sloppy Joe night. We used these napkins off and on for years. I know not from whence they came, but I assume their family of origin is the same as Christian toilet paper. (My friend Janice had Christian toilet paper at her house, and it always gave me stage fright during sleepovers. Thankfully, my own parents abstained from Christian toilet paper. To be clear, the tissue itself was not personalized—just the wrapper. *Still.* The more closely a Christian denomination ties God to the bathroom, the more likely its adherents are to experience PTCS. [Janice, if you're reading this, I started a Facebook support group. XOXO.])

My family may not have gone in for Jesus-themed toilet paper, but we had our own unusual traditions, like the Sunday afternoons of my childhood when my dad would swing a yellow baseball bat at Satan. The Bat was a plastic jobbie with post-it notes taped to it. On the post-it notes were Bible verses (handwritten by my mother because Dad had awful penmanship) urging all members of our household to "take up the whole armor of God, that you may be able to withstand in the evil day."

My dad would find The Bat and stalk about the house, reading the Bible verses and praying loudly as he went. In Pentecostal circles, this practice of exorcising the devil from your house is known as "spiritual warfare." As a child, I found the idea of Dad rebuking the devil simultaneously comforting and pee-your-pants frightening. On one hand there was a real, live Satan and he, the source of all evil, was lurking in our living room or possibly hiding directly under my bed waiting to snatch me in my sleep. On the other hand, my daddy was the boss of him.

A troop of kids ran through the Word Alive lobby, breaking my reverie about my childhood. I could hear the band warming up as I reached the sanctuary doors, and my hands went numb as I opened them. It looked so…dark. It was creepy—a three-thousand-seat church so dimly lit I wasn't sure if this was a worship service or a Halloween hide and seek. Only a hundred or so folks sat in the pews. Were the lights this dim for ambiance or because Word Alive—excuse me, "The Palms"—could no longer afford the electric bill? I walked to my family's former pew and realized the darkness had calmed me a bit, as if I were a church cockroach.

I looked around, breathing deeply to steady myself. Memories were everywhere in this building: ghosts of my former self sat in every pew, knelt on the steps to the altar, stood by the baptismal. The girl I was paced the balcony, praying. She sat in the Sunday school classrooms, learning. She was everywhere and nowhere, because I was not her anymore. When my faith broke, I was left staring into a kaleidoscope where there had once hung a mirror reflecting who I was, what I believed, and where I was going. My every memory was recast in fragmented light, the image of my future obscured. I had no sense of self apart from my faith because no part of my life was untouched by it.

The singing began; everyone stood and raised arms to heaven as they sang, "More of you Jesus," what seemed like fifty times in a row. I refused to stand. I sat with legs and arms crossed, casting a condemning eye toward an older tambourine player who was dancing through the aisles, banging her instrument to warm the crowd up for the Holy Spirit. The singing wore on for forty minutes, fraying my nerves as it worked the crowd into a tearful frenzy. Tears were something I remembered well. They were the vital sign of worship: if the Lord was really, really touching your heart, you'd better believe your eyes would be watering.

If my eyes were watering, it was because I could see my family past. In my memories, my dad was sitting next to me while my mother played her violin on the stage—her music so beautiful the angels seemed to sing along—and my twin sisters, Mary and Marcia, younger than me by five years, raised their chubby hands to Jesus.

A woman sporting poofy blonde hair, shoulder pads, and a jean skirt took the microphone and began spouting gibberish. Anywhere else this behavior would be labeled schizophrenic, but not in Pentecostal worship. This was speaking in tongues, the unintelligible words of the Holy Ghost, as though God couldn't communicate in English if he damn well pleased.

I raged internally against these bumper sticker people who enjoyed such weird displays of anything-goes worship. In my time I have witnessed a man pant like an animal because he was thirstier for God than a dog for water, a woman who faked a seizure because the Lord wanted someone in the audience to be healed of seizures, an entire congregation inspired to dance in the aisles and, on a separate occasion, the entire congregation overtaken by laughter—a case, Pastor Tom had said, of Holy Laughter.

In the pew, I fantasized about running up to the stage, stealing the microphone and yelling, "You people are bigots! You think you have the corner on truth! You shun anyone who doesn't believe what you do and send them to eternal hell! And, you, sir, *are barking like a dog*. That's not the Holy Spirit, that's *delusional!*" and then bolting straight out the back door and never looking back.

But this fantasy was exactly why I was there. I had to get rid of this ugly bitterness that made me want to knock the tambourine lady right over. Pulling my project list from my purse, I cross off Word Alive. *Only twenty-nine to go?*

Pastor Tom took center stage wearing…jeans? Growing up, jeans were not something you wore to Sunday church because, well, did we wear anything less than our best to visit Jesus' house? I think not. Apparently God had changed his mind.

"Do we want gays in our military, no!" shouted Pastor Tom, pacing across the stage. "Do we want gays raising our country's children? No! Do we want the sacred union of marriage to be compromised? Not unless we want the judgment of God to fall on this land like it did on Sodom and Gomorrah!"

His remarks were punctuated by a chorus of hallelujahs, and I threw up a little in my mouth.

Pastor Tom's sermon was interspersed with so much Scripture that it was confusing to see where God's word stopped and his began. Predictably, it morphed into an altar call. This was usually when people started falling down, televangelist-style. The one pointed failure of my young Christian life was always that I just couldn't fall down. I was *willing* to fall down. I was *waiting* to fall down, but despite my best horizontal intentions, I always remained disappointingly vertical when other people became like trees felled by the axe of the Holy Ghost.

"Deliverance is available to all through the blood of the Risen Lord Jesus Christ!" exhorted Pastor Tom. "All who need healing, salvation, and deliverance from all hell's demons, come to the altar for prayer."

Soon middle-aged men were prostrate on the ground before the altar and middle-aged ladies were rocking back and forth, hugging themselves and crying. Though I needed deliverance from the Sickness and healing from Post-Traumatic Church Syndrome, all heaven's angels couldn't have dragged me to kneel at that altar. Instead, I followed "all hell's demons" straight out the church's back doors, barely escaping the claustrophobic closing song.

Pushing open the doors, I breathed warm summer air like a diver coming to the surface. The fact that I had survived three hours at Word Alive without hives might have counted as a victory had I not limped out of there feeling worse than Word Dead.

I tossed my Thirty by Thirty list in the trash.

3

Dreams

"Can you pick me up for book club?" I slurred into the phone. "Hand surgery a few days ago. Percocet. Can't drive."

"Of course," Nadine agreed. An hour later, she eyed my cast when I climbed in her car. "How are you? It looks like it hurts."

"Not right now. The drugs are working." I preferred surgery to the Sickness; surgery gave me a break from the mental torture of wondering what was wrong with my body when my episodes hit.

"Did you read the book?" Nadine asked, turning down Jay-Z's "99 Problems."

"I not only read it," I answered, "I bought the journal. *Finding Your Own North Star* is my favorite pick yet. Speaking of which, Trent asked me on my way out the door, 'Why do you bother reading the book? Isn't it just an excuse for ladies to drink wine and gossip?' And I told him, 'Book club is group therapy plus wine and minus a certified professional.'"

We laughed because it was true. The women in our club knew about each other's bosses, birth control, eyebrow-plucking habits, weddings, evil co-workers, and childhood scars. The Sickness was the only thing my book club *didn't* know about me. Some secrets are simply too shameful to be shared.

When we arrived, Michelle—our resident book summarizer—was giving a recap. "*Finding Your Own North Star* by Martha Beck is a guide to living your ideal life. She says you do this by tapping into internal compasses that are always pointed towards your core desires—your own 'North Star.'" Michelle folded her notes and tucked her light brown hair behind one ear. "To me, this was a book about finding and following your dreams, so here's my question: Did this book make you think about your dreams?"

Since our typical book picks weren't self-helpy, the conversation turned from intellectual to personal in record time. We talked about our "North Star" dreams: opening a yoga studio, getting married, running for office, having children, getting over a broken heart. As everyone shared, I felt something slip in the room as it had in my closet: like the Godiverse was right there, lending weight and courage to our aspirations.

I told myself this woo-woo feeling had a name: Percocet.

Intending to retrieve my Kindle, I realized with dismay that I'd grabbed my workbag. *Thank you, loopy drugs.* I rooted around anyway. No Kindle, but from the bottom of my bag I pulled out a crumpled piece of paper.

My Thirty by Thirty list… What? How? I peered at it in bewilderment. *I threw this away.* I retraced my steps mentally: the limping out of Word Alive church, the tossing of the list, the driving home and sleeping for three days because the Sickness sucker-punched me.

Yet there was the list in my hand instead of the trash.

For the next half hour of wine and chatter, I couldn't shake the thought: *I didn't mean to keep this list, but it meant to keep me.* I clutched the paper, wondering what to do until I hit on a brilliant plan. *I'll let the book club talk me out of it!* These were professional, successful, well-educated women—pragmatic thinkers all.

Yes. The ladies would help my project rest in peace. Preferably in a trash can with a lid and a lit match.

"I'm thinking about going to thirty religions before I turn thirty," I blurted. There was a moment of silence; I assumed everyone was checking to see if I had lost my mind. Backpedaling, I braced myself to be talked off the ledge: "It wouldn't be actually thirty *religions*, because a lot of them would be Christian denominations…"

My book club ladies did not talk me off the ledge. They shoved me over that shelf so fast that I hardly had time to catch a breath on the way down.

Excitement palpable, they all spoke at once. "Would you do Scientology and Wicca?" "What about a mosque?" "You should totally be Amish for a day!" "What about Mormons?"

I glanced at my list. The decision felt made for me, a current that swept me up and carried me along. Very slowly, I nodded my head in assent.

"Yes," I said. "The answer to all the questions is yes."

The following Sunday morning, Andre rolled down his car window in our shared driveway. "Hey love. How's my Best Neighbor Forever? You look nice!"

I walked toward his Jeep. "Since I'm usually in sweatpants, the dress is a nice change."

"Where are you headed?"

"Tenth Avenue Baptist?" I squeaked. A fellow PTCS sufferer, Andre had disavowed the Baptist church when he came out at age nineteen. He and God weren't on the best of terms.

Andre was still sitting in his car, but he jumped anyway. "Church? *You*?"

"I'll explain later," I promised. "Hey, can I ask you a question?"

"Anything."

"Would Baptists who are African American object to being called 'Black Baptists'?"

Andre leaned out the window, his expression that of a teacher with a small child. "Reba. They're black. They're Baptists. It's a fact, not an opinion."

"Thanks for clearing that up."

"You know me," he offered cheerfully. "I'm your two-for-one deal. I can be consulted as your token black *and* your token gay friend. Hey, are you and Trent coming to my Pride party in a few weeks?"

"You know it wouldn't be Pride without my famous white sangria. Okay, I'm off to worship with the Black Baptists."

"Get ready to duck."

"Excuse me?"

He smiled. "To avoid all the hellfire and brimstone."

Nadine gripped my arm as we approached the stone entrance of Tenth Avenue Baptist. "Should we have worn hats?" she whispered.

I surveyed the ornate head coverings perched like butterflies atop the heads of the ladies of the church. They were dressed to impress in full Sunday best. Even their husbands and sons looked like dapper accessories in three-piece suits, ties, and pocket squares patterned with flair and lapel flowers. We passed an elderly woman in a wheelchair wearing full makeup, a bright pink dress and hat, hosiery, and high heels

"We probably should have worn hats," I whispered back, "but it's too late now."

In the narthex, a greeter with ebony skin and blue eyes stopped us. Her nametag read *Sister Maggie*, and it was more than her substantial size and feathery aquamarine hat that made her intimidating. She wore the look of a woman on a holy mission, God's own welcome wagon and security force.

Sister Maggie looked us up and down slowly, taking inventory of our shy smiles, pale skin, and linked arms.

"Y'all…visitors," she stated. The sentence was not phrased as a question. "Mmm-hmm. Fill out these cards."

Nadine, who had been so thrilled about my project that she volunteered to accompany me on this site visit, took a pencil and happily filled in her life story. I plotted to wriggle out of the obligation.

"May I please take it to my seat and return it later?" I asked sweetly, eyes downcast.

"No," boomed Sister Maggie, correctly guessing that I planned to stuff the card in the nearest hymnal. Her look said, *Don't you challenge me, little lady*.

I intuited that when in Sister Maggie's church, you did as Sister Maggie said, so I grudgingly scratched some minimal information.

In a solitary act of belligerence, I then stole the pencil, furtively stashing it in my purse.

We exchanged our visitor cards for programs, and Sister Maggie showed us to our seats—the last row of the first section. We shared our pew with a blind man who kindly stood to let us pass. "Welcome, welcome," he nodded his sunglasses in our direction, his guide dog lying calmly under the pew.

"I'm so excited," said Nadine in a low voice when we were seated. "I've never been in a church that isn't Catholic."

"Never?"

Nadine shrugged. "My family and friends were all Catholic. I didn't need to try anything else."

I looked around at the eager congregation, heard the riffs of the organist warming up, and saw the fifty-person choir file onto the stage, robed in purple regalia. *Oh boy.*

"Nadine," I warned, "I think you're in for a little culture shock."

On cue, a middle-aged black man with graying hair bounced onto the stage. He wore a full-length black duster over his suit, reminding me of Neo's costume in *The Matrix.* "Can I hear you make some *Holy Ghost noise* this morning?" he half-shouted, half-sang. The organist punctuated the man's words with decisive chords, signaling the congregation to rise en masse and issue forth a boisterous, joyful affirmation that included many *Hallelujahs, Amens,* and *Yes, Lords*!

"I came from a Pentecostal church," he said, clapping in time with the organist who had started banging the keys hard and fast. I flinched a little. "And we gonna be praisin' this morning—Pentecostal-style!"

Nadine nudged me in the ribs. "What does that mean?" she asked, understandably confused. She had a lifetime of exclusively Catholic liturgy working against her.

"It means that things are going to get loud up in here." And loud things got. On a Worship Enthusiasm Factor spectrum from one to ten, the *Matrix* music pastor was over the edge with an 11.5, maybe a 12.

He jumped for Jesus! He danced for Jesus! He may have even moon-walked for Jesus! The whole church seemed to be dancing along with him; our blind friend performed a few of his own moves in the pew next to us. Even the dog wagged his tail in time with the choir (which, by the way, could have hit the road as a touring act).

The music minister wiped sweat from his brow with a handkerchief that perfectly coordinated with his tie. I felt a few degrees warmer just watching him.

I snuck a glance at Nadine. Except for the fact that her hair wasn't blowing in the wind, she looked the same way I always do in those roller-coaster camera photos.

"What do you think?" I asked, my voice a normal level so as to not be drowned out by the praisin'.

"I *love* it." Nadine looked like she'd been riding inverted loop-de-loops. "I had no idea people acted like this in church."

By the time we sat down I was exhausted, and not only because the Sickness was pulling at my joints, begging me to go back to bed. Black Baptist praise time was a Zumba-worthy workout.

Sister Maggie shimmied her way to the front, and the *Matrix* music minister handed her the microphone. I glanced at the program, which announced that it was time for the formal GREETING OF THE GUESTS. The all-caps frightened me even more than Sister Maggie.

"We'd like to offer a warm Tenth Street Baptist welcome to our two guests this morning," she said, looking our way.

Four hundred people at this church, and we were the only Caucasians and the only visitors?

"Will Miss Nadine Smart please rise?" Nadine looked at me, slightly panicked.

Rise! Rise! I gestured. She rose.

"Welcome Miss Nadine," said Sister Maggie. The congregation applauded. "Miss Smart is Catholic and attends church at her local parish. She resides here in the city and enjoys yoga, the beach, and book club. Welcome, Miss Nadine!" Nadine waved excitedly to the crowd.

Sister Maggie cleared her throat and glared at me. Uh-oh. Only she and I knew about the train wreck that was about to happen.

"Will R. please stand up? R.?" Gulp. I stood. What choice did I have? "Welcome, R."

I waved weakly, cheeks flaming. *Why did I have to use an initial?* I berated myself, worried that the congregation would now show me the same cold shoulder I'd given the visitor card.

"It's time to fellowship with one another," boomed Sister Maggie. The organ started up and the crowd broke into groups, enthusiastically telling one another "Hell-o!" and "Don't you look fine this morning!"

Nadine gave me another questioning look.

"Prepare to be greeted," I intoned.

Within minutes Nadine and I were swept into the frighteningly enthusiastic embrace of the crowd. Never in my life have I given or received so many hugs in a fifteen-minute span. Fellowship time at Tenth Avenue was no cold, perfunctory, "Peace be with you, and also with you". This was not a greeting of limp handshakes. Fellowshiping at Tenth Avenue Baptist was a full-contact sport.

After fellowship time, two ministers took the stage, tag-teaming the sermon in a good-cop, bad cop routine that would have been funny if the bad cop (the older and shorter of the two) hadn't triggered my PTCS symptoms by yelling about the congregation's purported sins. In order of increasing decibel level, our collective sins were legion.

Why is he so angry? Nadine wrote on the program, scooting it under my gaze.

Some people think anger will scare a congregation closer to God, I wrote in reply.

Just as I thought I could take no more, the good cop stepped in to talk about dreams. He opened with Traffic Ticket Theology, which went something like, *If you have enough faith and pray hard enough when you get pulled over, God will get you out of a traffic ticket!* (The Trinity I was brought up to revere would want me wearing my seatbelt and driving below the speed limit.) He backed up this theology with the Old Testament story of Joseph, a favored-son-turned-slave-turned-ruler who was known for being a dreamer—a line of reasoning I couldn't follow, but enjoyed nonetheless, the same way I enjoy a winding drive in the country with no destination in sight.

But there was a destination in sight! "Let us bring forth the tithes and the offerings," the good cop pastor rejoiced, signaling the organist to play a rousing ballad and the ladies of the church to reach for their perfectly-accessorized handbags.

Nadine checked the time and leaned in. "I have lunch plans," she said, looking in Sister Maggie's direction.

I surveyed our options like a prisoner planning a break. The Tenth Avenue Black Baptists didn't pass the plate; they walked up to it row by row. "Here's the plan. We march up to the front with everyone else, put something in the plate, and instead of rounding back to our seats, we duck out the side door."

Nadine looked ill at ease. "Have you done this kind of thing before?"

"I've escaped from churches in more ways than I can count. I am the world's expert on the subject. Grab your purse."

We marched up the aisle and kept right on marching straight out the side door. As it was closing behind us, I overheard the good cop pastor say: "Jesus gave you a dream so you could give it back to Him. He can do exceedingly and abundantly more than you could ever imagine. Hand your dream back to Him."

I rolled my eyes. Thanks but no thanks. I preferred to keep my hands to myself and my dreams in my *Finding Your Own North Star* journal.

4
Tea

Going to the Buddhist Center felt deliciously illicit, like I was going to sneak around on Jesus and have a clandestine affair with the Buddha. Then again, Jesus and I were separated, so it wasn't quite an affair. Still, it was mildly thrilling, even if my new interest had a bigger belly than the world's favorite carpenter.

When I drove up to the meditation center, I felt briefly disappointed: it was a refurbished vintage church, which felt a lot like meeting my new date at my old boyfriend's house. Also, I never figured the Buddha as a grey aluminum siding kind of guy. I thought he'd be more into the stone-and-sand look. The only clues to the building's current Meditation Center status were the streamers of prayer flags draped over the former steeple.

I paused before entering the Center, checking myself for the remorse I'd been conditioned to experience should I ever dare to deviate from Christianity. Nothing. I took a deep breath and opened the red wooden door. I'm not sure what I expected…but it wasn't two sets of wooden stairs heading in opposite directions.

Following a small crowd gathering by the shoe rack, I copied their actions and removed my flip-flops. I mounted the wooden stairs going up, because, as with most life choices, up seemed better than down. I'd guessed correctly; a greeter ushered me into the center's main shrine room, formerly the church sanctuary. Absent of pews, the wooden floor gleamed under streamers and flags of every imaginable color. I'm sure the Buddhists weren't specifically after a rainbow-themed room, but they unintentionally achieved one. It's how Punky Brewster might have decorated a place of worship had she been given a free hand back in the 1980s. I loved it.

Purple cushions littered the floor, and I almost grabbed one before remembering that the shrine room was not my final destination.

"Where is the introduction to Buddhist meditation?" I asked a granola-type woman near me who wore a full linen outfit that stated, *I may not be in the Caribbean on the outside, but I have palm trees in my heart!*

"Over there," Ms. Granola pointed to a door to the right of the former altar. I made my way over, stepping around folks who were pre-meditating—not murder, just pre-meditating meditation.

Inside the door a wizened teacher sat on the floor—well, not quite the floor. His bum was supported by a short meditation cushion that slanted for easy rising. (If the cushion reminded me of the Liberator sex cushion beloved by the world's oldsters, I kept this thought to myself.)

The teacher motioned for me to sit on the floor beside three college girls sporting matching woven caps and broomstick skirts. I briefly wondered if they were members of a spiritually progressive sorority who preferred tranquility meditation to hangovers. I lowered myself with some difficulty as the Sickness did not take kindly to being ordered to the floor without the OTC painkillers I usually took prior to yoga.

"Let go of the past," the teacher breathed from his ~~Liberator~~ meditation cushion. "Let go of the future. Let go of the present. With a heart that is free, cross over to that shore which is beyond suffering. Close your eyes and breathe."

I closed my eyes. I breathed. I imagined myself in a small motorized rowboat, crossing over to the shore beyond suffering. Instead, I found myself on a regular old beach holding a coconut drink and wearing one of the unbearable swimsuits from the Victoria's Secret catalog, suffering because (A) I was not actually at the beach with a coconut drink and (B) No one looks good in those impossibly tiny bikinis.

My shore of suffering was interrupted by the sound of the door creaking open. I was…I was…a woman who completely lost her train of thought mid-sentence when the damn near hottest guy I had ever seen waltzed in like he owned the place. Six-foot-gorgeous, two-hundred pounds of muscle, blissfully disheveled blonde hair, baby blue eyes—Mr. Hotness walked over and sat down next to me like all the air hadn't just been sucked out of the room as he rendered every female meditationally challenged.

"Hey," he whispered in my general direction. The college girls swooned. I stared at him, blinking. *Pardon me while I remember how to speak.*

"Hey," I squawked belatedly, voice cracking. He smiled. The angels wept with joy.

Do I even need to mention how poorly the session went after this?

It was terrible. I was terrible. A hopeless mess of non-tranquil, non-meditative sitting.

Not that I blamed Mr. Hotness; I was a bad meditator under the best of circumstances. My ability to remain motionless and think about nothing while sitting cross-legged on the floor rivaled that of a class of kindergartners with ADHD. Whenever I tried to quiet my mind in yoga Shavasana, it filled with dinosaurs and sasquatches yelling well-meaning advice.

Mr. Hotness, by contrast, dropped right off into meditative la-la land. I know because I watched him furtively. (Reba Riley, the peeping tom-ette of Intro to Buddhism tranquility meditation.)

At some point the practice mediation finished and the lesson began, but I missed most of it because I was busy chastising myself for forgetting to wear deodorant.

"...*Ehipassiko,*" the teacher pronounced. "It means, 'Come and see.'"

Well. That phrase certainly arrested my wandering attention. It was a piece of Christianese—the language of Evangelical Christians and therefore my native tongue. Due to my background, I speak Christianese beautifully: I can catch and throw idioms and deftly season whole conversations with Scripture. It's like a secret verbal handshake, so Evangelicals can instantly recognize one another regardless of the setting.

In Christianese, "Come and see" referred to the calling of the disciples in John 1 and meant: "Come meet Jesus. See the one true Truth, and then get saved, preferably with many tears, and forever fellowship over potluck suppers." *Come and See* inferred that everyone who came to Jesus would see the same thing. *Come and See* left no room for people like me.

This was not a phrase I wanted to hear in Buddhist mediation class.

"*Ehipassiko,*" the teacher looked over the group and reiterated his statement in a Zen-like tone that was the precise vocal opposite of the Baptist bad cop pastor's shouting, "is a part of the Dharma, the Buddha's teachings. Come and see."

The elderly teacher's gaze landed on me. "Your life is a laboratory for the Dharma. Test the teachings. Question the teachings. Truth exists in the value it brings to you—not in an idea someone told you, or in a holy book someone wrote. Let your experience inform your spiritual life."

My heart beat faster, and not just because I caught a whiff of Mr. Hotness's cologne. Ehipassiko. No corner on truth. No believe-it-all or believe-it-none theology. No hard-and-fast rules. No black and white. *Come and see for yourself.*

Something opened up inside me, but just as quickly slammed shut. *It can't be that easy.*

"Please join us for announcements in the main shrine room and tea in the meeting hall downstairs," the teacher invited, closing the class.

I stopped briefly in the shrine room just long enough to hear the announcements—*Wait, Buddhists have bake sales, too?*—before going downstairs for the Buddhist tea, which sounded much more exotic than it actually was. The regulars clustered together discussing whatever Buddhists discuss while the visitors paced near the walls. After shifting to and fro, I moved to a couch where I assumed someone would speak to me eventually. No one did.

Except Mr. Hotness.

I reasoned that it had little to do with me; in any randomly nerve-racking situation, one is drawn to others who appear to be in the same state. Mr. Hotness introduced himself; we small-talked while I wondered if I had remembered to brush my teeth.

"So," he said, twisting his mug. "Will I see you here next week? Maybe I could get your number and we could have a drink and discuss our spiritual journeys."

Oh…my…Godiverse. Was Mr. Hotness was trying to pick me up? In the basement of a Buddhist temple?

Why, yes. Yes, he was.

With a highly eloquent, "Ummmmm…" I faked a double cough and covered my mouth with my left hand to display my marital status.

"Ummmm…" Mr. Hotness said, equaling my eloquence. "I…need a refill. See you around."

Ehipassiko, Mr. Hotness. Come and see my wedding ring.

"Mom," I said into the cell phone tucked between my cheek and a hotel pillow, "A healthy person's dream weekend is a sick person's nightmare. How am I going to make it through four full days of sightseeing in Chicago without collapsing on the sidewalk?"

"*You're* in Chicago?!" my mother squealed. "*I'm* visiting Chicago!" This was such good news I almost forgot how bad I felt. I was just a short train ride away from my mom, the woman who can solve almost anything with a steaming mug of tea. Remember the dad in *My Big Fat Greek Wedding*, the one who fixed everything by spraying it with Windex? That's my mom and Earl Grey Decaf. Skinned knee? Earl Grey. Broken heart? You guessed it.

That is why we met for tea the following day at The Drake Hotel's Palm Court while Trent was interviewing and my mom's fiancé, K.C., was working.

"We're so fancy!" I whispered to Mom, who delicately dabbed her mouth with a cloth napkin. Everything from the lush palms to the burbling fountain in the middle of the court to the china, sterling silver service, and teensy sandwiches, screamed: "Mother-Daughter Bonding with an Elegant Twist!"

"This napkin has a higher thread count than my sheets," Mom whispered back. Then she lifted her teacup in the air and said in an English accent, "Why, yes your Majesty. We'd be *delighted* to come to the palace!"

We were having such a good time that I felt hesitant to bring up my project. Though my mother is my biggest fan/cheerleader/life coach and the person most likely to help me clean up a murder, we'd barely discussed the topic since I had first mentioned my project in May.

I'm pretty sure that when I had said, "I'm trying to get rid of this Post-Traumatic Church Syndrome thing," she'd heard, "You and Dad reaaally messed me up with all that speaking in tongues stuff and ten thousand hours of Christian education, but I'm moving on! Watch me, moving on! In a really bizarre fashion! Woo-hoo!"

"You mean you'll be visiting other religions? Like other than Christian churches?" she'd asked in that strangled, supportive-of-my-adult-child voice, similar to the voice she might use if I, say, ran off to Vegas and got married, then Facebooked the photos before I mentioned the wedding to her.

My mother has a talent for bringing out the best in people. A gifted musician and teacher, she once adapted *Rudolph the Red-Nosed Reindeer* for a special-needs preschool class, and cast a highly autistic boy as Rudolf, being pulled in a carriage by the reindeer. She brings out the best in me, too, with one exception: when it comes to spiritual matters she is equal parts inspiration and hindrance. She is the voice in my head singing, "Jesus be close to me," when I go to sleep, and the voice in my phone urging Trent and me to "really find a church home already."

Since I'd first mentioned the project, Mom wasn't asking and I wasn't telling—which was out of character for us both. I took an easy segue: telling her about the prior day, when Trent and I had been sightseeing and I'd begged to stop and sit in the Fourth Presbyterian sanctuary. "I told him it was for my Thirty by Thirty project, but really, it was because I didn't think I could walk another step."

"Oh, honey," she said, patting my hand, but not taking the conversational bait. I took a breath, figuring it was now or never. We couldn't spend the whole year not talking about it.

"Mom, why don't you ever ask me about my project?"

She winced a little and cleared her throat. The peaceful strains of harp music floating in the air seemed at odds with the tension the question created; distance that had not been present a moment before now stretched between our teacups.

"I don't understand why you would feel like you need to go looking everywhere when you already know The Truth." My mind capitalized her words: two presses of the Shift key standing between me and believing. "Jesus is the Way, the Truth, and the Life. No man cometh to the Father but by Him," she quoted.

"You shall know the truth, and the truth shall set you free," I quoted back. "But Mom, that truth didn't set me free. It imprisoned me. That truth is keeping me *away* from God because I can't buy into all the church crap. And I can't understand a God who would send people to a fiery pit for eternity. That's not a God I can believe in. That's not a God I *want* to believe in. Period."

I might as well have taken the silver butter knife in my hand and twisted it in her gut. She looked tearful, and I immediately felt sorry. Why had I brought this up?

"The Bible says, 'Train up a child in the way he should go and in the end he will not depart from it,'" Mom recited softly. "What does it say about me as a mother that you've turned away from everything we taught you, and now you're running all over creation, visiting all these religions? It makes me think I must have gone terribly wrong. Was it the divorce? If Dad and I hadn't gotten divorced, would you be doing this?"

This was not the question I'd expected. Their divorce when I was nineteen had changed my life, certainly. It had broken my ideas about God and family and the world, but its impact was not a loss of faith: my grief caused me to dig deeper into faith. It was only later—when I realized I didn't, I couldn't, believe in the primary tenets of Christianity—that I walked away. And it was the walking away from everything I knew that caused The Breaking.

I didn't blame my parents; any system of belief built like a Jenga tower is breakable. If you must believe x to believe y, and y to believe z, and x, y, and z to believe in God, it only takes a crack in one area to bring all of faith crashing down. My parents didn't break my faith; they had given me a faith that was inherently breakable.

"Oh, Mom," I said. "I'm sorry for bringing it up. You didn't do anything wrong."

"But you're always talking about how 'hurt' you are by religion— the religion I taught you. And when you say 'Post-Traumatic Church Syndrome,' how could I not feel like it's my fault?"

I decided to razz her a little—mostly to de-escalate the conversation.

"Well, I mean, you *did* encourage me to dwell on the gory sacrifice of Christ. I lived in terror of being left behind, alone and hungry, in the potential bloody aftermath of the Rapture, and I wasn't allowed to watch the Smurfs."

She exhaled deeply. "We were just doing the best we could. Did we scar you all forever?"

"Maybe." I replied with mock drama. "I do sell nails for a living. And I hang out in hotel bars. But I'll forgive you if you'll go to the 3D Smurf movie with me when it comes out in the fall."

"Done," she said.

I thought we had moved on until she sighed. "I'm so afraid you're going to end up more lost than you already are, and fall off the deep end and start following a guru."

"A guru?" I spotted my exit to the conversation and grabbed the opportunity like a life preserver. "Mom, do you really think I'm going to run off to India and take up chanting?" I closed my eyes and pretended to chant. "I don't even have the energy to sightsee in Chicago."

I looked up; she was smiling again, and we dropped the Project Thirty by Thirty topic in favor of a trip around the corner to the American Girl store.

When it came time to say goodbye, my mom held my shoulders and looked at me. "I will support you whatever you do, but I don't understand your project, and I don't like it. I want you to remember your calling, remember the prophecy over your life."

How could I forget? I was thirteen when the traveling revival minister stopped speaking mid-sermon, almost mid-sentence. Sitting in the pew, my hands began to shake, and that's how I knew before I knew: *He was going to say my name.* From the pulpit, he said: "Is there a Rebecca here tonight? Rebecca? Where are you?" I stood, feeling tingly all over. He proceeded to give a long and powerful prophecy over my life, detailing my special calling: I would serve God in ministry and be a healer. Prophecy like this was not something taken lightly in my family or church.

I had accepted my calling that night, and every day and night after the Breaking I'd walked further away from it. My mother's reminder made my guilt palpable, heavier than the weight of her words. I nodded that I did remember, even though I'd tried to forget. A tear ran down my cheek and she wiped it away.

"It looks like you need more tea," she said, pulling a package from her purse. "Good thing I brought you some." She handed me a box of Earl Grey.

"I'll be praying for you, honey," she said, kissing me. "And I'm going to look for the tape recording of that prophecy. God doesn't send a word that big if you aren't going to need it."

5

Communion

*L*eaning against a wrought iron fence near the park, I inspected the Gay Pride parade passing by. "You know the best part about the Short North?" I asked Andre as we watched an array of scantily clad men strutting down the street in rainbow boas, neckties, and Speedos. "The stunning display of abs. I didn't even know you could have that many."

"Look—that lady has a twenty-four pack," he answered, pointing to a woman riding a motorcycle in the next procession.

I called to my husband, who had gone to retrieve more drinks. "Hey Trent, can you snap a picture of me and Andre?"

"Hang on," Trent balanced three red cups on the grassy hill and grabbed his phone, capturing an image that showcased our funny grins, a host of half-naked people mid-march, and a contingent of angry protesters on the opposite side of the street holding up handmade signs that said, "Repent!" and "God hates fags!"

"Ugh," I said, looking at the picture, "The Reba of the year 2000 would have been on the other side of the street with the protestors."

"I guess you traded in communion with the saints for sangria with the sinners," Trent joked.

"And she wouldn't have it any other way," Andre side-hugged me.

We turned back to the parade. "Andre!" I grabbed his arm. "Are those church floats coming our way?"

"Yeah," he said, as though this was normal. "Some of the churches come out to support Pride every year. A few synagogues, too."

Aghast, I watched fifty people march around King Avenue United Methodist's float, tossing candy to the crowd. The protestors went ballistic against the church group, screaming all manner of vile things, the fully dressed people in church t-shirts appearing to offend them even more than the half-naked transgendered marching band.

"Stone Village Church," I read the print on the next, smaller group's t-shirts. The protestors ratcheted up their discourse another decibel, so I covered my ears to avoid symptoms of PTCS at Pride. Stone Village. I turned the name in my mind; it sounded more like a place that would be holding protest signs, yet they strolled, smiling, past the protestors—a graceful display of acceptance in the face of graceless rejection. They looked like saints who might drink sangria.

King Avenue Methodist cut an impressive figure on the corner of Neil and King, and I wondered how I'd missed this place all through college. Once I noticed, it was hard to ignore the rainbow flags sticking out from the stone façade of the beautiful early-twentieth-century structure.

Entering through large wooden doors that reminded me of a storybook castle, I felt a little shaky at the scent of the place. (What is it about churches? They all smell the same—like all old ladies in the world made a pact to wear the same perfume, make loads of stale coffee and walk around fanning the scent into the walls. "Pearl, Gladys—we need some more perfume over here!") The sanctuary was lovely: all arched ceilings and stained glass and old wooden floors under thick-piled maroon carpet.

I sat in the farthest possible corner from the pulpit, smooshed at the end of the last pew. I grabbed a few hymnals and stacked them in the seat next to me, barricading myself from overly friendly passersby. I didn't want to talk to anyone. I may have appreciated the members' role in the Pride march, but that didn't mean I wanted to meet their eyes.

"Please stand for our opening prayer and hymns," invited the minister, a woman wearing a robe. I wasn't ready to make that kind of commitment, so I sat very much like I had at Word Alive, aka The Palms, the very picture of closed body language. I imagined one of those TV body language "sexperts"—like the one who diagnosed Brad and Angelina with romantic problems based on the fact that he was turning his head to cough—and what they might have to say about my body language. "Aha! Note her closed posture: arms crossed and legs crossed means she is distinctly uncomfortable, as if her date just told her he'd like to eat her brain." (That actually happened to me once on a dinner date courtesy of Match.com. He'd looked me straight in the eyes like he was going to confess love, and said in a low voice, "I want to taste your brain.")

A second pastor—this one a man sporting an impeccable white linen suit, blue tie, and flesh-toned ear microphone—delivered a homily that started in Matthew 10, detoured into a touching story about a closeted lesbian, and ended with an exhortation to Love Everyone, regardless of gender, sexual identity, nationality, ethnicity, family/economic status, and physical/mental/emotional ability. It took him less time to preach than Pastor Tom at The Palms had spent condemning the gay political agenda. Come to think of it, the entire fifty-minute service could have folded up nicely into the carry-on suitcase of my Word Alive experience.

Performing a quick emotional inventory during a post-sermon hymn: everything was surprisingly okay…until I noticed "Communion" listed next on the program.

My palms began to sweat. Communion and I were not on friendly terms. It seemed impossible that one cup could be weighted with so much guilt, and one morsel of bread with such anger, but for me these sacraments were the heaviest elements in the universe.

If communion wine and crackers were listed on the periodic table of my life, the chart would hang sideways. At various points since the Breaking, I had dipped the bread in the wine. But as oft as I had done these things, I had done them in memory of loss that had nothing to do with "backsliding" and everything to do with having nothing left to slide away from.

As the "righteous" went forward to receive, I cowered in my seat, as though the simple words, "This is my body, broken for you," could break me all over again. I closed my eyes in fake prayer until it was over.

The robed woman minister dismissed the congregation with the exhortation to, "Greet those strangers around us and make a new friend!"

I did not want to make a new friend. I wanted to make a hasty exit. But an older woman in a watermelon hat (complete with painted black seeds on the ribbon)—stopped me for a handshake.

"That is a very refreshing hat," I complimented, hoping to sidestep further conversation with her and her partner, a P.E. teacher-type with hip glasses and a crew cut. No luck. They chatted me up, and I half-expected Ms. Crew Cut to blow a whistle when she noticed my hand, still bandaged from physical therapy after my hand surgery.

"How did you hurt it?" she inquired.

"Wrong side of a closing door," I explained wryly.

She empathized with her own finger-smashing story. "It can take a long time to heal. Give it all the time it needs."

"Come as you are…in your car…" I recited the church billboard advertisement as Trent drove us toward Lake Erie for a summer holiday weekend with his parents. Smiling goofily at the idea of a drive-in church, I imagined it as a 1950s movie, with a pastor headlining instead of a film star, and communion wafers in place of popcorn.

"A drive-in church? This I have to see," said my mother-in-law, Becky, stirring her famous mojitos on the porch at sunset.

Calm and cheerful, Becky is the mother-in-law everyone wishes for; in seven years, I had never seen her angry. Incredulous that someone could be so calm, I once asked Trent if she ever lost her cool when he was growing up. "What about the time you filled the gas tank with water? Or took apart the computer? Or drank gasoline?" Nope. She was petite, with shoulder-length blond hair that had never been colored because, even at sixty-one, she had fewer gray hairs than I did. My theory was that she had good karma returning to her in the form of hair, perhaps from a former life as the Dalai Lama's favorite kitten.

"Hey Becky, if we put down the convertible top, we could go to church topless!" I laughed after she poured me a mojito.

"Here's to getting a tan at church," she said.

On Sunday morning Denny, my father-in-law, was calmly drinking his coffee and reading his Sunday paper when Becky and I started jabbering about the drive-in. He partially lowered his paper and said with an air of good-natured sternness, "You two better not become Holy Rollers on me."

"It's too late," I informed him. "In less than an hour we'll be holy rollin' right into church."

Denny shook his head and went back to the Cleveland *Plain Dealer*.

Dressed in bathing suits, cover-ups, and flip-flops, Becky and I climbed into the convertible and put the top down.

"Don't forget the sacrament of sunscreen," I reminded her, pulling an emergency bottle from the glove box.

We donned our sunglasses and set off for the bar parking lot/church. I drove, enjoying the feel of the hot July sun and the smell of summer: a heady mix of freshly-cut grass and tangy lake breeze. As we waved to sailboats when the bridge went up, I thanked the Godiverse that the Sickness had granted me a measure of independence for Independence Day—not that I was ever really free. Every day of activity came at a price: a number of days spent in bed in pain, often too exhausted to roll over and lift a glass of water. The Sickness never told me the cost in advance; it sent me a bill after the fact, payable immediately upon receipt. Still, I tried not to think of the bad days coming and appreciate the good times I was given, even if those days were tainted by joint pain and bearable (instead of debilitating) fatigue.

"Turn right here," Becky directed when we got close.

I was surprised to see a long line of cars backed up off the main road, inching forward for admittance. "I guess we aren't the only weekenders who appreciate a church where the dress code is, 'no shoes, no shirt, no problem.'"

A caddy look-a-like greeted us at the entrance. "Welcome," he boomed. "If this is your first time, turn your radio dial to 88.1 AM to hear the service, and instead of clapping, toot your horn. Here are your programs." He handed me two booklets and motioned where we should park.

After pulling into a spot, I fiddled with the radio dial, getting it right just in time for the pastoral greeting. If a tricked-out, camper-jobbie married one of those county fair food vendor carts that specialize in elephant ears and heart attacks, their love child would be this altar, er, stage. Distracted from introductory remarks by the sheer strangeness of sitting in my convertible, in a bathing suit, in front of a fold-out stage, I couldn't help but feel that cloggers were going to riverdance out, right over the pastor, in keeping with the county fair setting.

I privately hoped that fried Twinkies on a stick would be passed from car to car in lieu of the standard church meet-and-greet. Though fair food never materialized, all that was required to pass the peace was a quick wave to a neighbor through the windshield. "Church with a built-in shield," I observed to Becky.

After we sang two hymns, the pastor began his message. "Church need not be entertaining to be beneficial," he said through the radio.

"Bummer," I deadpanned. "I came for the fireworks display."

Throughout my church tenure, I'd encountered Christian jugglers, stand-up comedians, magicians, clowns, dancers, actors, mimes, puppeteers, strong men, fighters, musicians, and bands of every variety— heck, I'd *performed* four or five of those functions in church. Singers, acting troupes, acrobats, skateboarders, whistlers, motivational speakers... if the Christian label could be even vaguely applied to it, I'd seen it done.

It's not that I didn't enjoy such entertainment growing up, but looking in my rear view mirror at the drive-in, I wondered why everyone felt so compelled to make Jesus sing and dance, play rock 'n' roll, be faked-nailed to a cross, and transfigured via crane into a *papier-mâché* sky every Easter. If Jesus had to be dressed up so much, how would you recognize him if he walked in quietly through the back door?

Finishing his message, the pastor called for communion. *Communion. Two weeks in a row, ugh.* At least there wasn't the usual public shame in refusing communion at a drive-in; the car offered the benefit of privacy. Soon a small army of caddies dispersed amongst the cars, ferrying single-serving communion cups. In well-practiced order they approached each window, offering the communion in one hand and the offering plate in the other.

A single-serving communion packet, drive-in style, initially presented like a tiny coffee creamer. A thin, clear plastic layer embossed with the words, "He is Risen!" covered a cross-emblazoned cracker sealed between the plastic and the foil layer beneath. The foil peeled back to reveal a teaspoon of purple juice.

Fascinated by the ingenious little thing, I wondered aloud, "Who holds the patent on this and what is its official product code? 'Single-serve Jesus'? 'Individually-wrapped Christianity, conveniently packaged for the on-the-go believer'?"

Becky took communion while I stowed my souvenir in my cup holder. I didn't know it then, but that single-serving communion cup would be my constant companion for the remainder of my project, riding with me to every religious visit. Communion's meaning would do somersaults and back-flips, turning me upside down and—eventually—right-side up.

6

Persevere

"Sorry I'm late," I apologized to Bill at the street-level entrance to the Scientology center. I failed to add that my tardiness was his trendy religion's fault; after I saw the huge, vertical "Scientology" sign, I'd had to circle the downtown block for twenty minutes.

"No problem," Bill mumbled. He looked twenty-three, max, a fact belied by premature baldness. From his starched shirt to his shiny shoes, Bill wore black, reminding me of an undertaker at a very chic funeral home.

He ushered me into a loft-like, glass-enclosed space. Two-story windows flanked a front desk and seating area. An imposing bust of Scientology founder L. Ron Hubbard dominated the center of the room, while books, audio recordings, and DVDs by L. Ron Hubbard lined the perimeter. It's what Barnes & Noble would look like if there was only one author in the world.

Without pleasantries, Bill thrust a personality test, scantron sheet, and pencil into my hands. "I'll be back," he said, pointing me toward a desk in the corner.

I squinted at the 200-question test, trying to answer questions like: *Do you often make tactless blunders?* (Yes.) *Do you browse through railway timetables, directories, or dictionaries just for pleasure?* (Yes.) I was totally acing this "Oxford Capacity Analysis"!

The moment I finished the test Bill returned, prompting me to wonder if the desk had a convert cam for new recruits. Probably. He looked at my paper and said, "Follow me." He led me down a hall to an uncomfortably warm, windowless theater room that looked perfect for extended make-out sessions…or brainwashing. He fed my test into a machine that spit out a report. "Let's go over your test results," he said, emphasizing "test results" in the same tone a clinician would say "genital warts."

"These lines—" Bill indicated two descending curves with a pencil, "—show that you are irresponsible and depressed."

I looked at my scores in alarm. "A few minutes ago I could have sworn I was responsible and reasonably happy!" (Sickness and PTCS excluded.) He shrugged. It was all there in black and white: my personality was not only in bad health; it was practically at death's door.

"Exactly how accurate is this test?" I asked suspiciously. The test showed my physical energy levels as off the charts when at that very moment I was struggling against the urge to collapse into a pile of drool.

"Over 90 percent accurate!" Bill looked offended.

I cleared my throat and changed gears. "Why are you a Scientologist, Bill?"

"Simple," he said, jumping from his chair and circling the room in excitement. "Most people wander around their whole lives, confused about everything, but Scientology teaches you the straight line." He changed from pacing circles to figure-eights, and I had to turn my head to keep up with him.

"The straight line through life?" I sank deeper into the couch.

"Yup," he nodded. "Scientology helps you expand your personal power!" Bill made a large gesture, illustrating his personal power expanding. If he'd looked like an undertaker before, he now took on the manner of a casket salesman showcasing velvet-lined wares. "Scientology helps you be all you can be!"

Like the army? I imagined a parade of uniformed Scientologists saluting L. Ron Hubbard's marble bust.

"And how does Scientology help you do that, exactly?" I inquired, pen poised.

"Through the auditing process. It helps you overcome your deficiencies—" he pointed to my frightfully deficient Oxford Capacity Analysis—"and reach a state of clear."

Bill launched into a wandering tirade of explanation about "auditing" and "clear," much of which was incomprehensible. I pieced together that "auditing" was a little like psychotherapy without a licensed practitioner, and "clear" was when a practitioner traded in painful life traumas for the mental power of Einstein and the sex appeal of Marilyn Monroe.

"And how long does it take to become clear?" I asked, thinking how much I'd always admired Mr. Einstein's brain and Ms. Monroe's body. I could do some serious damage in a state of clear.

"At three sessions a week," he calculated, "it should take me about twelve years."

Yikes. I'm all for therapy, but twelve *years*? This guy was barely out of puberty; how could he need nearly two thousand hours of therapy? (I didn't dare ask the cost of becoming clear. I had the feeling if you have to ask, you can't afford it.)

"There are so many problems in the world," he exclaimed, pounding an overstuffed chair for emphasis. "Human trafficking! Drugs! War! Murder! Illiteracy! Scientology can help them all!"

"This has been very enlightening," I interrupted when Bill paused for a breath, "But I'd like to try out auditing for myself to really get a feel for Scientology."

Bill appeared to rein in his mental horses. "You can't just 'try out' auditing," he said, falling back into undertaker mode with crossed arms and a sour face.

Scientologists, it seems, don't just let you sign up for auditing willy-nilly. For the privilege of being audited (which, like drugs, is free the first time and expensive thereafter) I would need to commit to the following preparations: watching a two-hour video, sleeping a full eight hours, eating a healthful diet, and remaining drug-and-alcohol-free. The regimen sounded a lot like New Year's resolutions. We all know how well those go.

I squinted at him. "Does drug-free include medicine for a medical condition?"

"What kind of medical condition?" Bill asked skeptically.

"I'd rather not say," I would have gladly told him—if only I knew.

Bill pressed the issue to the point of extremity, asking me in four different ways what was wrong with me, getting closer to my face each time. A stranger who asks inappropriate questions should be prepared to be lied to.

"Gonorrhea," I declared. (I had never suffered from the condition and had been happily monogamous for years.)

Bill blinked twice and backed away. "Uh, okay...I think antibiotics are fine."

We set a date for my audit. "You really have to be seeking the truth," Bill advised.

"Oh, trust me," I assured him. "I am."

Two weeks later I found myself in the same theater room, watching a long-form Scientology video that reminded me of a college look-book; everyone seemed too serene, maybe drugged. The video implied that Scientology could give me everything from riches to love. "We have all the answers!" the narrative seemed to sing. "Follow us to fame and fortune!"

I feared I might fall asleep and wake up as, well, Bill. To keep myself awake, I jumped up and down on the couch a la Tom Cruise, just to see how it felt. (Just kidding. But wouldn't it have been cool if I had?)

I heard a staccato double-knock at the door, and an older gentleman entered. "I'm Al," he said in a heavy brogue. "I'll be conducting your audit." Al wore wire glasses; he had grey, curly hair and an unassuming manner. He was missing a few teeth; apparently a state of "clear" didn't come with a dental plan.

We walked down a long hall to an elevator. Scads of professional-looking people buzzed about, toting notebooks as though going to class. I noticed several women wearing colorful head scarves with tribal prints.

"Who are those ladies?" I whispered.

"They're Muslims on a weekend retreat to practice co-auditing," Al explained.

"You can be a Muslim and a Scientologist?"

"Oh, yes. Scientology is a complimentary practice to any religion—or no religion at all."

We arrived at another windowless room, this one much smaller than the theater. In the manner of a crime-drama police interrogation, Al and I sat facing each other on opposite sides of a desk. I wondered if he would pull out a spotlight and demand, "Where were you at 6:31 p.m. last Thursday?"

Al explained the auditing process: I was to sit with my eyes closed while he read instructive statements to help me channel my memories of painful traumas. As I recalled details of these memories, I would recite them aloud.

"Are you ready to begin?" Al adjusted his glasses.

"As ready as I'll ever be," I felt a curious mix of excitement and fright.

"Go to your earliest memory of discomfort or pain," Al said.

I assumed the present moment wasn't early enough.

"Go to your earliest memory of discomfort or pain," he repeated.

I latched onto the discomfort idea and remembered aloud, "My mom is pulling me from the bath. I'm cold." Al instructed me to describe the scene with sensory detail. What did I see/smell/hear/see/touch in the memory?

Dude, I was three years old, I thought. I *barely even knew what my toes were.* But I played along, describing the scene once. Al told me to go back to the beginning of the memory and start over, describing it again, and again, and again with more layers of detail each time. I did my best, but knew I was fabricating things just to please him. By the twelfth go-around with my faux memory, I became a smidge angry. This was a waste of time.

"I'm making all this stuff up!" I opened my eyes in frustration.

"Eyes closed!" he barked. "Back to the memory."

I decided to go with it—how much longer could it last, anyway? I closed my eyes and relayed the pretend memory a thirteenth time: the floor was still hard and cold; my mom was singing; I felt droplets of water clinging in my hair.

"What color are the shower tiles?" Al asked.

"They're yellow," I snapped. "The tiles are light yellow." Without ringing any internal warning bells, a new memory—a darker one—surfaced. Inexplicably, tears formed and rolled down my cheeks.

 Why are you crying?" Al asked.

I don't know. Is this a real experience, or have I just been cooped up in this building for too long?

"I'm in a different bathroom," I stumbled.

"How old are you?"

"Eighteen."

"Go toward your memory of the pain, and tell me what you see."

I've been home from my freshman year of college for two weeks. I'm in the bathroom in the house where I grew up. The air is hot and sticky. My sister Marcia is in the shower, and I'm leaning against the sink, dreading what I have to do. I have to tell her our parents are getting divorced. I don't want her to find out alone; I want to face this with her . . .

Al interrupted, "What do you smell?"

"Shampoo. My sister's shampoo," I recalled in more detail than I'd prefer. Even though it had been years since I'd accessed this memory, I definitely wasn't making it up. I wanted to open my eyes, extract myself from the interrogation room and the memory, run down the hall, and bang the elevator's down button. But I also wanted to know where this audit was going. Curiosity won.

"Go on," Al encouraged.

Marcia turns off the shower. She steps out wrapped in a towel and sees my stricken face. Even at twelve, she is so little. I want to protect her.

"I told her about the divorce. I hugged her and we slid down the bathroom wall together, sinking to the floor in tears." Eyes closed, I felt the experience all over, just like it was happening again. When Al told me to go back to the beginning of the memory and start again, my eyes flew open. "No way."

He removed his glasses and rubbed his eyes.

"You're free to leave, but based on my experience, you're near a breakthrough. Close your eyes and go back."

I backtracked a second, third, fourth, and fifth time. On the sixth recitation, something resolved, a key clicking in a lock. The discomfort of the memory was replaced with calm.

Al noticed. "What just changed?"

I answered honestly. "The memory isn't forgotten; it's just…different. I can see through it to the before and after. I see it made me stronger."

He smiled. "I think we're all done here. How do you feel?"

I felt unsettled. Though eminently professional, a dude I didn't know had just been all up in my stuff. Emotional and physical fatigue threatened to overtake me.

"I'm surprised, more than anything. Auditing feels real, raw." I paused. "But it's not something I plan to repeat."

"That's too bad—you did very well, especially for your first time." (If that was doing well, I didn't want to know the definition of "bad".) "It gets easier. If you persevere, auditing will be the best thing you ever do."

I didn't share my private thought about more auditing sessions: *Quitting what drains you is the only way to persevere.*

"Hi! How are you, honey? I had this dream last night…" my mother babbled when I answered my cell in the car. She was upbeat as usual, but I emitted a strangled guttural noise that she correctly translated as, "Mo-om, help!"

"Rebecca Lynne, are you driving? I can hear you driving. Pull over right this minute!"

A greater person than I might have been thankful to be able to drive to the doctor after being in bed with the Sickness for a full week following my Scientology audit, but I was not a greater person. I was a sick person who would've been throwing a Texas-sized hissy fit if rage wasn't so damn exhausting.

I pulled over. My mother is a loving woman, but you do not cross her when she uses your middle name, even if you are twenty-nine years old and hundreds of miles away.

"What happened, sweetheart?"

Her voice unstitched me. "I'm so tired," I cried, tears falling so hard and fast I couldn't squeeze out any other words. I collapsed over the wheel, choke-sobbing.

"Mom, I'm so tired that I can hardly roll over in bed," I managed to force out. "I've been wearing the same clothes for days; there's food rotting on the dishes in my sink. I'm on my way to see to another doctor who is just going to tell me there is nothing wrong with me. He's just going to say I'm depressed. Then I'm going to start crying because I'm not depressed, but then he won't believe me because I'll be crying. The only thing I'm depressed about is not being able to stay awake for more than a few hours at a time. Why can't anyone tell me why I'm so tired and in pain?"

My mother made supportive noises. I wiped my face on my sleeve, leaving behind clumps of days-old mascara.

"I can't do this thing, Mom, I can't do this project. There is no way I'll be able to finish it feeling like this. I'm quitting the project. I'm quitting my job. I'm quitting *everything*."

I waited for her usual motherly sympathy, but she was silent. When she finally spoke her voice was stern and a little too quiet for comfort. "You're not quitting anything. You are going to persevere."

"Persevere? *Persevere?* Are you serious? I can barely work, Mom."

Her voice softened. "I know honey, but you're going to get through this. There is a Great Cloud of Witnesses cheering you on." *Oh boy, here we go. Mom's busting out the Bible, just what I need.* "You remember that verse 'since we are surrounded by so great a cloud of witnesses, let us also lay aside every weight and run with endurance the race set before us'?" (How could I not? The entire Bible was drilled into my brain prior to eighth grade.) "Like I was saying, I had this dream last night, which is why I called you. Your Grandpa Dally was in a packed stadium, running a race. Just as he was crossing the finish line, he looked at me and said, 'Persevere. Keep running. Cross the finish line. Persevere.' I think that dream was for you."

It was my turn to be silent. Despite the Bible verses, something about the dream felt otherworldly and smacked of truth. I stopped crying long enough to ask, "If the dream was for me, why would you have it?"

"I don't know, honey. Why don't you ask God yourself?"

When I hung up the phone, I was already fifteen minutes late to my doctor's appointment and figured I had nothing to lose by following my mom's advice.

"Fine," I spat toward the roof of the car when I got back on the road. "If you're going to run around giving my mother dream messages, I'd like a sign. An unmistakable sign. A sign that is obviously for me. I need a sign, Godiverse. Got it?"

A short while later, at the doctor's office, I waited at the check-in window. When no attendant appeared after ten minutes, I searched for a way to alert the staff, finally deciding to crack the office door and call for someone.

"Excuse m—" I started, but my voice halted mid-phrase.

Directly in front of my face was a dry erase board. Written on the board in blue marker, underlined twice, and in all caps—as though the Godiverse was yelling at me—was one word: PERSEVERE.

"Miss, are you all right? Miss?" I heard the worried nurse, but it was like she was speaking under a deep sea from which I had just emerged.

I couldn't have answered her anyway. I was too busy staring, slack-jawed, at my sign.

7

Knocking

ap-rap-rap. Three loud knocks on my driver's side window woke me. Disoriented, I remembered where I was: a rest stop parking lot in West Virginia. I'd fallen into a dead sleep over my steering wheel.

"You okay, miss?" a guy with shoulder-length dark hair asked me through the glass. He wore a ball cap and shirt that identified him as the rest stop's janitor. Between the outfit and his transparent green eyes, he didn't look too threatening. I rolled down the window.

The janitor took in my ashen face, the imprint of the steering wheel on my cheek. "Are you going to be okay to drive home? Do you want me to call someone for you?"

"No," I said, smiling a fake smile. "I'm okay."

He shook his head in disapproval, dark hair moving in the wind. "I hope you don't mind me saying so, but it's not safe for you to be sleeping here like this, even in broad daylight. Does your mom know you're out here all alone?" He checked my hand for a ring. "Or your husband? I don't think he'd like it much."

"Thanks for the advice. I'll be more careful."

"You do that," His eyes searched my face in concern. I felt he could see everything I was so busy hiding from the world. "I'd hate to see you get hurt."

Too late, I thought, rolling up the window and starting the car.

Winding my way from the rest stop in West Virginia through rural Ohio for the remainder of the day, I stopped at lumberyards to hawk my lubricated nails. Running only on coffee and resolve to make it back to my own bed, I followedUrsula the GPS's electronic directions listlessly, barely registering my surroundings until near dusk, when the roads began looking familiar even though I was still two hours from home.

Bridgeville. My heart flip-flopped in surprise, *Bridgeville Christian School*, where Josh the bartender and I had learned to spell, do math, and follow Christ. Where I'd learned from my teachers and friends and parents exactly what it meant to be a Bible-believing, Holy-Spirit-filled Christian who lived out her faith every day in every way.

"Better to not know the truth than to know it and turn away from it," they'd all said. "Turn away from the truth and God will spit you out of His mouth." The original text in Revelation 3:16 indicated God would "spew" or "vomit" out those who turned from the truth, as many a chapel speaker had explained ominously.

To me, Revelation 3:16 had always seemed the sad corollary to the love and life everlasting in John 3:16, the final, disgusting resting place for everyone who didn't believe. It's not a place I'd ever intended to end up.

How could I *not* stop, *not* turn into Bridgeville's deserted parking lot?

Rays of sunset lit up the school's red metal roof like a beacon, illuminating the empty sign at its entrance. All the sign's large block letters had been removed or stolen when the school had closed its doors for the last time in the wake of a bad economy.

Looking at the blank sign, I felt love and loathing in equal measure. Love because this had been such a beautiful, safe, almost charmed, place to grow up; loathing because all the beautiful memories were distorted by the idea of a God who would be disgusted at the person I'd become, even to the point of vomiting.

Getting out of my car, I walked a slow circle around the school's brick façade. In the dying light, I noticed dented fences, growing weeds, peeling paint. Cupping my hands against the windows, I peered down empty hallways. I saw the girl I once was: pigtails and braids and perms and bad bangs and chunky layers. She was always praying. Praying God would never leave her, never dreaming that she would leave God.

I knocked on the metal red doors of the chapel, even though they were chained. It seemed that if only these doors would open, everything could rewind; I could go back to before the Breaking—when I believed with the faith of a child.

When the doors didn't open I banged on them with both fists, as if someone inside could unlock my way back to peace.

There was no one but me.

Too exhausted to stand any longer, I sat on the blacktop. The dusk grew until I was crying in the dark. I looked out into the night through my tears as moonlight reflected off Bridgeville's empty sign. I stared at it for a long time, until I realized I no longer wanted to rewind the tape to find what I had lost.

I wanted to change the ending.

When I found a Christian Spiritualist church that advertised, "Spiritualism meets Christ Consciousness," and promised a day full of Christian energy work and a light lunch, I couldn't resist. All that and a side of hummus? Sold!

I checked in at a table in the church kitchen. Incense and patchouli overruled kitchen bleach to create a scent that was distinctly hippie—minus the pot smoke. "Here are your change and your number," an elderly woman said over her reading glasses, handing me a paper slip bearing a #107 stamp—(*Like the deli counter?*) "The number is for your fifteen-minute readings," she explained. "You sign up for different energy workers in the sanctuary; they'll call your number when they're ready for you." She shooed me toward a wooden door that I assumed led to the main activity.

The sanctuary itself was traditional enough: stained-glass windows framed by white walls that soared into arches supported by dark wooden beams, and a huge pipe organ front and center. But the activity—well, I tried not to look shocked, but my eyes widened anyway. Around the central wooden pews, all manner of psychics* and energy workers sat at small card tables using Bibles, tarot cards, and crystals to impart spiritual guidance to seekers. I'd entered an alternate dimension, where divination and Christ combined to create a haven for all things spiritually strange to me: one fortune-telling nation, under God, indivisible, with liberty and communing with dead relatives for all.

The same painting of Jesus that hung in my mother's bathroom (Jesus as a divine shepherd, surrounded by lambs) adorned the altar, but this Christian Spiritualist Jesus, whom I quickly termed *Psychic Jesus* in my mind, was not part of the Trinity I grew up with. That Trinity frowned upon divination, Ouija boards, alien abductions, and crystals of all kinds because they fell neatly under the label *Witchcraft*.

Truth be told, I'd always found something incongruous about Jesus in Mom's bathroom, but seeing Psychic Jesus amongst crystals and mediums was a whole new level of cognitive dissonance. I had never imagined a Christianity deep and wide enough to hold both Pentecostals and psychics.

---

* I later found out many Spiritualists would not refer to their gifts or practices as "psychic" in nature.

I rolled with Psychic Jesus, though. I personally had nothing against the practices that used to get people burned at the stake—and still might get you exorcised of demons, depending on where you went to church. Frankly, I was curious about the whole psychic/medium/energy healing thing because (A) if there was any actual healing going on, the Sickness and I were so there, and (B) several years earlier I'd started feeling an Energy (for lack of a better term) when the nerves in my scalp, neck, and shoulders began occasionally to tingle and buzz like someone was stroking my skin there. It came in waves, bouncing off random strangers at odd intervals: a grocery store clerk, the sandwich delivery guy, a girl in a cell phone store. Though feeling the Energy had become a regular occurrence, it was unpredictable. I'd lackadaisically hoped to run into someone—anyone!—who could explain what the Energy was and what to do with it, but it's not the type of thing you go around telling people about, is it?

Maybe I'll bring the Energy up with the Christian Spiritualists, I thought. *Given the amount of leather fringe and gemstones in my immediate vicinity, I'm sure no one will judge me.*

Desiring to have the full Spiritualist experience and get my fifteen dollars' worth of fifteen-minutes sessions, I signed up for everything that had availability. Reiki healing? Check. Mediums? Check. Qigong? Check. Dream interpretation, "angel whispers," Tarot reading? Check, check check.

"Number 107," shouted someone from the rear of the sanctuary. I turned around and raised my hand. The shouter was a strapping guy, maybe nineteen, with a huge amount of hair circling his head. (If I had that kind of volume, I'd be a Pantene model.) He wore jeans belted around his knees, and boxers featuring cartoons. His hulking frame easily filled out an oversized tee. He approached me, heavy gold and diamante chains clanking together.

"Are you ready for Reiki?" he asked, towering over me but sweet as pie. His nametag read "Maverick" in bold print. I nodded and trailed behind him.

Friends, when I signed up for Reiki I never imagined following Maverick into a little room off the sanctuary; nor did I envision said room to contain two of Maverick's closest bad-ass looking buddies (Goose and Cougar?) and a massage table covered with a woven blanket.

Goose slammed the door shut with a Cheshire cat grin.

"Please sit on the table and remove your sandals," Maverick asked.

I gulped. *First the shoes...* "Ummm," and stumbled to do as requested, reasoning that I was in a church, and they were *probably* former altar boys.

"Now, lie down, close your eyes and relax," Goose said, moving toward me. I lay down. I squinted. I did not relax.

"You're so tense, lady," Cougar admonished, waving his hands over my forehead. "Are you under a lot of stress or something?"

Why yes, gentlemen. As a matter of fact I am.

"I'm infusing healing energy into your foot chakra," Goose whispered soothingly, moving his hands closer to my bare feet.

Just as I determined that this spiritual adventuring had gone too far and plotted to flee the scene, an angelic, white-haired oldster rose and emerged from a far corner. She was so tiny I hadn't seen her before.

She hobbled over and hovered her hands over my forehead. "I'm channeling energy into your crown chakra," she said. "Relax." I relaxed— almost. *Nothing truly awful could happen to me in the presence of Reiki Grandma. Right?*

Over the next quarter-hour, Grandma, Maverick, and Co. infused all my chakras, sometimes one a time, sometimes in tandem. For the finale, they surrounded me on all sides. It was a very long few minutes.

"Namaste," said Goose with a slight bow at the conclusion of my session, meaning: *The Divine in me bows to the Divine in you.*

"Namaste," I replied, meaning: *I would like to leave now.* I gathered my sandals and went back to my pew, resolving to evermore avoid small rooms where the men outnumbered me three to one, even if there was a grandmother involved.

Waiting several minutes for my next session, I imagined what might happen if my dad circa 1990 walked into this sanctuary. I thought he would likely swing the yellow plastic bat around and throw everyone out, in the manner of Jesus and the money changers in the temple. From the armchair (or pew, as it were) of the future, it seemed inevitable that uptight, overprotective, über-religious Dad of twenty years ago would eventually morph into easygoing chill Dad circa 2011, but I doubt anyone would have predicted the shift back in his demon-rebuking days. If Dad had a soundtrack back then, it would have been a military march, Soldier of the Lord edition. But by 2011 he'd become much more Kenny G than dictator.

I attributed this change in large part to Franciscan monks, bless their celibate hearts. A *Monks, Live!* CD came into my father's possession when I was nineteen, right around the time he and my mother divorced. He went through a phase where he listened to chanting during his hour-long commute. I think we can all agree that, among other life changes, piping fifteenth-century religious chants through Honda speakers soothes the heart and starts one on the mellow path. Dad married my stepmother Edie, whose fun-loving, upbeat attitude probably helped even more with his serene vibe. It wasn't that Dad stopped being religious (whenever I visited him and Edie in Indianapolis I invariably ended up at a Bible-study potluck); it was just that the carnage left in the wake of how the church reacted to a Christian divorce toned his religiosity down about three hundred notches.

He may have lost his yellow bat, but he still had the Word of God for a sword, his faith as a shield, and one righteous mustache. (Everything else may have changed, but Dad's mustache would remain the same forever and ever. Amen.)

"Number 107," called a man in a striped pirate shirt and red bandana. Approaching his table, I mentally added an eye patch, peg-leg, and shoulder parrot to his look.

"Your angels are saying you need to 'Dance more'!" he informed me.

"Like a jig?" I questioned, desiring celestial clarity. If my angels were into dictating dance moves, I didn't want to offend them with the wrong ones.

The pirate tilted his head to hear their heavenly missive. "Dance the disco, baby," he relayed, demonstrating a seated version of Saturday Night Fever. "You're going to dance the *disco*."

I thanked him and excused myself, privately wondering if this particular disco-dancing pirate had {taken one too many nips below deck} or {ingested too much seawater}.

Shortly after my next session, during which a woman wearing a pentagram necklace told me, "I may be Wiccan, but I'm a Jesus fan myself. Jesus rocks!" and flashed me a double thumbs-up, as though Jesus had earned excellent movie reviews, I decided to leave. The incense/patchouli was giving me a headache. I was gathering my things when Pastor Judy, a hip, middle-aged spiritualist minister with short dark hair and a kind smile, called my number. She beckoned me toward the altar.

"Sit down," she invited, gesturing to the folding chair opposite her.

I sat, noticing that her table was placed directly in front of the Psychic Jesus painting. It seemed Psychic Jesus was watching over me placidly, petting his lambs and saying: *There, there, Reba, there's nothing to be afraid of.*

Between Pastor Judy and me was a closed black Bible, as though our session was normal pastoral counseling instead of a metaphysical encounter.

"I'd like to open in prayer," Pastor Judy stated. *Uh-oh.* Praying—both in general and out loud—was soundly in PTCS territory. My hands began to sweat. Pastor Judy offered hers, waiting expectantly. I felt like Psychic Jesus was looking over my shoulder, like, "Get on with it already," and I was so discombobulated that I mentally gave up my resistance. I wasn't going to pray myself, not out loud—no sir—but maybe I could let Pastor Judy pray for me.

The second before we touched, I was surprised to feel the Energy emanating from her hands. I bowed my head, only half-listening to Pastor Judy pray out loud and mightily, because I felt the familiar tingle buzzing through my arms, over my scalp and back down again, like a fountain cycling water through my nerves.

Pastor Judy's eyes snapped open, as if in psychic surprise or bad Botox. As she cocked her head and studied me, I had the eerie feeling that the whole Godiverse surrounded the two of us. It was like there were angels and—heck—maybe even a few ghosts standing at attention for what she was about to say.

"You are a Healer," she proclaimed, with an authority that stretched beyond the stone church and into the infinite. "You will heal with your words. You will heal yourself and you will heal others." She stopped, closed her eyes, and listened to a Voice I did not hear.

I waited, riveted by the energy flowing through my entire body, stronger than I'd ever felt it.

"You will be transformed like a phoenix," Pastor Judy foretold. "It has something to do with…huh." She stopped again, appearing to check her facts. "It has something to do with the number thirty."

Now there was nothing around us except her words; the altar faded, the chatter of the spiritualists quieted.

"The energy you feel is part of your healing medium; you are a gifted healer." Pastor Judy opened her eyes, shook her head at me and laughed a little. "Honey, if you're not using what you've been given, you're missing out."

I wanted to laugh and cry at the same time. *A gifted SICK healer? What kind of cosmic prank is that?*

She sensed my discomfort with the message. "A phoenix doesn't have it easy. It has to be burned up before it gets up." Pastor Judy peered at me. "Transformation. Rebuilding. These are the words for you. If you persevere, you'll be an entirely different person. Reborn."

Persevere. That word again.

She smiled broadly, patting my hand. "Please visit one Sunday; we'd love to see you for Fellowship."

And with that invitation she stood up, excusing me like we'd just finished having a nice chat over tea instead of an encounter that tipped my existence on its axis.

Part 2
Autumn

8

Kneeling

"You waiting for somebody?" asked a guy sitting two bar stools over.

"I'm waiting for a whole group of somebodies," I answered, looking his way. From his artfully waxed brows to his indoor sunglasses, he bore a striking resemblance to Mike "The Situation" from MTV's *Jersey Shore*. I consulted the restaurant's clock. "I don't think they're going to show, though. The meeting was supposed to start fifteen minutes ago."

"Vinnie," he offered by way of introduction, sliding himself and his Red Bull & Vodka over next to me.

"Reba."

Flexing one artificially-tanned arm, Vinnie swigged his drink. "What meeting? Sorority or something?"

"Ha. Funny guy. I'm waiting for the Omnipresent Atheist Society. According to the Internet, they meet here every Tuesday."

He clapped his hands and laughed like I'd made a joke. "Sounds like their version of a ritual is drinking beer. Maybe the atheists don't believe in being on time."

A passing waitress overheard our conversation and stopped. "The atheists? They changed their meeting to every other Thursday night."

"Okay, thanks." I turned to Vinnie. "That's my cue to go. Nice to meet you." I slid off the stool.

"Wait a minute—I'm confused. You don't look like an atheist."

I couldn't resist engaging. I enjoy any line of reasoning that equates physical appearance with religion, especially when issued by a guy who looks like his own faith might involve fist pumping and Jell-O shots. "Tell me, Vinnie, what does an atheist look like?"

He studied the ceiling. "Um, I dunno. Angry or something? I think of them protesting shit and burning bras."

I cleared my throat. "I think you've got your –ists mixed up."

Vinnie shrugged. "I'm Catholic myself. Not practicing, mind you. But you know how it is: once Catholic, always Catholic." He gave me an aggressive once-over. "To me you look more Catholic than atheist."

I couldn't help myself. "What does a Catholic look like?"

He didn't miss a beat. "Guilty."

"You're saying I look *guilty*?"

Vinnie drained his glass. "You look guilty as sin, sweetheart."

I laughed. I had to hand it to a guy who could deliver a compli-sult with a straight face, especially when his jeans were tighter than my own.

"Vinnie, I'm visiting a Roman Catholic church this weekend. Do you have any advice for me?"

He leaned in close and looked around like he was about to share a secret. "Listen. You find yourself an old lady, or a couple of old ladies, and sit right behind 'em. That way you can watch 'em, so you'll always know what to do, even if you aren't paying attention."

Vinnie sat back, looking very pleased with himself.

I considered this stacked wisdom. "Find an old lady and follow along… I'll try it."

I named this strategy Vinnie's Rule, and it works every time with every religion. If you ever use Vinnie's Rule and it saves you embarrassment, light a candle for him. Thanks, Vinnie, wherever you are. Have a Red Bull & Vodka for me.

"This is a confection of Christianity!" I said to my mother-in-law, Becky, on the sidewalk outside the Catholic cathedral downtown. "It's so pretty that even if it was your famous triple-chocolate cake, I wouldn't eat it."

Heads back, we stared up the Gothic Revival structure of grey and light brown stone. I counted six stained-glass windows reflecting morning light.

"Let's see what the Internet has to say about this building." I queried Google. "Completed in 1872, stone quarried from local counties… Oh, this is interesting: due to design changes, they had to tear down the original brick foundation and replace it with stone. Also, there were supposed to be two bell towers, but neither one has been completed."

"It does look a little lopsided with the tower on the left," Becky said, "but it's still pretty."

I looked up. Now that I'd seen the lopsidedness, I couldn't un-see it.

"Let's go in," Becky said. "I'm a little chilly."

"Whoa," I breathed when we entered the building with its massive main sanctuary. "If churches were beauty pageant contestants, Catholics would win evening gown every time."

I scanned the pews. "Do you see any little old ladies?" I whispered. Becky snickered; I'd already told her about Vinnie's Rule.

"There!" she spotted a grey-haired crew toward the front. We slid in the pew just as angels started singing above us. Okay, they were just regular, everyday people harmonizing in the pipe organ loft, but a pleasant shiver ran down my spine at the beautiful music. The Latin helped; I had no idea what they were saying, so I could just float along the melody.

As the processional and service started, Becky and I followed the grandma crew: sit, stand, sing, sit, kneel, pray, stand, sit, kneel, repeat—a process which felt a little bit like religion-themed Simon Says.

"Are you *smelling* this?" I checked in with Becky when incense assaulted my nostrils.

She looked a little wan as she pointed up. "You can see it!"

A mist of incense hung over us, thick as clouds gathering for a storm. I am allergic to a great many things, incense among them. This worked in my favor at Ohio State (post-Christian college, post-Focus on the Family). Since I couldn't inhale much more than a waft of scented candle, I never got into drugs. But it worked against me here at church. I started to hack, like Oxley after he has eaten forbidden garbage.

My mother-in-law patted my back as the old ladies looked to see who was making such a ruckus.

"It will diffuse," Becky promised. Diffuse it did, right into my lungs.

"Inhaler," I wheezed to Becky, who handed me my purse. I took a fast-acting allergy pill, a puff of inhaler, and covered my nose and mouth with the end of my long sweater, mimicking a child whose classmate has just ripped a foul one. I couldn't continue the religious Simon Says, so I sat back and let church happen around me: the priest gave a homily; people kneeled and prayed and crossed themselves. I watched, not moving but also not bothered by the proceedings, no more attached than if I were in a corporate lecture suffering Death by PowerPoint.

I could remain detached because I lacked any ties to Catholicism, unless you count the premarital counseling weekend required by our wedding officiant. The blessed Catholic weekend event was named the "Engagement Encounter," and we encountered our engagement in several poignant ways: soul-mate letter-writing, hours of listening to speakers followed by hours of discussion, and a seminar titled "The Effectiveness of Natural Family Planning."

Imagine a room full of young professionals—who value career building, sex, and happy hours—and you'll get an idea of the effect of this talk on our collective consciousness. Men were loosening their collars. Women were squirming. The doctors were rolling their eyes. At the break, I leaned into the girl next to me and said, "Can you believe this?" She gave me the evil eye, and I realized my mistake. *I had spoken to the only Catholic virgin in the room.* "My fiancé and I plan to use Natural Family Planning exclusively!" she huffed in the manner of a future PTA Mean Girl.

I answered with the best defense I could muster on short notice.

"I'm…Protestant!"

"Oh," she said. "*That* explains it."

In the pew, I smiled behind my protective sweater mask at the absurdity of that weekend, but at least it was a direct experience. As I looked back on my religious life at the narrative I'd been taught about Catholics— they may or may not be saved, their saints are too close to idol worship, there is no value to be gained in vain repetition of liturgy, their rituals get in the way of a relationship with God—I uncomfortably realized the Engagement Encounter was my *only* personal experience with the world's largest religious organization.

Catholicism was about as far away as I could get from the church of my childhood and still have Jesus at the front. If a full Catholic mass was an evening of food and wine pairings at a fancy restaurant, the church I grew up in was the kind of casual joint where you throw peanut shells on the floor and go home with balloon animals. *Which is why I'm not reacting with PTCS here,* I thought. *Catholic rituals aren't my triggers.*

This insight hit me just before the congregants flowed up to take communion, a Catholic ritual with more than enough trigger power to override any spiritual inspiration. Communion felt like divinely-approved discrimination. The idea that humans could use God to sanction rejection galvanized me with anger.

"Let's go," I whispered to my mother-in-law. Others shuffled forward; we shuffled out. "Sorry, Becky." I breathed the crisp air outside. "I couldn't handle any more incense."

Well, that's what I said. What I meant was: "I couldn't handle communion."

Which made me wonder: how often have I told myself I was escaping one thing only to realize I was running from another?

"Hi, Mom," I spoke into my cell while walking quickly from our house to the restaurant where I was meeting a friend. The days were getting shorter, so the evening was brisk.

"Hi, sweetie. How's your project? What's your next visit?"

I cringed. "The Omnipresent Atheists?" It might have been my imagination, but I think she thumped her head against the wall.

"The *atheists*?" I definitely didn't imagine the maternal guttural noise that translated: "Why God, why?"

"You're taking this project too far, Rebecca. Growing up wasn't so bad. What about all the good people, the good memories, the positive lessons?"

I should have stayed quiet, but instead I got mad. "What about the collateral damage to my identity and my faith? What about the religion that I crash into every time I go looking for God? Why do you think I have to do this project in the first place?"

Walking faster now, I tromped through the small piles of leaves gathering on the sidewalk.

"Maybe there's something else you need to face," Mom continued in a soft voice that took the force out of my anger. "Maybe something is keeping you from seeing the good things about church and how we raised you. I think it's easier for you to pin everything that went wrong on religion—than to think about what might be inside you."

"I'm trying, Mom. But it's hard to see a good cause where there are bad results."

"Stop. The results aren't *that* bad. You're successful at work, happily married. You have to remember not to throw the baby out with the bathwater. There are good things about church and religion in general, things you know firsthand."

"Uh-huh." I arrived at the restaurant and ground the toe of my leather boot on its brick foundation, kicking loose flakes of old mortar.

"It's easier to hang onto your hurt and bitterness than to work through it. There's a valid time and place for spewing garbage, but if you sit in the garbage long enough, it will poison you. Do you have reasons to have garbage? Absolutely! We all do. But then we have a choice. Do we stay where we are, or do we move on?"

"I'm trying to use this project to move on, Mom, but you're judging me for it."

"I'm not judging you. I'm trying to figure out how to entrust you to the Creator. Every time you tell me you're at one of those crazy places, I have to take a deep breath and tell myself, 'Continue to put her where she already is: in the palm of God's hand.'" Mom was quiet for a minute. "You may have been a victim, but you don't have to stay a victim for the rest of your life."

I remained taciturn, chipping more pieces from the restaurant's foundation. I didn't love what she was saying, but I knew my mother's words didn't come from an insulated bubble of Christendom. She was speaking from experience.

Mom had her own PTCS of sorts from her California years spent in an overbearing version of Christianity that required devout service, like cleaning the pastor's house, and unquestioning obedience. My parents were even told to delay having children for several years so they could better serve the ministry. But even these things didn't test their faith; that happened when the church attempted to cover up the sexual abuse of children by a congregation member who frequently babysat during services. The church's leaders didn't want to investigate to find out how many children might have been hurt, or to involve the police. They just wanted to keep up appearances. My parents and others who knew about the situation would not be silenced. They fought the church leaders and strong-armed them into prosecuting to the fullest extent of the law.

Even though their effort was successful, my parents were disillusioned. They moved across the country to disentangle themselves from the church. The events threw my mother into a crisis. She would kneel by her bed, growing more bitter by the day. "God, how could you let this person hurt kids?" She pounded her fists and cried into a pillow. "How could you let people in charge hide it?"

One day while kneeling in prayer, she had an epiphany. She saw that if she didn't choose forgiveness, she was only punishing herself. Somehow, my mother was able to recall the wonderful relationships and moments she had had in that church, and remember how many times God had touched her heart. Those things were real to her, even more real than the crimes. She didn't understand why God had allowed the abuse, but she also knew God wasn't a part of it. She had a choice: to be bitter or better.

And now she was offering that same choice to me.

I'd read that holding a grudge is like drinking poison and then waiting for the other person to die, but I'd never considered how complicit I might be in keeping myself bound up by PTCS. Did I like being angry? Was my grudge against bad theology and harmful churches shielding me from a greater truth—that there were things about myself that needed to change, too?

"Rebecca--are you there?"

"Yeah, I'm here," I said. "I'm at the restaurant and I need to get going. Let's talk tomorrow."

"Can you *please* try not to become an atheist in the meantime?"

"I'll try."

"And Rebecca? Thankfulness is the antidote to unforgiveness. Maybe you should give it a try. When you choose grace, grace chooses you."

Hanging up the phone, I looked down at my boots, which were now covered with flakes of mortar and dust. I kneeled to clean them off and found myself thinking of the Catholic cathedral I'd attended; its foundation had to be torn down so it could be reconstructed in stone.

Was I like that? Did the beliefs my parents taught me about God, the ones that were stacked one on top of each other Jenga-style, have to be destroyed so something stronger could take their place? And what about all the anger and bitterness I'd stacked on top of those beliefs?

I thought of the cathedral's towers that were never finished, and how I couldn't un-see the lopsidedness of the building once I had noticed it. Maybe faith was like that. If I could choose forgiveness, might I be able to rebuild something different, something better?

9

Expectation

"To the Omnipresent Atheists," said the guy at the head of the bar's lodge-style table, clinking drinks with his neighbors. The lights were low, and a stationary disco ball hung above , glinting light over all the room. He saw me enter and looked over, bringing everyone else's gaze with him.

I felt like a middle-schooler with braces, thick glasses, and a unibrow walking into the lunchroom (aka, Reba circa 1993). It's amazing how quickly certain situations can reincarnate much younger, less fashionable, and more tweezer-challenged versions of ourselves.

"Hi…" I gave a small wave. "I'm here for the Omnipresent Atheist meeting?" I gulped, remembering how I'd protested atheists' demonstrations and argued against them in creation debates. I'd joined hands with classmates and prayed for atheists' deliverance from their so-called logic. I'd tried to "help" them, and now here I was hoping they could help me.

"Welcome, fellow atheist!" cried a girl.

Um…not quite. I stood awkwardly, unsure what to do until the guy who had given the toast walked over.

"I'm Daniel," he stated, pushing his glasses to the top of his head. "The president of the group. Why don't you sit by me?" *Yes! An invite to the cool kids' table!* I thought. In his early forties with close-cropped dark hair and a heavy five o'clock shadow, Daniel did not strike me as the kind of person who smiled goofily for photos. He struck me as the type who would want to have a Deep Intellectual Conversation. An older gentleman scooted over to make room for me on the bench seat.

As we sat, I became physically incapable of holding in the truth.

"I'm not an atheist," I rushed, stumbling over the words. "I'm doing this yearlong religion project, and, well, I didn't think I should leave out the flip side. Atheism is the yin to religion's yang, you know?" Too late, I realized that I had just used a quasi-spiritual metaphor.

"We welcome everybody," said Daniel.

"We welcome everybody *open-minded*," corrected a young blonde gal mid-table, who was busily knitting a red scarf. "A couple of times, fundamentalist Christians showed up at our meetings wanting to 'save' us, and we gave them the boot." She stabbed her knitting needles at the air to demonstrate.

"As long as you're not here to convert us, you're good," added the older gentleman.

"I'm definitely not here to convert you. Hell, I wouldn't even know what to try to convert you to."

"What are you drinking?" Daniel asked.

"Vinho Verde, Pinot Grigio, house white. Whatever they've got, really. At home I drink the stuff from the box out of a mug, so I'm not really that picky."

Everyone laughed, which broke my internal tension. I thought back to Vinnie, who had said that atheists looked angry, and realized I'd expected anger too. Though there was a lively conversation going on about theists, no one seemed mad. It could have been any pub theology group, swapping out religion for science.

"Why did you decide to do a religion project?" Daniel asked.

"Post-Traumatic Church Syndrome," I sighed. "I'm trying to get over it."

He hooted. "Hey guys," he called. "This girl has Post-Traumatic Church Syndrome. Anybody else?"

The little crowd started laughing as several hands went up.

"I guess I'm among friends then!" I said.

"So, tell me about your journey," invited Daniel. We discussed our backgrounds and the places I'd visited. After about forty-five minutes, he sat back and looked at me. "My father would have loved your project," he said. "He was a Lutheran minister for over forty years. He also turned out to be an atheist, something I only found out shortly before he passed away in 1994."

"A stealth atheist?" I was aghast.

"I was shocked! I asked him how he reconciled not believing in God with his profession. He told me: 'To the old, infirm and dying, I can bring comfort. To the young, I can bestow rational thought. You know, one thing people never consider about atheism is that it gives us even more of a reason to be good people. This life is all we have. No second chances.'

"I've never thought about it that way," I responded. "I've always heard people use the argument that atheists can't have morals because they don't believe in eternal consequences."

"Hogwash," Daniel shifted in his seat. "If there's a reunion in the sky, none of us knows. It's all wishful thinking. But we *can* be a positive force right now."

"What if you're wrong, and there is a God or an afterlife?"

"That would be great," said Daniel, which was not the answer I'd expected. "I'd be glad to be proven wrong. Our point is—there's no way to know this side of a heart attack."

A girl with hipster glasses and a carefully distressed t-shirt interrupted our conversation, directing a question at me. "Did you ever consider that there might not be a God?"

"No," I answered truthfully. "The idea of a great big void isn't any easier for me to swallow than the concept of, say, an eternal, fiery hell."

I thought someone would immediately attack me for this view, but the discussion just moved on to what it was like to be an atheist in a theist society. It wasn't long before the Sickness exhausted me, so I said my goodbyes.

"I'm so glad you came tonight," Daniel said. "Even if you believe in God, you have an open mind and that's something we value. You're welcome any time. Let's connect on Facebook."

The next day I posted on Facebook about the atheists, and my wall blew up in a debate about my project. I called it "Team Reba vs. Team Jesus." Team Reba—my secular friends, book club, and everyone with a case of PTCS—sent supportive comments with messages that read like elementary-school grading stickers: "Way to go!" "Awesome!" and, "Wow!"

Team Jesus—hardcore believers and extended family members who will remain unnamed—was on a mission to expose my folly and make sure my "spiritual exploration" (a phrase in quotes, as if it were an alleged crime) ended at the foot of the cross. They sent messages that read like the PTCS-trigger handbook: "I am prayerfully concerned about the status of your salvation, Sister." "The Lord still loves you." "Repent!" and my personal favorite, "You are being deceived like Eve."

"Trent," I yawned,. "I found a great way to experience PTCS. I don't even have to leave the bed. I can just open my laptop."

"My wife, always finding the most efficient solutions," he said.

"You know what's weird? Some friends I thought would be behind me aren't, and others I expected crap from are supportive. I did get one interesting message from my seventh-grade teacher—remember I told you about her, Mrs. Easton? She wants to have dinner. I'd like to see her, but I'm afraid she going to try to 'save' me."

"There's only one way to find out."

I clicked reply and stared at the blank white screen. My mom had said thankfulness was the antidote to unforgiveness. Maybe being thankful for Mrs. Easton would be a good place to start.

I waited at a table by the restaurant's windows, overlooking a grove that blazed red and orange and yellow—trees dressed in fall finery before the nakedness of winter. A gust of wind blew, and leaves fluttered to the ground like colorful snowflakes.

"Ah!" Mrs. Easton cried when she spotted me, "my favorite student." After folding me into a long hug, she held me at arm's length. "You're not in middle school anymore."

Her hair was my first shock. I knew Mrs. Easton (Susan, as she quickly corrected me) as a short-haired redhead, but she now had long hair, pale as a moonbeam. If not for her heart-shaped face and huge, "I haven't seen you in fifteen years!" smile, I might not have recognized her. Instead of the dress I always pictured her in, she wore jeans and ample turquoise jewelry.

"I'm glad to see you, too," I said, hoping behind my smile that I would not live to regret this lunch. With the Sickness pulling, I didn't feel up to a conversation about my eternal salvation. If Susan tried to save me, I'd pray the Sinner's Prayer just so I could close my eyes and rest my head on the checkered tablecloth.

"Why don't we order, then catch up," I suggested. "Do you mind if I order a glass of wine?"

This question was an unscientific test. Susan had belonged to an even stricter congregation than my own. This kind worshiped Homeschool Jesus, who favored long skirts, especially denim, paired with white socks and athletic shoes. If your Jesus thinks the road to hell is paved with playing cards, you *know* alcohol is taboo.

Susan made a dismissive gesture. "Get whatever you want. If I wasn't driving, I might have one."

Hello, shock number two. We perused our menus, giving me a few minutes to reconcile this relaxed Susan from the rigid Mrs. Easton in my memory. In the museum of my middle-school self, I kept Mrs. Easton under glass alongside every belief and Bible verse I'd memorized at Bridgeville Christian School. She was a symbol for all the teachers and preachers who were disappointed in how I'd turned out. She was *not* the living, breathing person across from me who said:

"You must tell me about this project of yours. I am so interested. I want to know everything! Scientology, Buddhism, the drive-in church."

"W-What?" I stuttered, reeling as though someone had come into that middle-school museum and shattered the exhibits. The shock showed on my face.

Susan laughed. "Did you think I was here to try to change you?

"I, um…yes?"

"Oh, *please*," she drew the word into a sentence. "Honey, I've been through a lot in the past decade. What did you call it on Facebook…Post-Traumatic Church Syndrome? I have that and then some, but I still love Jesus. Do you still love Jesus?"

Being sassy to avoid answering, I retorted, "I don't know. What version of Jesus do you love?"

"I love a Jesus who has tattoos. Not only that; the God I love has *sleeves* of tattoos."

From Homeschool Jesus to Tattoo Jesus? My brain blinked: Unable to Load Mrs. Easton/Susan Version 2011.

Something cracked open inside me as I sat there staring at the teacher who represented a cacophony of voices telling me I was "a backslider fit for being vomited out of God's mouth." I was furious with these voices because they had taken my spirituality hostage. Looking at Susan, I realized the voices were no more real than a pre-teen Reba. I was letting shadows of former people hide out in my mind and tell me who God was or wasn't, who I was or wasn't, and what I should or shouldn't do.

Susan grabbed my hands and leaned in. "Rebecca, even in seventh grade you had this light inside you. For most of my kids through the years, faith was something their parents put on them, but with you it was different, almost like you were glowing from the inside because you were so connected to the Spirit. Wherever you've gone, whatever you've done, that light and that connection are still in there—even if you don't see it. So tell me about your fascinating journey."

"Mrs. Easton," I said, forgetting to use her first name. My eyes filled with tears. But these were not angry tears; they were thankful ones. "You're not at all what I expected, but you're exactly what I needed."

10

Saved

The driver next to me honked his horn six times in quick succession. Annoyed, I looked his way. "Miss, Miss!" He rolled pointed to my car's rear. "You've got a tire going flat."

"You've got to be kidding me." I opened my door to take a peek. *Inconceivable. This has to be a Guinness Book record.* At the nearest repair shop, I asked, "How fast can you fix this? I'm still a ways from home."

"Rush job?" he scratched his chin. "Under an hour. But it'll be $350.00."

"Charge it," I said wearily. "Whatever saves me from sleeping in a hotel tonight."

Pouring myself stale coffee, I retired to a cement-floored waiting area that smelled of motor oil and B.O. I'd been resting my head against the wall for the better part of an hour when a bell jingled with another waiting customer.

"Hi," I greeted, less because I wanted to and more because the small area made it uncomfortable to avoid him. He was a sturdy guy who looked like he had been a linebacker in college before retiring to desk life.

"Hey," he tried for a smile, but I could tell he was having a bad day.

"What are you in for?"

"Break-in. They smashed both windows and stole my stereo and phone."

"That sucks," I sympathized.

"The worst part is that I was parked in EmptyTomb Church."

"Really?" I asked. "Are you a member of EmptyTomb?"

He grunted. "Used to be. I even worked there as a videographer until the pastor tried to force the staff to tithe on our paychecks by telling us that was "God's will." He started firing people over it, so I quit. It's just one big production, a money-making machine."

"I hear you." He had no idea how much I understood, but I was too tired to tell him.

The mechanic jingled the door. "Reba Riley? You're ready to go."

"Good luck," I told my new friend. "Don't let that break-in break you."

"Is this a church or the United Nations?" I questioned through the windshield. The EmptyTomb Church was so massive it looked like Elton John could give a concert there. (Not that this church would host Elton John, no sir.)

I regretted my decision to add EmptyTomb to my list as soon as I walked into the lobby, where I could hear the ginormous praise band rehearsing and see the tables laden with books by megapastor Rick Smith. If Rick's politico smile on his many book covers inferred anything about the God he served, that God must ooze panache and eat Grey Poupon.

A menagerie of people—from babies to the elderly, with skin tones in every shade—crowded the halls. Their clothing style varied wildly, which made me wonder if some of the folks were confused about where they were going that morning: a pack of teenage boys with Justin Bieber hair and grunge clothes looked like they were heading to a concert straight from the service, while one sporty-fresh lady wore a pleated skirt and sneakers as if to say "Jesus is my doubles partner." A handsome black fellow in a throwback Shell Station uniform and blue jeans chatted up a dame who sported a cheetah-fur-trimmed jacket over knee-high leather boots.

I stepped into the main sanctuary, unprepared for how large it would be: rows of blue chairs stretched like an ocean. I chose a seat in the middle section near the camera guy, wondering if he had to tithe out of his paycheck.

Projected on huge dueling PowerPoint screens, a service countdown clock unnerved me. *Church was beginning in two minutes ten seconds, nine seconds, eight seconds…* I felt like I should be disarming a bomb. Between the screens a massive stage was set up like a Broadway musical, complete with a light bar that looked more expensive than my college degree.

At T-minus two seconds, the lights went down and creepy music filled the auditorium. I'm not talking PTCS-spooky, but full-on *horror music* spooky. A frightening voiceover of Psalm 23 began. Now, I've never considered "The Lord is my shepherd" to be an alarming verse, but when paired with an angry voice, sinister music, and a dark room, it became terrifying. I was frozen in place by the weirdness of it all, barely breathing.

The words, "Experience the terror… Feel the horror… Face your worst nightmare" flashed over both screens, with images of red eyes, a woman screaming, and children singing "I know a secret." This megacreepiness was followed by an advertisement for an anti-Halloween theater production.

If this church's goal was scaring people into heaven, it was doing a bang-up job.

The spotlights flashed on. The pianist gustily played a riff, bringing the congregation to its feet and signaling the huge choir—I counted nearly seventy members—to sway for the opening song. "Jesus!" the sopranos floated; "Jesus!" the baritones echoed; "We're here for Jesus!" they harmonized together. "Are you here for Jesus?!" the music minister yelled jubilantly, as if verifying the reason for our attendance.

I remained seated, feeling more nauseated by the minute.

A muscle man to my left was excitedly raising both hands to the heavens, trading high-fives with the Holy Ghost. To my right, Leopard Coat Lady stepped out of her pew to spin when the Spirit and music so moved her. A guy in front of me did an improvised "Pharaoh-Pharaoh" dance. "Satan be gone from here," he commanded with authority, as though Satan had been trying to block his dance moves.

The buildup went on for half an hour before Pastor Rick Smith graced the stage. From the thunderous applause that greeted his arrival, you'd think he was Jesus resurrected.

"How many of you believe five thousand people will be saved at the coming revival?" Pastor Rick shouted. The crowd roared.

"I believe!" yelled a short, middle-aged brunette to my left, punctuating her words with large hops. Her daughter, who looked about eleven, sat directly next to me. As the pastor talked on the mother grew visibly more excited, alternating between speaking in tongues and shouting "Amen!" The daughter visibly shrank into her seat.

I had the urge to grab the girl's hand and run to a place where she could order ice cream and I could have a very strong drink.

"Hell is REAL!" Pastor Rick yelled. The tween was now practically curled in a ball. If she hadn't been next to me, I would have bolted. But I felt protective of her, as though by simply sitting there I could shield her. I felt the PTCS symptoms all over: elevated blood pressure, rising nausea. I couldn't help but be reminded of the guy whose windows had been smashed in this church's parking lot; I felt like the pastor was taking a sledgehammer to me personally.

The pastor stomped around with a red face, the huge dueling screens rendering him the world's biggest, scariest oompa-loompa. "You must be SAVED!" he shouted.

I agreed with him; I needed to be saved, all right. Saved from his service.

"Take out a paper and pen!" he decreed. Pockets rustled. "God told me each person in this congregation needs to save twelve people from hell this year. Make a list of everyone you love and look hard at this list. Every person on that list is going to *burn in hell* if you don't do something today!"

That did it. I grabbed my purse and ran to the bathroom, mentally apologizing to the girl for leaving her there alone. But even in the bathroom I couldn't escape the pastor's voice piped in on high volume. "If you don't invite those people to church, they're going to hell. And their *blood is on your hands!*"

I barely made it into a stall before I threw up my breakfast.

"How many people are you going to *save* this year?" Pastor Rick yelled through the speakers as I sank to the white tile floor in the stall, shaky from heaving.

One. I thought. *I hope to save exactly one.*

"You know, for a holiday that's supposed to be about attracting the goddess of wealth, Diwali sure seems to be repelling money right out of my bank account," I muttered to Erin on the phone while clearing my wine bar to make room for an altar. "I had to spend forty bucks to prepare for today's Hindu New Year."

"Isn't it a little early for the New Year?" Erin asked. My roommate at Ohio State, she had moved to Tennessee after college. I loved her in spite of the fact that she looked like Giselle the supermodel and had more energy than Tony Robbins on Red Bull. We talked as often as we could.

"Different calendar. Hey, I have to get going. I still have a bunch of preparation to do before going to the temple tonight: buy fireworks, trace *Rangoli* on the floor, decorate my shrine…"

"Who are you and what have you done with my best friend?"

"No time to chat. The sari store opens in an hour. Talk tomorrow!"

Since Diwali was a labor-intensive holiday, I was thankful the Sickness had given me a good day. (I'd been awake for a full four hours in a row!) I felt the same joy and excitement of preparing for Christmas with one notable difference: the goddess Lakshmi was a bit more terrifying than Sweet Little Baby Jesus. I mean, this woman had the power to give or take away my wealth and came equipped with more breasts than hands, so I did my best to please her:

1. **Clean my house.** Partial check: I only got to the kitchen and living room.

2. **Place mustard oil lights around my home to attract Lakshmi.** Partial check: improvised. I smeared yellow mustard on candles.

3. **Set off fireworks.** FAIL. Problems: A) Lack of readily-available fireworks in Ohio in October. B) Setting off fireworks downtown is illegal. C) My leftover July 4 sparklers failed to ignite. Instead, I watched authentic Diwali fireworks on YouTube.

4. **Trace *Rangoli* (lotus patterns) on the floor with chalk and fill with powder.** Partial check. Sidewalk chalk did not work on wood floors, so I put a piece of paper on the floor and drew on it. Since "powder" was not otherwise specified, I grabbed chili powder, which caused Oxley to sneeze violently and spread chili dust all over the living room.

5. **Open doors and windows to let Lakshmi in.** Partial check: windows only. It was chilly and Oxley might try to escape.

6. **Decorate shrine to Lakshmi to attract prosperity.** Check. I created a lovely altar on our wine bar, hoping Lakshmi would enjoy a glass of chardonnay on Diwali like Santa enjoys cookies. My altar included candles, fruit, flowers, cash, and mustard. I am nothing if not thorough.

7. **Finalize all account books to be ready for the start of the new financial year.** FAIL. No holiday is worth that much effort. Instead, I exerted the powers of online bill pay.

8. **Exchange gifts of nuts and sweets.** Partial check. We did not have nuts, so Trent and I exchanged granola bars.

9. **Wear new clothes.** CHECK! But this one took a little more doing. I fell in love with a satin and chiffon sari that, while entirely impractical for work, made me feel exotic and sexy and… temple ready? The kind sari shopkeepers assured me that I was. The woman who dressed me murmured instructions about the elaborate pinning in a heavy accent, "Thirty-five pins…get all out before take off!" I stood perfectly still to avoid the pins while a second woman fussed to arrange my sari just so. The first woman draped me in jewelry and bracelets while I half-heartedly protested. *What am I going to tell Trent?* I worried. *"The outfit was cheaper than a trip to India?"* But it was all so incredibly lovely . . . and the shopkeeper said she would give me a discount . . . and then I was taking out my credit card.

I twirled in front of the mirror, thinking how I had always envied sari-wearing Hindu women for their tantalizing lack of body shame about baring their midriffs at the mall. Toned or ample, supple or saggy, they promenaded in public wrapped in gauzy fabrics, strutting their stuff like colorful butterflies, stomachs exposed between the sari top and skirt, as if to say: *So what if I've had a few kids! Stretch marks are a point of pride!*

My midriff was bare under the gorgeous sheer wrap, and my sari's intricate blue-and-red beadwork glittered and sparkled madly. I was an exotic princess. I was a Bollywood movie star. I was Hindu Bride Barbie. I was…shockingly overdressed.

As in, wearing-a-tuxedo-to-wash-the-car overdressed. I furtively surveyed the people in the temple parking lot, who were all wearing *jeans*.

But I had already spent the money on my outfit, so I pulled myself together Scarlett O'Hara-style, and marched my bejeweled behind right through the temple door while giving myself a pep talk: *I am fierce. I am fearless. I am…* totally unsure whether to wash my feet in the little foot shower in the coatroom.

Okay, so the pep talk fell apart as soon as I got through the door. Since I knew I would soon lose my nerve, I tore off my shoes and dashed around the corner, nearly colliding with a short, stout, shirtless Indian gentleman wearing a loincloth. It was a long loincloth—to his feet—but "loincloth" was the first word that came to mind. Well, that and "Buddha," because he looked exactly like one.

"Welcome!" he beamed.

I explained that I was the woman who had called ahead, and could he please direct me to the priest?

"Speaking."

"Is my dress okay? I wasn't sure what to wear…"

"Traditional dress is perfect," he smiled.

I was so relieved I almost hugged him. Instead I took him up on his offer of a quick tour, and within two seconds, I felt like I'd stepped straight through to India, minus the twenty-four-hour flight and jet lag. There were more shirtless men in loincloths, a few in outfits that resembled white togas with decorative sheets thrown over one shoulder, and several wearing traditional "everyday" garments. Many, including my guide, Shri Kyran, had markings on their foreheads—like a more elaborate version of what Christian churches do on Ash Wednesday. "To signify the gods we follow," he explained, adding that this temple served a wide range of devotees from all over the world. I tried and failed to imagine a single Christian church in India that could meet the needs of the gazillion brands of Christianity.

"How many gods and goddesses are there?" I asked.

"Ah, very good question. Many Hindus will say there are ten or a hundred or a thousand or 330 million, but there is really only one God."

"One?" I said, baffled, because there were at least ten statues of different deities in my direct line of sight.

"Only one."

The temple was set up in an octagon, with each wall housing a different god/dess behind a glass wall, like a very large jewelry display case. If there were only one God, why were there eight walls? And two extra statues? And a fountain? On our tour, we had walked counter-clockwise around the perimeter to greet each god/dess, and devotees were doing the same, bringing gifts (like on my home altar!) and bowing, even prostrating, before the statues.

"It certainly looks like they are worshiping multiple gods."

He reflected for a minute. "The gods and goddesses are different faces of the one God, like different personality aspects of God. You are familiar with Catholic saints, yes?"

"So...like how some Catholics relate to Mary as the divine mother, some Hindus relate to the goddesses?"

"Yes. People need different representations to relate to the Divine."

I considered Shri Kyran's words as we continued greeting the gods, which I accomplished with a reverent bob of my head and slight bow. He explained that many people had trouble with the idea of God as a father, especially people who had endured drop-out dads or abuse. I was struck by the idea of a female God; there seemed something terribly lacking about a patriarchal male God who was ever-ready to smite you but also the embodiment of Love.

I liked all of the god/desses once I got used to their snaky arms, squat hips, and multiple appendages. But my hands-down, write-a-postcard-home favorite discovery was a little room with a fountain in the center and just enough space for us to shuffle single-file around it.

"What's this?" I whispered to Shri Kyran as we approached.

"This is our monument to the invisible God who cannot be seen, who is too vast to be contained."

Well. Knock me over with a feather: This was a God I once knew very, very well. "Hello," I said mentally to the God Who Could Not Live Behind a Glass Wall, whom I did not expect to encounter here, in a Hindu temple.

Devotees walked into the little room and around the fountain. We fell in line behind them and I carefully copied the actions of the people in front of me. *(Walk halfway around the fountain. Stop. Bow head. Pick up ladle. Dip into fountain. Pour water over top stone. Dip hand in fountain, touch water to forehead. Kiss hand.)*

I realized that my attitude to this God had softened enough that I could kiss my own hand in his honor and…could it be? Almost enjoy it.

Was I worshiping the God I once knew while performing a Hindu ceremony? Holy cow, I was! (Sorry. The 'holy cow' thing just seemed appropriate, given the setting.)

So it was there, in the Hindu temple, performing a Hindu ritual, that I realized it was possible to honor the God of one religion through the rituals of another.

It was also at the temple that I asked myself a question my heart seemed to already know the answer to: Could it be that all religions were like these statues in the room, different representations of a God who was too vast to be contained? Could it be that the God of my childhood, this Unknown God, was another face I could learn to celebrate?

As I stood there mid-thought, a tiny girl escaped her mother, bounded into the little altar room, and jumped right into the fountain. She splashed me, soaking herself and laughing gleefully, as if playing in the fountain of the Unknown God was the very reason she existed, the very reason we all exist. Time seemed to slow down as I took in her wet dress, lacy socks, and tiny shoes. Her exuberant brown eyes met mine and she lifted her tiny arms to me. I picked her up. Before I handed her off to her apologetic mama, I realized, *She is me; she is all of us.*

It was late when I bid Shri Kyran a heartfelt goodbye. He pushed a fragrant container of leftover dessert *Gulab Jaman* into my hands on my way out the temple door. "Enjoy, Reba. Happy Diwali!"

As I drove away, I saw teenage boys setting off fireworks at the edge of the property. *Guess I get to check fireworks off the list after all,* I smiled. Though exhausted, I wouldn't have wanted miss the experience.

Until the drive home, that is. It was inky black on the back-country roads that Ursula the GPS instructed me to take, making me hopelessly lost in the process. It began to storm, sheeting rain and wind that had me gripping the steering wheel with white-knuckled hands. Near midnight, I put on emergency flashers and drove slowly, but as I turned a sharp corner, I saw two large headlights coming straight at me far too quickly. A truck was hydroplaning in the center of the road.

I didn't know what awaited off the road, but I knew I had to go, now.

I heard the awful sound of truck brakes and skidding. I felt the bumpy crunch of gravel and dirt beneath my car as I veered to the shoulder of the road. The moment was suspended in a wordless prayer: *Please, not now. Please, not when I've just started to find You.*

I don't know if the "You" I meant was God or me or both, but the truck whooshed past, rocking my car but not touching it. My headlights illuminated a wide tree, and my wheels skidded to an uneven stop mere inches away from it.

Saved, I thought, shaking with thoughts of what could have been and almost was. *I'm saved.* I sat in the weighty silence, crying terrified and thankful tears. I turned on the interior light to call Trent, but the force of the turn had spilled my phone and the contents of my messy passenger seat all over the floor.

Bending over the console, digging through church programs and religious tracts of multiple faiths, I took stock: I was wearing a sari and holding a New Testament, a Quran, and a synagogue's Yom Kippur announcement. On the floor, my single serving communion cup and tea bags from the Buddhist meditation center had spilled over my medical files and "Dummies Guide to Wicca" bookmarked with a printout about Native American spirituality.

I started to laugh. *If I had died tonight, who would they have called for last rites?*

11
Quitting

$\mathcal{J}$ crutched into the joint where I was meeting Erin for our first breakfast together since she'd moved back from Tennessee the prior week. She was planning on accompanying me to a church that morning, but wasn't expecting me to be injured. Her green eyes widened when she saw me.

"What happened?" she stood up to help me into the two-person booth. I sat down heavily and scooted in while she leaned my crutches against the wall.

"It was so stupid. I turned my heel on loose gravel in a lumberyard parking lot. It felt broken but the x-ray says it's just a bad sprain—hugely swollen and fourteen shades of black and blue."

"Ick. I'm sorry."

"At least it's not broken." I tried to be positive. "And it's my left ankle, so I can still drive." I put my head on the table and groaned. "As if I ever want to drive to another lumberyard. Don't get me wrong; I am really thankful to have a job, but…"

"…But you never want to see another lubricated nail in your life?"

"Exactly." We grinned at each other with the understanding of friends who had cheered together at the sidelines of high school football games, held each other's hair back when sick (and drunk) in college, and proofread each other's first post-collegiate résumés.

"Erin, I am so glad you are back! You can make new friends, but you can never make an old friend."

Over omelets and pancakes, we discussed her transition back to Ohio and I caught her up on my project. Erin didn't have any PTCS issues, but she was a hundred percent behind me, even to the point of accompanying me to church after breakfast that day. "There's just one thing I don't get about you," said Erin when the waitress brought the check.

"Just one thing?" I snorted. "There are about three thousand things I don't get."

"I mean one thing about your project. If you no longer believe what you grew up believing about life, what *do* you believe?"

"You're getting so deep, and I haven't even finished my coffee," I teased. "My best guess is that maybe we choose our lives on earth like we are choosing a major in school. I'd like to think that instead of God just plopping us down, we agree to come here and put up with all this crap because we know our souls will learn from it and we'll be better in the end."

"So, you don't believe in Jesus? You're not a Christian?" asked Erin, perplexed.

"I don't know," I said honestly. "I know I don't believe in him or Christianity the way I was taught, but maybe I believe another way. I'm just not sure."

"I think you should keep going until you figure it out," said beautiful, blonde-haired Erin, Champion of Goals. "It's like exposure therapy. You know how people who are afraid of snakes just keep making themselves be around them until they're not afraid anymore? That's like you and church."

"Speaking of which, are you ready for this church?" I asked. I felt I needed to prepare her. "The congregation we're going to meets in a basement beneath a storefront, and their sign has a Homer Simpson quote on it: 'Well, I may not know much about God, but I have to say we built a pretty nice cage for him.'"

"I don't know about a church that quotes the Simpsons," Erin said, helping me out of the booth, "but I'm ready to help you cross a visit off that list."

When we arrived at the "Basement Church," as I was calling it, the sign in the window had changed since I had last driven by. It now read: "Many people are leaving the church and going to God."

"I assume Homer Simpson didn't say that," I observed as we made our way down the concrete steps to the basement. It was a slow process due to the crutches.

Downstairs, we faced orderly chaos: an exposed coat rack and a messy half-kitchen, fifty folding chairs, the remains of a potluck breakfast on a table by the back wall, and a haphazard set-up of microphones and sound equipment. As the whole place was only a thousand square feet, the audio components were entirely unnecessary.

I poked Erin in the ribs. "Did you know I once witnessed the exorcism of a church camp sound system that looked like that one? The system was behaving badly, and it was clearly no ordinary power surge. Demons had infested the equipment to keep fourth graders from hearing the message of salvation for the twenty-seventh time in six days!"

Erin didn't flinch. This is the type of statement she had come to expect from the friend who could recite all sixty-six books of the Bible without taking a breath (even after multiple shots of tequila) (and blindfolded) (and balancing on one foot). "Demonic speakers, huh? Where do you want to sit?"

The pastor strode over to welcome us. A compact man in his late forties sporting prematurely graying, if well-spiked, hair, he wore blue jeans and a button-down shirt with rolled-up sleeves as if to announce, "I'm here to do some heavy Bible-lifting today."

"Jesus bless you for coming this morning! We're going to have a sweet time of fellowship," he boomed, inches from to our faces. If I hadn't been on crutches, I might have cowered in the face of his close-talking Christianese. (Also? He needed a breath mint.)

"Thanks," Erin rescued me from having to speak. "Glad to be here." She smiled encouragingly when he walked away. "If it's too bad, we'll just leave, okay?"

I nodded uncomfortably and crutched my way to a seat. "Oh no," I whispered to Erin as the two-man praise band floated the first strains of a far-too familiar worship song. "This is not good." I felt claustrophobic when the singing started. Everyone was so earnest and worship-y: closing eyes to see things I couldn't see, raising hands to a God I did not feel.

When the title of the sermon flashed on the projection screen, I couldn't breathe. "Place your identity in Christ," the pastor yelled into the microphone.

"Placing your identity in Christ" is lingo for church-approved codependence: you allow your church's brand of Jesus to dictate what you do or don't wear, eat, read, discuss, watch, and listen to. You let your church's Jesus pick out your lipstick and your friends, run your bank accounts, and prescribe your wardrobe. Having my identity in Christ was the problem, the entire reason I fell apart when I could no longer believe. When I left my faith, I didn't have anything of my own. I was exactly like a woman who allowed her husband to make her every decision; I'd let the principles of the Bible (as taught by my brand of Christianity) govern everything from my finances to my schooling to what I would and would not do with my lady parts.

As the pastor continued on, I remembered the very last person who had told me to put my identity in Christ: Amy. I was twenty years old, in

Starbucks with my young women's small group. All of us were part of The Furnace, an intensive megachurch ministry-training program in Colorado Springs. (For the record, it was Ted Haggard's church, pre-scandal.) We were tight. These were my only friends for hundreds of miles; they knew nearly everything about me. They knew about my recent traumas, and that I was recovering from deep depression. They knew I was alone, so very alone; they were my only support system, the last string tethering me to the church, to God, to myself.

And yet they tossed me out.

"Your identity just isn't in Christ, Reba," said Amy, the leader of the posse and the last to speak. She shook her head sadly, as if the next part was breaking her heart instead of mine. "We've voted and think it's best for you to no longer be in our group." Amy was everything I hoped to be one day: beautiful, sure of her faith, a happily-married mother of five. I'd been at the hospital for the birth of her youngest son; that's how close this group was. I couldn't believe she was saying this, doing this.

Amy and the others spent the last twenty minutes going around the circle. One by one they shared how my doubts and failures were *bringing down their walk with Christ*, and they were *so sorry* but they were going to have to ask me to leave the group because *I wasn't serious enough about God*. They were *just concerned* about me, they soothed, *just speaking the truth in love*; their chastisement was intended to *give me the wake-up call I needed* so that I could *come back to the fold*, when I was ready to fully *place my identity in Christ*.

Without hugs or goodbyes, they left me there all alone, sobbing in a Starbucks, hands clutching my arms so tightly that I had eerie finger-shaped bruises for days, like someone had grabbed hold and shaken me hard.

Here in this odd basement church service, I felt the spasms of PTCS along with the memory. My heart contracted as if it hadn't been almost ten years ago, as though I hadn't been doing Project Thirty by Thirty for months, like I hadn't made any progress at all. *If we don't leave I'm going to puke,* I thought.

"We have to leave. Now. *Right now*," I told Erin with urgency, even though the pastor wasn't even halfway through the sermon.

We made quite a ruckus in the small room, my crutches banging against the metal chairs. The pastor and congregation looked puzzled, and I could feel the eyes of the small congregation on our backs as Erin helped me ascend the stairs. We burst out into the cool sunshine and I inhaled freedom with deep breaths.

"That was a little weird," she said reasonably—right before I began to cry.

"I hate this project," I spat. "I hate it!" Actually, I hated that I could not look at this evangelical service with the same open-mindedness I afforded Diwali. I hated that I turned into an angry, mushy, crying mess with the mere mention of the harmless-sounding phrase "identity in Christ." Mostly I hated that I was still sick in body and in spirit, even though I'd been trying so hard to get better.

But that's not what I told myself. I channeled everything into hating the project; if there was no project, there wouldn't be any extra triggers to tear apart my emotions. If there was no project, I would have more energy for dealing with the Sickness. Things would get better.

"I quit," I announced to Erin. "As soon as I get home, I am tearing my list off the fridge. I am *done*."

"How's your project?" my book club friend friend Michelle asked when she picked me up a week later.

"I quit," I said miserably, trying to adjust my ankle to a comfortable position. I was no longer on crutches, but it was still wrapped and achy, prompting a hefty limp in the evenings.

I thought Michelle was going to pull over the car to shake me. "Quit?! You can't quit!"

"I can and I did."

"Then why are we going tonight?" Michelle asked. She had invited me to this evening's Forum on Religion a month ago; it was a panel discussion with several authors of note. Thinking it would be a good supplement to my project, I'd RSVPed, crossing my fingers that the Sickness would give me a reprieve. I hadn't counted on either the sprained ankle or the quitting.

"Guilt," I sighed heavily. "I would have felt bad if I'd made you go alone."

The Forum was packed, standing room only. When I limped in, the room was abuzz with energy, and despite my discomfort I found myself a teensy bit interested in the discussion, especially when the panel of authors mentioned interfaith work. "Interfaith," Michelle whispered, "that's like what you're doing!"

"Correction: what I'm *not* doing," I replied. "Besides, it was less interfaith and more 'spiritual sojourn without leaving home.'"

I realized I was speaking of Project Thirty by Thirty in the past tense and felt a twinge of regret; I'd already poured so much time into it. *Too bad that was all for nothing,* I thought, just as Michelle whispered, "Do you think you could do just one more thing for the project before you officially quit?" Her eyes were luminous in the semi-dark auditorium. "I think you should ask the panel about your project during the Q&A," she prodded. "I want to see what they'll say. C'mon!" She actually elbowed me. "It'll make a really good story at book club."

And that is how I found myself in the spotlight, goaded into limping up to a microphone in the middle of a packed auditorium, my Quasimodo look projected on a huge screen. Five hundred people, two noted authors, and one famous mediator stared at me from the darkness. The light felt too bright on my face, like the police trying to force a confession. I nearly forgot my question, but as I started talking into the mic, I heard my voice echoing through the auditorium: "Post-Traumatic Church Syndrome... thirty religions..."

Something went sideways, just like it did with Pastor Judy under Psychic Jesus' watch: I was talking, but also watching myself talk. Whether it was the stress of public speaking or the Godiverse at work I may never know, but when I finished speaking and the panel answered, I wasn't really listening to them. I was listening to my heart, which was beating *don't quit, don't quit* in a nervous flutter.

I thanked the panel and stepped away from the mic, content that I had done my duty by Michelle and the book club. I limped away, teetering on the Quit/Don't Quit edge. The flutter was enough to make me reconsider my decision, but not enough to shove me back into the project. A woman tapped my shoulder.

"Excuse me," she said, her face aglow, "but I wanted to ask you: are you writing about your Thirty by Thirty experiences?"

I shook my head weakly, thinking, *I'm not having any more experiences.*

As the woman pulled out her business card, the room tilted even more. "I'm Sue Goodwin, the executive producer of *Talk of the Nation* on NPR, and this is one of the most original concepts I've seen in three years. Listen, you need to do a blog. There are so many people who would want to read about your project."

As she spoke, I felt dizzy, like at the doctor's office with the "Persevere" sign. This time, the Godiverse was sending me a telegram in all caps, courtesy of a messenger I couldn't ignore. It could not have been more clear, in fact, if Ms. Goodwin had knocked on my door and started tap-dancing while singing: "*This is your singing telegram...ba-da-ba-doo-da-ba!*"

DO NOT QUIT (STOP) PERSEVERE (STOP) THIS IS BIGGER THAN YOU (STOP)

Sue and I stepped into the hallway to discuss our spiritual paths: hers from fundamentalism to mindfulness, mine from fundamentalism to Project Thirty by Thirty. The room never righted itself. Throughout the half hour we talked, the Energy coming from her was so strong that it tingled down my spine, making me shiver. Even though Sue wasn't religious—and she certainly wasn't prophesying—I couldn't shake the feeling I'd had with Pastor Judy at the Christian Spiritualist Temple, like the whole Godiverse surrounded us.

I sent up a quick telegram of my own to Psychic Jesus, who I imagined must be smiling "Gotcha!" over my shoulder while petting his lambs.

GOT THE MESSAGE (STOP) WILL NOT QUIT (STOP)

and—just for good measure—PLEASE HEAL ME (STOP)

The decision to pursue the Project felt made for me. Again.

In the car, Michelle smirked, "I knew you needed to ask that question."

"You were right." She had earned smirking rights for at least six months of book club. "But how did I go in two hours from 'I quit' to starting a blog?" I felt a little spiritually stoned, as if I had smoked a peace pipe with the Transcendent Telegrapher in the sky. I was almost afraid to try to quit again; what would the Godiverse do then? Mystical Morse Code? Psychic pigeon post? Seraphic skywriting? Would Psychic Jesus himself appear to me in a burning bush? *Holy Toledo.* I realized that if I started a blog I was committing to the project even if it *got* me committed—or killed. Between the backside bruises, broken/deformed pinky finger, sprained ankle, Sickness, and car breakdowns, I seemed well on my way to an untimely demise.

When I got home, I found the Project Thirty by Thirty list and taped it back on the fridge while telling Trent the story.

"NPR, like National Public Radio?" he said, eyes wide.

"Uh-huh," I answered, proffering Sue Goodwin's business card for his review.

"Wow," is all he could muster.

"I know, right?" I answered, taping her card right next to the list. "If I ever say I'm going to quit again, just point to the card."

Oxley was the only member of the family to remain unimpressed; he just sat primly next to the fridge waiting for a treat as usual, as if I hadn't just been bested by the Godiverse.

"I may not be the wisest man in the nativity scene, Ox," I said "but even I know when I'm beat."

12

Redemption

"*C*hronic urticaria," diagnosed the allergist cheerfully. "That's doctor-speak for hives that won't go away."

He adjusted his bowtie; I gritted my teeth. It's much easier to be cheerful when you're not the one who has been dealing with daily itchiness for six weeks. "Could this be related to my other symptoms?"

"It's more likely stress-related. Let's see…" He flipped through my chart. "Since there's nothing actually wrong with you from a medical perspective, I recommend you see a psychologist."

I congratulated myself for not using my pen as a weapon. "A counselor. *Excellent* idea." Failing to catch my dripping sarcasm, the doctor scribbled some referrals. This is how I found myself on Darla's office couch once a week, asking the same questions over and over. *What's wrong with me? How am I going to live like this?*

"One minute at a time," Darla would say, but sometimes I could only get through seconds in therapy before breaking down.

"When Erin moved back from Tennessee, I was too tired to even call and ask if she needed help," I wailed. "I hired a housecleaner and said it was a housewarming gift, but it was really an I-suck-at-life gift… The only way I'm keeping my job is lying: to my boss about where I was, to my customers about why I'm not seeing them often enough, to my friends about why I can't make it to parties or book club. I called my human resources department about medical leave, but I can't take it because we wouldn't be able to keep up with the mortgage and the bills. I even pretend with Trent because I don't want him to look at me as a sick person. Sometimes I get up and dressed only to fall back into bed the second he leaves the house, and I don't wake up again until I hear his key in the door."

The project was just one more thing I was failing at. Sure, I crossed more visits off the list—Christian Science, Unitarian Universalism,

Sikhism, Seventh-Day Adventism—but they barely registered because I didn't have the energy to research or get into the services.

I barely had the energy to dress myself.

"How do I keep going, Darla?" I asked from the couch, stretched out on my back because sitting up the whole hour was too tiring.

"Don't think about everything ahead of you, just the next thing," she advised. She had become a fan of my project. "You're becoming more spiritually healthy with each visit, and the importance of that can't be overstated."

"Redemption of my spiritual health one step at a time," I grumbled. "It seemed like a good idea."

If I *was* becoming more spiritually healthy, my body didn't know it. Though it was only two p.m. when I left Darla's office, I drove home and went straight to bed. For nearly a week. On the fifth night, I stumbled into the bathroom around three a.m. My joints felt painfully gummy, as though I'd been hanging from my hands and feet instead of curled up in a ball. Half my body was covered in a fresh rash of itchy welts; I had at least 150 unanswered work e-mails, a full voicemail box, and a disgustingly dirty bathroom. With oily hair and smelly frog pajamas, I was the poster child for slumpadinkas everywhere. I sank to my (dirty) red bathmat and ugly-cried.

A composite memory bobbed to the surface of my mind: the hundreds of times my dad had sat on the edge of my bed when I was sick as a child, stroking my hair while he prayed for me. Sometimes he prayed in a rush of holy tongues, but mostly it was regular old English words that seemed powerful when coming from his mouth, as though a fever or the chicken pox had to disappear when he mandated it in Jesus' name.

I was in bad shape, kids. Bad enough that I did something I never could have imagined a few months prior. I went into the closet and called my dad, Former Commander of The Bat. He may have retired from workaday yellow-bat spiritual warfare, but once a prayer warrior, always a prayer warrior. I didn't really think praying would make a difference, but what did I have to lose?

Dad answered, groggy. "Hello? Are you okay?" I could almost see him on the end of the line, looking like the Italian restaurateur from *Lady and the Tramp*, except with his hair sticking out every which way from sleeping. I filled him in on the situation, leaving out the part about how I hadn't showered for…I couldn't remember how long. There is a limit to how much information one's father needs at 3:05 a.m.

"Dad, do you think you could…pray for me?"

He didn't seem surprised that his twenty-nine-year-old daughter, widely known to avoid supplication, needed urgent divine assistance. As he prayed, loud and mighty, using all the words that several months prior would have thrown me into a PTCS panic, I slipped into my little girl self and let my daddy tell my Sickness exactly where to go. Instead of shivers of PTCS, I felt comforted.

"You know, Rebecca," Dad said when he was done, "I'll always pray for you, but you know how to do it yourself."

"Thanks, but no."

He yawned. "You have all the tools; you just need to use them."

"Thanks, Dad. I love you."

We hung up the phone, and I knew the Sickness hadn't left. Not that I'd really expected it to, but a girl can hope, right? Or, maybe a girl can (gulp)…pray?

Out loud in my closet, my voice a hoarse whisper, I revived words that had been dormant for years. I suspected this was a knee-jerk reaction based on my childhood and too many healing services. But still:

I prayed.

I skidded into the synagogue parking lot twenty minutes before service time, worried I might already be too late to snag a seat. But instead of the sea of cars I'd expected, policemen were setting up orange cones in an empty lot. I'd read that Yom Kippur—the Day of Atonement—is like the Christmas Eve of Judaism when it comes to attendance: everybody shows up for Grandma, whether they like it or not. *Did I misread the start time?*

"Happy New Year!" greeted a policeman when I exited the car.

"Happy New Year!" I responded, thinking he must be referring to the Jewish New Year, Rosh Hashanah, that had occurred ten days prior. Turning toward the synagogue door, I noticed a lady taking tickets from an older couple.

"Am I supposed to have a ticket?" I asked the policeman, who guffawed like I was joking.

"You forgot your ticket? Good luck getting past Dinah!"

Before you judge what happens next, please consider I was not only *awake* and *out of bed* on a Saturday morning; I was dressed in my best conservative attire and had driven thirty minutes. Dinah or no Dinah, I was not leaving without the full Yom Kippur experience. I surveyed my options.

- Option 1: *Talk Dinah into letting me in*. I mean, I sold stuff for a living! And I once talked my way into a sold-out event where best-selling author Elizabeth Gilbert was speaking. Surely I could sneak into a free* religious service. While I was thinking this, Dinah turned away two people.

- Option 2: *Go in the back door*. Policemen were everywhere; I did not want a full synagogue experience that began and ended with me in handcuffs.
- Option 3: *Find an ally*. This possibility presented itself in the form of a hobbling old man. He looked like he needed help walking; I needed help walking in. *Perhaps we could come to an arrangement?*

The elderly gentleman greeted me joyfully in Hebrew; I muttered something under my breath that might be construed as Hebrew before brightly adding, "Happy New Year!"

"So nice to see such a pretty young lady, coming to synagogue early!" he said, patting my arm. "G-d" forgive me, I took the opportunity to grab his elbow just in time for Dinah to see us.

"Moses!" she waved. "It's so nice your granddaughter came with you!"

(Yom Kippur was the Day of Atonement; my slate was already pretty dirty—what's a few more chalk marks before repenting?)

He didn't hear; I kept quiet and flashed a demure smile that I hoped communicated "just another nice Jewish girl helping Grandpa." He handed off his ticket while I pretended to fumble for mine.

"No ticket?" Dinah knit her brows.

"No," I conceded miserably, sure I was about to be ousted.

"No problem," she winked. "You take good care of your grandpa."

I settled "Grandpa" in his seat, then followed Vinnie's Rule, slipping into the fourth row on the right side directly behind an old lady—who immediately decamped as if my sitting had offended her. *Now there was no one in front of me; who was I going to follow?*

No one, apparently, because even the people behind me weren't paying attention to the praying and reading happening at the front; everyone was just milling around, taking their time, chatting with friends on the way, apparently disregarding the rabbi's speaking and singing. I assumed this was normal and began taking notes. *Lovely stained glass—looks very much like a church, except with Hebrew writing everywhere...*

Almost immediately, a gentleman pounced. "Put that pen away! What are you thinking, writing on Shabbat?!"

"Oops..." I tried to apologize, but he threw up his arms in a disgusted, "Kids these days—who needs 'em?" gesture.

---

* I discovered much later that it was *not* a free event; many synagogues charge money for a seat for the High Holy Days. My apologies to the rabbi.

A young guy—"A doctor!" he quickly informed me—plopped into the seat next to me: Did I come here often? Was I meeting my family later? Would I like to get married? He was joking, but there seemed to be a little desperation behind his glasses. He was a handsome fellow, if you're into dark, wavy hair and liquid brown eyes. *This cannot be happening again!* I thought back to the Buddhist Meditation tea. *Does Project Thirty by Thirty broadcast spiritual pheromones?*

"I'm already married," I shifted uncomfortably, realizing I had forgotten my ring on the bathroom counter.

"Oh," he laughed it off. "Too bad!"

"Can I ask you something, though…?"

"Joseph," he supplied his name. "Sure."

Confession time. "So…I'm not Jewish." His brows shot up. "I thought today would be a good time to experience the synagogue, but the thing is, I've been so sick that I didn't do research on Yom Kippur—or Judaism for that matter—beyond what I know from growing up."

My former brand of Christianity maintained a complicated relationship with Judaism, sort of like a boyfriend they'd broken up with but couldn't ever get rid of because they had a baby together. (That baby is Jesus, which makes God the baby-daddy.) It takes fancy theological river dancing to sidestep the "Are God's chosen people in hell?" problem. This same set of Christians respects any Jew who plays for Team Jesus so much he even gets his own VIP title: "Completed Jew," which is someone who is Jewish by heritage but Christian in belief and practice. This term always bothered me, like the Jew in question was only half a Jew before accepting Jesus into his heart, like in that famed movie scene—"[Jesus,] you complete me!"

"Cold or flu?" Joseph asked, all his doctor-y antennae up. He appeared to have heard nothing I said after the word "sick," and I feared he might pull out a stethoscope and a tongue depressor from under his seat.

"Both," I sidestepped the question. (I needed zero more doctors in my life, even cute ones.) "Anyway, I know Yom Kippur is the Day of Atonement, but what's it really all about?"

It was Joseph's turn to be uncomfortable. His collar appeared to be choking him. "Uh, I may not be the best person to ask. I'm Jewish but not religious."

Hmmm. Maybe PTCS is really PTRS—Post-Traumatic Religion Syndrome?

Joseph cleared his throat. "I'll do my best. Yom Kippur is a day of fasting where you repent of the old and promise to be better. It's about making peace with God and others, but it's also about staking a claim to the generations of people who came before you, to the religion of your people."

I nodded. "Why are you here if you're not religious?"

"Aside from the fact that my mother would kill me if I didn't show?" He laughed wryly. "I guess for me, it's about connecting with my family and my heritage. You can't change the religion you were born with, so you might as well learn to celebrate it."

"Especially if your mother will kill you if you don't?"

"Yes! Especially then." He caught a glimpse of someone behind me. "Speaking of my mother, there she is. I better get going."

"Thanks, Joseph," I said. "Happy New Year."

I looked around the rapidly filling synagogue, wondering how many of the people were practicing Jews, and how many were culturally Jewish— here for Grandma, as it were. I also wondered how many of them had some form of PTRS. Joseph had said that if you can't change your heritage you should celebrate it, but I felt a little jealous that he was able to claim the family and community aspects of his heritage without all the religious stuff. Joseph was still Jewish whether he practiced or not. *If only I could be Christian-ish,* I thought.

Christianish.

The idea was so big that it knocked my mind out of the way of my feet, which propelled me to the ladies' restroom. I locked myself in a stall and took out my pen and journal.

> What if instead of constantly warring with my religious past, I think of Christianity as my country of origin? Could I claim everything helpful as my heritage, my birthright, and get rid of the rest? Could Christianity be the bedrock of my transformation instead of something to overcome?

I heard my mother's voice in my head.

"Don't throw out the baby with the bathwater." *Was this Christianish thing a way I could keep the baby, dry it off, and adopt it, while still getting rid of the dirty water?*

"Thankfulness is the antidote to unforgiveness." *Could being Christianish allow me to be thankful for people like Mrs. Easton and forgive all the spiritual bullies?*

"When you choose grace, grace chooses you." *Could being Christianish allow me to choose grace?*

I sat back. I didn't know the answers to all these questions, but I knew this was a Day of Atonement, even if I was in a bathroom stall breaking the Sabbath rules. To me, atonement meant redemption: the redemption of everything bad for good. Christianish.

I tested my Christianish theory by thinking about atonement in the parlance of my childhood: *Redemption is like exchanging beauty for ashes, gladness for mourning.* These words from Isaiah 61 were the best ones I knew to talk about atonement, but ten minutes prior I wouldn't have used them because they were too churchy, too PTCS-triggering. But now…I remembered something Elizabeth Gilbert had said at that event I talked my way into. "Take whatever works from wherever you can find it, and you keep moving toward the light."

Beauty for ashes. I thought the words of the Bible verse again, mentally moving toward the light. It felt awkward, like a baby colt trying to walk.

But it sure as hell didn't hurt.

"I'm going to test the Christianish theory by going to the Vineyard," I told Trent over chocolate frozen yogurt topped with strawberries. Even though it was so chilly that we needed heavy coats, fro-yo was a weekly ritual.

"Are you sure you're ready for that?" Trent asked, spooning his peanut butter and toffee combo. The Vineyard was the same church that had caused the hives right after college.

As I considered his question, I looked over Ohio State's campus oval. There were hardly any leaves left on the trees now; winter was closer every day.

"I'm not sure," I confessed. "But there's no other way to find out. Plus, I already have hives regularly. What's the worst that can happen?"

We looked at each other and started laughing. Who knew what awful things could befall me at a church that sounded like it belonged in Napa Valley?

"I'll be on standby while you're there," Trent promised, "like a spiritual ambulance team. Except with wine instead of IV fluids."

I sat in the parking lot staring at The Vineyard, which looked more like a Super-Walmart than a church. The last time I'd been here, I'd placed myself in the last row of the back balcony. It was dark, which I knew would hide my inevitable tears. I'd hoped the distance between me and the altar would give my soul space to breathe; instead, the place had nearly given me a panic attack. And now I was going to walk in there again, sit in a pew, and deal with whatever came up.

Hopefully, what comes up will not be vomit, I thought wryly before steeling myself to open the car door. On the long walk—the parking lot also resembled Super-Walmart—I gave myself the pep talk I'd practiced earlier that week:

Christianish means my old religion is my past, not my present or my future. It means my old religion is not allowed to define who I am today, who I will become tomorrow. It will not dictate how I feel about myself or the world. Christianish means my former faith will no longer keep me from seeking or finding new faith.

I didn't believe a word of it, but I recited *Christianish* in my head over and over anyway. I said it as I breezed past the greeters and through the glass doors into the atrium. I repeated it so loudly in my mind that it almost covered the familiar PTCS-triggering taunts from the people and theology of my past:

"You can never find Truth because you already left it behind. You have no identity and no future. Your rejection of your faith is a disappointment to your parents, your church, and most of all, to God. You are worse than someone who didn't ever know the Truth because you turned your back on it."

The two competing soundtracks were in stereo as I took a deep breath and entered the sanctuary, as if they were warring for my soul, and possibly for the contents of my stomach. So I reminded myself of Mrs. Easton; the voices on that soundtrack had existed only in my mind. I simplified the chant I was trying to dub over my past. *Christianish. Christianish. Christianish.* I chanted it like a meditation, clinging to it exactly the same way I had grasped onto each of my Project Thirty by Thirty visits. Each word gave me the next tiny thing to do, each formed syllable prompting one little step toward peace.

It worked. PTCS was afraid of this new soundtrack. The radical Christianish idea—that my past was not my future, that I had power to change the storyline—seemed to scare it off. I Christianish-ed myself all the way to the very front row.

I did not stand for the singing; I did not hum along. I stared straight ahead, concentrating on this new voice in my mind, waiting for a negative physical or mental reaction that—shockingly—never came. When the singing and the sermon concluded, I was still in one piece mentally, emotionally, and physically. No hives. No puke. No need to call my husband to come get me.

I knew better than to think this meant I was cured, but I also knew this meant my project was helping me make progress.

It's good enough for today, I thought, waiting impatiently for the service to be dismissed. Just because I made it through didn't mean I wanted to stay a second more than necessary.

But the service wasn't dismissed. The music minister paused his guitar playing and whispered into the microphone. "The Lord's presence is here this morning…"

Gag me. This guy was an archetype of every suave worship leader I'd ever known: a little too handsome, a lot too soulful. The lights were low; his eyes were closed; the piano strained softly behind him. This dude wasn't feeling the presence of the Lord; he was feeling the adoring stares of a few hundred women who were ready to swoon over his spirituality.

"There is someone here today who needs healing," he intoned, his voice sending a low buzz of Energy over my scalp.

I tried to shake it off. *Uh-uh, no way, not into feeling Energy waves from music ministers.*

"This is someone who has been sick for a long, long time," he continued. "Someone who needs answers. You know who you are. The Holy Spirit is working on you this minute, prompting your heart to come forward for prayer."

I didn't feel the Holy Spirit, but I certainly felt the Energy. It was circling my body like a swarm of friendly bees, teasing my nerve endings. In my head I knew this cold call for entries to the "Be Ye Healed!" lottery was applicable to many people in this audience, but in my heart I felt it: *I am exactly the person to whom this worship leader is speaking.*

Absolutely not! replied everything in me…everything except the part that moved my muscles to stand and my feet to walk the short distance to the altar. I kneeled at the lowest step and started sobbing. I'd barely made it out of bed today, let alone to church. I was sick. I was painfully sick, and had been for a long time. This was not a PTCS breakdown, but a different breakdown altogether: I needed to do something with this Sickness, to put it down somewhere else, in front of other people. I needed Divine help.

This is what it means to be Christianish, I thought, as gentle hands alighted on my head, back, and shoulders. Soft prayers surrounded me like a blanket. "Lord, help our sister," the voices prayed, their kindness drowning out the voices from my past. "Heal our sister with your power, in the name of Jesus." More hands on my head, more weight off my heart.

I could not abide their theology. I did not agree with their politics. I didn't even like their God. Heck, I still didn't even like the *word* "God." But in that Christianish moment, it didn't matter.

In that moment, I grasped exactly what I needed from my past, yanked it into my present, and offered it to my future. Redemption.

13
Tears

Becky phoned me the morning of Thanksgiving. "Can you please bring a salad?" she asked. A super-hostess, my mother-in-law never requested that I bring anything.

"Of course! I'd love to!" *This will be the salad to end all salads, my contribution to the holiday, my Salade d'Resistance!* I thought, trying to pep-talk my way out of bed. Instead, I fell back asleep, awakening with barely enough time to trade my pajamas for clothes.

I forgot the salad. The thought squeezed me as I pulled up to Becky's house alone because Trent had gone ahead of me. I was so tired that I wasn't sure how I was going to walk into the house, let alone produce a salad out of thin air. I wish I could tell you I did the reasonable thing that normal people would do in this circumstance: go to the grocery store. But I was not a reasonable person. I was a sick person. And chronically fatigued people make chronically fatigued decisions like buying salads for a crowd at a fast-food drive-through window.

"You want *how* many side salads?" the attendant exclaimed through the intercom.

"Fifteen!" I shouted. "With packets of balsamic and Italian dressings." (*Why not full-size salads?* The reasonable reader may wonder. Well. Nothing says drive-thru *Salade d' Shame* like rubbery hard-boiled eggs and crispy chicken.)

I'm not sure that there is another image that captures the lengths I would go to disguise my sickness—and seem like a normal, functioning person who could do normal, everyday things—than the picture of me parked in front of my mother-in-law's house with fifteen side salads, crying over a bowl and tongs I'd stolen from her kitchen cabinet. I dumped the salads and all of the dressings in the bowl in the passenger seat, tossed it together, walked in through the garage and placed my *Salade d'Shame* on the buffet table.

"This salad is delicious!" said my father-in-law, Denny, a little while later, his plate heaped high. My shame grew exponentially.

"Reba brought it," said Becky.

"Did you make it?" Denny asked.

"I threw it together," I said modestly, because I *did*.

Even though I'd done the drive a hundred times, I took a wrong turn on the way home from Thanksgiving dinner. A really wrong turn. I ended up in a neighborhood I wouldn't visit in the dark, not even with Trent and pepper spray.

On one side street, I passed a tiny stone building: St. Lydia Eastern Orthodox Church, the sign proclaimed. The "orthodox" part stopped me because I'd been trying unsuccessfully all month to figure out the Greek Orthodox service times. According to a Greek friend, the time of church meetings is a Big Fat Greek Secret. "If you don't already know," she'd teased, "no one is going to tell you."

Interesting, I thought about St. Lydia. The steps and small garden were filled with loitering people—several of whom looked pretty scary. I clicked my locks, sped off, and determined to keep calling the Greeks.

I made the same wrong turn a few days later—and wondered if the Godiverse might be trying to tell me something. Maybe it was the *right* turn.

"I'm thinking about going to a service by Smith Park this Sunday," I told Trent.

He looked mildly alarmed. "You'd better leave your wedding ring at home and drive my car." Trent's ride was Old Lady Buick, circa 1993. We loved her and hoped she'd survive through law school, but no one in their right mind would try to steal her.

Before I even got out of bed that Sunday I felt an energetic pull, a phenomenon I named the "Siren Song of St. Lydia." As I dressed for the service, I wasn't sure exactly what was going to happen, but the day felt significant somehow.

The pull helped me exit Old Lady Buick and stride quickly and purposefully to the church's entrance. The red wooden door was ajar and the service had already begun. I crept into the sanctuary of this stone jewel-box of a church. With only twelve wooden pews, six on each side, it was maybe twenty-five feet from the front door to the altar.

The calm I experienced just inside the doors did not match the fear I'd felt outside. Maybe it was the incense. (Could it be? An incense brand I wasn't allergic to?) Maybe it was the lighting—sun cascading through stained glass, bright flecks of candle scattered around the front. Or maybe it was the holy hush of the thick, worn carpet under my feet and the soft background soundtrack of monks chanting. But for the first time since beginning the project, for the first time in nearly a decade, something within me stirred in recognition in a church. *Peace be still,* It whispered, and—also for the first time in a long time—I was.

I slipped into the second row on the left. There were only ten people present; I was the only Caucasian until the priest appeared from a side room, dressed in ornate robes. From the church's website, I knew this priest was a professed monk who lived here in the church "dedicated to serving the poorest of the poor in the inner city." He was absorbed in the preparations for the service and helped by a teenage boy who—also robed—looked like a handsome, dreadlocked angel. I couldn't see most of what was going on because it took place behind a partition, but when the Urban Monk (as I immediately named him in my head) came to the front, he faced away from the tiny congregation, as if leading us directly to God.

The pageantry of the service—the use of color and incense and ritual—felt Eastern; though it was decidedly Christian, it reminded me much more of the Buddhist meditation center I'd visited than any church I'd ever been to. The whole service was elegant, even though people seemed to stream in and out as they pleased. Time moved slowly, but in a good way, like the wax dripping from the candles on the altar. As the Urban Monk sang and chanted long prayers with his back to the congregation, I realized what felt different. This place was *real.* There was no separation between the church and the community: the front door was open straight into the sanctuary. There was no vestibule, greeter, or program. The liturgy, incense, and candles lent a surreal feeling to the hour.

Eventually the Urban Monk turned around, and I found myself smiling. He looked just like Santa Claus: long white beard, red cheeks, wire glasses, jolly grin. "Welcome," he beamed to the eight of us still there. As he transitioned to the homily, our eyes met briefly, and the Energy sent a shock down to my toes. *He's important,* the Energy told me.

The Urban Monk spoke without preamble. "Zechariah the priest, father of Saint John the Baptist, questioned God. His wife Elizabeth, mother of Saint John, questioned God. Sometimes we question the ability of God to come in and change things."

As he spoke, I knew what had stirred when I walked into St. Lydia—*my heart,* I realized with a jump of recognition, perhaps like John the Baptist's in Elizabeth's womb, when he recognized, even before he was born, the arrival of his salvation.

"The Scriptures tell us to 'come and see' the goodness of the Lord. Come and see for ourselves. Not because it's what someone else told us, but because we have firsthand experience."

I flashed back to the wizened old teacher at the Buddhist center. "*Ehipassiko*," he had said. "Come and see. Your life is a laboratory for the Dharma. Test the teachings. Question the teachings. Truth exists in the value it brings to you."

My heart fractured wide open. Tears streamed down my face because I felt as though the Breaking, Project Thirty by Thirty, and my whole life had brought me precisely to this moment, to hear exactly this:

"We may not recognize it," the Urban Monk said, looking straight at me. "But the moment we ask the question is the moment the miracle happens. The answer comes with the question, the miracle with the asking."

Part 3
Winter

14

Boot Camp

The siren song of the Urban Monk's church called to me the entire week following my first visit.

I heard its strains in the doctor's office, even when the newest white coat scribbled on a pad with a self-satisfied expression, as if he'd solved the Sickness with one sentence. He ripped off the prescription and handed it to me.

"Get more exercise in the morning?" I cocked my head in puzzlement. Was it my imagination, or was the doctor actually smirking?

"You just need to reset your circadian rhythm," he explained in a clipped voice, my fatigue an annoyance. "Getting your heart pumping is the best way. I recommend an early-morning exercise class, maybe one of those boot camp-inspired programs." He glanced at the clock and capped his pen. "One tip: if you pay in advance, it's harder to sleep through." Then he *laughed*.

The calm I'd felt at St. Lydia the previous Sunday was the only thing that kept me from wadding up the prescription and throwing it at Dr. Jerktastic. As the door closed behind him with a metallic click, I leaned my head against the wall behind my chair and looked at the ceiling. I imagined I was back in the Urban Monk's tiny, jeweled sanctuary and instantly felt a current of connection to the Godiverse.

How could I not return the following Sunday?

Parking across the street, I noticed St. Lydia looked like something out of a storybook. With its red arched door, small stained-glass windows, and heavily sloped slate roof perched atop a stone exterior, it reminded me of a church you might find slumbering in my mother's ceramic Christmas village atop cotton-ball snow.

"Be careful with the church," my mother always cautioned when we decorated for the holidays. "The village won't look right without it."

Inside, a candle was burning on every sill, as if the windows could hum along with the Monk's worship. I thought of the twinkling Christmas lights that used to illuminate our toy village, how I'd sneak down to the living room at night just to see them glow. Here, the village church had come to life.

I easily fell into the cadence of the service, noticing that every detail created sacred space. From the lovely icons adorning the sides of the altar, to the well-worn books stacked on the piano, to the unique timbre of the Urban Monk's voice as he intoned the liturgy; everything fostered the mysterious peace I'd felt all week.

When the Urban Monk led the Lord's Prayer, he sang in baritone. Usually a PTCS trigger, I followed the familiar words layered on the unfamiliar melody without any discomfort—realizing even as I did so that although I couldn't say the Lord's Prayer in a Baptist church without flinching, I could easily harmonize with it here. Changing the context removed the trigger.

Maybe that's a PTCS survival hack, I mused. *Sing what you can't say.*

A few minutes later, the Urban Monk's eyes briefly met mine as he talked about Jesus going into the desert to fast. "Jesus did not know what he would find in the desert, but he must have believed it would be exactly what he needed," he explained. I felt like the Monk was talking to me. I'd gone into my project having no idea what I would find. Heck, I *still* didn't know what I would find, but maybe walking into the desert of my own heart was already an accomplishment.

The Urban Monk reminded me of that old show *Touched by an Angel*—where God's messenger would light up right before delivering a heavenly message. I almost expected him to light up and say, "God loves you more than you can imagine," before disappearing to a harp soundtrack. He didn't glow or vanish, but he did bless every parishioner with the sign of the cross before closing the service. They went forward one by one; I waited until everyone else had gone, then went forward by myself.

"My child," he said, eyes shining as he drew the sign of the cross over me and took one of my hands in blessing, "Something wonderful happened for you last Sunday." This seemed a counterintuitive thing to say to someone who had snotted her way through an entire box of Kleenex the prior week, but I nodded in assent, somewhat surprised that he remembered me. Then again, based on the attendance I'd witnessed, parishioners weren't exactly knocking down his door.

"I'm not sure what happened last week," I offered, "but I felt like I needed to come back. I can't explain it, really."

He waved his hands dismissively. "No need to explain. Everyone who walks through my door is brought by God."

We made formal introductions, but the words felt worn out as soon as they were spoken, like the Urban Monk and I had been acquainted for a long time. My friend Jan, a global missionary who has met many new-old friends through her travels, has a good phrase for this new acquaintance–old friend phenomenon: *déjà-forward*. "Déjà-vu feels like we've already been somewhere, done something," she'd explained to me upon our first meeting twelve years ago, when we'd become insta-friends in spite of our age gap. "*Déjà-forward* is remembering what our heart already knows in the future."

I felt major *déjà-forward* standing there with the Urban Monk. "Do you think we could meet sometime?" I asked. "I'd like to find out more about what you do at the mission." (That was a lie. I wanted to know what it was about this man and his church that turned my PTCS on its head, why I felt like I knew him before we'd even had a conversation, and why I felt an inexplicable draw to this place.)

"Of course. I'd be delighted! I have to serve lunch right now." He gestured toward a door that I assumed led to the mission. "But if you can come back around three o'clock, I'll have time then."

Promptly at three, I knocked at the side door as the Urban Monk had instructed.

"Well, hello! Welcome back!" he beamed, ushering me into sanctuary. During the service he'd been wearing a large hat and satin robes, but now his dress was more monk-casual: still all black robes, but more cotton. If his service dress was akin to a tuxedo, maybe this getup was his equivalent of khakis and a button-down.

A mite of a girl ran from the back of the church, beaded braids flying behind her. She stopped short to inspect me. "Are you the new piano teacher?"

I bent down to her level. "Nope, sorry. I didn't practice enough when I was your age. Do you play?"

"Yes!" she bobbed her head with enthusiasm. "My teacher comes to church every Monday!" Her grin lit up the room before she hopped back to what I assumed was the mission's kitchen.

"That's Julie," the Monk explained. "I bring in university students to teach music lessons for the kids every week… Julie's mother has been in and out of jail since she was born. Prostitution, drugs, you name it. Sometimes she lives with her grandmother; sometimes an aunt. Very unstable situation. But she certainly loves the piano."

He opened a door off to the side of the altar. "Please make yourself comfortable in my 'office.'" He laughed as he said it, and I soon saw why: the tiny space tripled as office, living quarters, and overflow church storage. In the farthest corner, a small brown mutt was curled atop the one pillow on a neatly made twin bed. At first the set-up surprised me; I wouldn't normally enter a man's bedroom. Then I realized he had to sleep *somewhere*, and as the main church area featured only two rooms, where else would he lay his head? I stepped inside.

The dog jumped up to growl at me, fur standing on end, and barked so loudly that I wondered if the window might shatter.

She looked at the Urban Monk for guidance. "This is Reba," he whispered to her. "Go make friends." She rolled over and offered her belly for scratches.

"Please, take a seat," he invited, gesturing to a worn office chair opposite his desk. I recognized the screensaver of green-and-black code falling vertically across his outdated computer screen.

"Are you a fan of *The Matrix*?"

He looked at the screensaver. "Ah, yes. The film is a wonderful allegory, reminding us that this life is a transient illusion."

"My favorite scene is where Neo stops the bullets. There are a lot of days I wish I had that kind of power."

He looked at me over steel-rimmed glasses, his expression serious. "You do have that power."

I just looked at him. "Um…"

"Meditation is how you learn to stop bullets. Meditation is where God separates truth from illusion. Would you like some tea?" I nodded, trying to digest his words as he flipped on an electric kettle near his keyboard.

Someone knocked on the "office" window. "Father? Father?! You in there? I need your help!"

"Excuse me," he apologized. "Please watch the tea."

The Monk stepped out, but I could hear the beginning of a conversation with a guy who sounded young and angry. "Someone stole the bus pass you bought me, and now I can't get to work!"

"We can get you another pass, but right now you need to get to work. Here's bus fare. Call when you're done and I'll come pick you up. I've got someone in my office right now."

"Thanks, Father!"

"You're welcome. But no more bus fare until I see your homework done." I could almost see him wagging his finger at the kid. The monk stepped back in as the kettle whistled. "Sorry," he smiled. "That was the acolyte, Devon. Did you notice him this morning?"

I thought of the handsome, dreadlocked angel-boy and said yes. "Good kid, rough situation. I try to help him all I can." He rubbed a tired hand on his forehead. "Right now I'm just hoping he'll finish high school."

The Urban Monk poured us both tea and leaned back in his chair, getting comfortable. It seemed as if he was readying himself for a story—mine.

"You said you wanted to know more about the mission." His look was friendly, yet piercing. I imagined it to be the same "No-B.S.-in-God's-house" expression he'd just given Devon outside. "Why are you *really* here?"

Uh-oh—busted. I started to speak…and immediately all my spiritual garbage came up and out. For two hours my words spilled over each other while the Monk alternated between handing me tissues, patting my hand, and freshening my tea. If my tirade was the spiritual equivalent of bending over a toilet in a bar after too many shots of tequila, the Monk was a kind stranger holding back my hair. Aside from murmuring encouragements, he spoke only once, when I mentioned Post-Traumatic Church Syndrome.

He issued a deep belly laugh. "PTCS, eh? I think I have a touch of that myself."

I talked until I was hoarse and had nothing left to say. When I was finished, we were both silent. Me, because I was mortified that I'd allowed myself to be so vulnerable with a member of the clergy; him, because he was in prayer—or at least seemed to be. If he hadn't been thoughtfully stroking his beard, I would've thought him asleep.

I squirmed in the stillness. Maybe the *déjà-forward* was wrong; maybe this visit was a really bad idea. Sure, the Monk seemed accepting, but everything I'd just said was a roundhouse kick to the gut of traditional theology—at odds with every iconic Christian painting, symbol, and sacrament in his little Orthodox church. I calculated how fast I could get to the car. Two minutes? Three?

He opened his eyes and began to speak in a voice that was velvety smooth and impossibly strong, like a yoga teacher giving a presidential address.

"Reba, God loves you more than you can possibly imagine."

(Aha! My *Touched by an Angel* moment.)

"There is nowhere God isn't. Even when you thought you were running away from Him, you were always running toward Him. He has never let you go, not for a single moment, and He never will let you go. Nothing you can do or not do can keep you from Him."

"But…" I objected. "But I don't even *like* God most of the time. Or at least not the God I grew up with. I can barely even use the word. I use Godiverse." He looked more amused than scandalized.

"Go on."

"I don't believe in hell or the inerrancy of the Bible. I don't know what I think about Jesus or God." It felt important that he know all these things up front, so there wouldn't be any confusion later. "I'm not interested in being converted or 'brought back to Jesus,' whatever that means. I don't want to substitute one religion for another. I'm just looking for peace."

Surely *now* he would tell me to get out of his office and take my blasphemy with me; I cowered in my chair, bracing for the blow like a dog kicked too many times.

He shrugged. "It matters not." For someone with seventeen saint icons on the other side of the wall, he seemed very unconcerned about my sacrilege. "Religion is simply a tool to put God's love into words and symbols. Doctrine is only useful to the extent it enhances your understanding of that love. God doesn't care about your religion. He cares about your heart."

Whoa. This was one very unorthodox Orthodox monk. I liked him. I liked him a *lot*. I liked him even more when I found out that in addition to the whole Christian monk-thing, he had spent time in India studying Buddhism under the Dalai Lama.

"I have taken the vows of Enlightenment," he performed a seated half-bow. "*Bodhisattva*, at God's service." The Urban Monk was also a former scientist, businessman, inventor, and—for one year in the mountains—a hermit. He was a Reiki master, student of world religions, and an interfaith activist. He seemed to have been everywhere and done everything before landing in the inner city to serve the poor and homeless.

He answered all my questions seriously, in a voice filled with the peace that radiated around him. I'd never met anyone like him. If I could see auras, I imagined his would be a cool, blue pillar stretching from floor to ceiling. The ambience around him was so calm; it seemed as if he might actually be able to stop bullets with his mind.

"The only true religion is love," said the Urban Monk when dusk fell around the little church. I became conscious that I wanted to come back here, possibly tomorrow.

I want to learn from this man. The thought stunned me. I'd always assumed that Project Thirty by Thirty was a solo activity, like reading a self-help manual or tweezing my eyebrows. But here was someone right in front of me who possessed what I'd been seeking: *Peace*. Peace that was much bigger and wider than I'd imagined it could be, even if it involved religion.

The Monk seemed to read my mind. "Would you like to learn to meditate?"

I didn't need time to think about it. "Yes! But I have one question. Buddhist meditation or Christian meditation?"

He smiled. "There is no difference whatsoever."

The first morning my clock buzzed at 4:45 a.m., I hallucinated. "Trent!" I shook him. "The house is on fire!"

Sleepily, he shook me back. "No, it's not. That's your boot camp alarm."

I remembered with a groan. In an act of Sickness desperation, I had followed Dr. Jerktastic's advice: I'd signed up—and paid for—an expensive boot camp that met at 5 a.m. I lay back on my pillow, weighing the dollars I'd prepaid against my heavy limbs. *Ugh. But how many times in my life would an Urban Monk—who was once blessed by His Holiness the Dalai Lama!—issue an invitation to teach me meditation?* Since I had to get up for that, I decided not to waste my boot camp money. Dragging myself from bed, I threw on my gym clothes and exited into the winter cold.

Including me, six ladies assembled for boot camp. (If you were imagining chipper soccer moms with matchy-matchy fitness ensembles, you would be correct—except for me. I looked like last week's pot roast.)

"Drop and give me twenty!" shouted the instructor, a buff character I quickly nicknamed the Torturer. He herded us through frantic exercises with a shrill whistle. We ran bleachers and stairs; we did sit-ups and push-ups and leg-ups and pull-ups. When the wretched hour was over, I trudged through a light snow to my car, exhausted but buoyed by the thought of starting meditation training.

I shivered in my car. Reaching for the heater, I accidentally hit the radio dial and the stereo blared.

How did the Christian station get on? I wondered. One errant phrase could set off a torrent of PTCS. Before I could change the station, strains of singer Mark Schultz's "I Am" surrounded me: "Come and see…follow me…I am…the healer of the broken. I am the One who even knew you before your birth…" My heart caught; I remembered singing these words in high school chapel, hands raised high in praise.

I flipped off the radio in a huff.

It was still dark when I pulled up to St. Lydia. One of the large wooden doors was propped open, releasing light like a beacon. I ran up the stone steps; the cold rushed in with me, but dissipated quickly in the warmth of the entryway. I unwound my scarf as I walked up the short aisle. A faint smell of freshly lit incense hung in the air along with the scent of snuffed-out matches. A soundtrack of Tibetan singing bowls played softly from somewhere in the rafters, and candles burned near the altar and on a few windowsills. The light I'd seen from the street shone from above, illuminating the altar table.

I almost didn't see the Urban Monk at first; he was tucked in a chair at the altar's far left, face half-shadowed by a cloak worn around his head and shoulders like a hood. But for his glasses, he could have stepped straight out of a monastery in an earlier century. Robin the dog curled at his feet. A small table to his left held one burning candle, a Bible, a prayer book, and a golden bell.

He greeted me with a gentle nod, and I took a seat on the wooden pew nearest him. The whole world seemed silent except for the sound of my own breath and the singing bowls until he spoke.

"Meditation means stilling your mind enough to let the light in. In the discipline of doing nothing and thinking nothing, we reach a state of peace that surpasses our worldly understanding. And in the silence, we allow God to do His deepest work: redemption. Redemption of our mind. And how do we meditate? We close our eyes." He closed his eyes, so I did as well. "We begin to breathe: slowly and deeply." We breathed for a few minutes. "We may remain silent, or we may use a mantra." He spoke-sang his mantra: "Lord, have mercy on us. Christ, have mercy on us."

The phrases pulled me out of relaxation, and my eyes flew open. "I can't use that mantra!" The idea of mercy made me think of God as a harsh judge sentencing a criminal, then knocking a few years off for good behavior, and the name "Christ" unnerved me.

"How about 'Jehovah'?"

"No." (Too Old Testament.)

"Maranatha?"

"No." (Too many praise songs with that label.)

"Agape?"

"No." (Too reminiscent of studying the Bible's Greek.)

Any normal person might have been frustrated, but the Monk didn't even open his eyes. "No mantra, then. God will give you your own when you're ready. We will simply sit in quiet." He didn't say for how long, or set any alarms (which alarmed me). He simply rang the golden bell, and we began.

I sat. I was silent. I even avoided squirming. No meditation was forthcoming. After about thirteen hours (or maybe it was seconds), I admitted to myself that I'd avoided the whole "training" concept of the meditation; I'd imagined skipping all the tough stuff and waltzing straight on through to enlightenment. I hadn't even *considered* there might be work involved.

I think we sat for about fifteen minutes, and by the end I felt so mentally drained that all I could think about was getting home to bed. Granted, the Sickness was also calling me back to bed, but the post-meditation fatigue was a different type of tiredness altogether. That first, miserable attempt to meditate felt like the mental equivalent of my boot camp—except I was both the Torturer and the tortured. I felt I was running bleachers and steep stairs inside my mind, then blowing the whistle at myself because I was supposed to be sitting quietly and not thinking. Then I was chasing myself around with the whistle and yelling at myself to work harder at being quiet, but I kept escaping.

The Urban Monk rang the bell to close our session, and we both opened our eyes. He smiled beatifically, as though he'd just come from a relaxing spa treatment. I looked like my hairdresser had accidentally dyed my hair purple.

"What do you think?" he asked.

"I think I have a lot of work to do."

15

Truth

"What are you doing, babe?" Trent asked the following Sunday morning as I sat clicking away on my laptop.

"Recon. The place I'm going today is called Aletheia—that's Greek for 'truth'—and I need to know what I'm walking into."

Aletheia promoted itself as "a church of broken people seeking to live lives transformed by the gospel by the power of the Holy Spirit." *Broken, check*. But that last clause with too many prepositional phrases? Ugh. It was Christianese code words for what I called Spiderweb Theology: first we lure them in…then we *eat their souls*.

Sure enough, the first page of the church's website was all: "We're open! We're friendly! We heart broken people!" But when I dug down to the Membership Covenant, the Spiderweb appeared: "I covenant to follow the biblical procedures of church discipline, and submit myself to discipline if the need should ever arise." This was followed by Scripture references, as if the agreement was backed by God himself.

I felt queasy instantly. I'd seen the "S" word (submit) used to control more people in more ways than I could count. Yuck. It reminded me of every time the fear of God was put behind the words of human beings, of every covenant I signed, vowing my chastity, sobriety, money, time, and (of course) my total and unquestioning loyalty to doctrine disguised as Jesus. I counted them in chronological order: one contract for high school, at least three for various youth groups, two virginity pledges, one for Christian college, one for the Focus on the Family Institute, one for the Furnace's discipleship program. Though never explicitly stated, it was always understood: *If you break this covenant, you're crucifying Christ all over again*. I may as well have signed those agreements in his blood.

I pulled into the Aletheia parking lot with the same enthusiasm I might muster for pouring hot sauce in my eye. (I did that once at the beginning of my career to prove to my customers that I was a "man." It turns out I'm less man and more screeching hyena.)

The building was a large, squat, concrete structure that used to be a manufacturing facility before the warehouse district was abandoned. I entered though double-glass doors, and a greeter enthusiastically shook my hand, issuing a hearty, "Welcome! Welcome!"

I tried very hard not to imagine him as a spider welcoming me to my own demise, but what can I say? His looks improved with the addition of six more legs.

I hung my coat and rounded the corner into a large, crowded area with painted concrete walls and industrial carpet. Half of the industrial space opened into a lounge with couches, tables, and a small coffee bar; the other half featured chairs and a stage. A blaring Christian soundtrack mingled with snippets of Christianese spoken around me. ("How's your walk with God?" "Have you surrendered?" "You're heavy on my heart.") The familiarity startled me, and my internal floor dropped out beneath me. The resulting spiritual vertigo made me dizzy.

I still might have been okay if I hadn't noticed a girl on a couch in the corner. She wrote earnestly in a journal—face glowing, so full of believing; she reminded me of the person I once was and the light Mrs. Easton had reminded me about. As I looked around, the whole church filled with imaginary Rebas of days past. The angry Rebas shouted but were easy to discount; it was the sad ones that made me want to bolt from Aletheia. I tried the silent chant that worked at the Vineyard—*Christianish*—but no dice. I tried to find a meditative breath, but it was too loud for quiet.

In my imagination, I caught a glimpse of a possible older Reba; I envisioned her face glimmering with hard-won belief and peace, but not the kind that surpasses understanding. Peace that exists only *because* of understanding. I guessed peace that stopped bullets could be mine, but my former selves stood between the person I was and the woman I wanted to become.

They were warring factions; my future was the disputed land, and this Spiderweb Church was the battleground. This was serious. This was important. This was…a great time to hide out in the nearest bathroom.

I took refuge in an empty stall, but could still hear the angry Rebas in my mind, condemning me for the many promises made in blind faith. Sad Rebas reproached me for all the covenants I'd broken; they poked me with thorny Bible verses and filled my mind with all my spiritual failures. They held up a much younger me as evidence of my many sins—*look how much you've disappointed this little girl who loved Jesus so very much*. I couldn't breathe, couldn't think. So, hands interlocked behind my neck, nose squished into my knees, I whispered a one-word prayer, but not to God.

I spoke to the woman I hoped to become.

"Please," I said, waiting—for what exactly? I wasn't sure until the commotion faded into silence, as if my future self raised her hand for quiet and pressed the mute button on my self-condemnation.

She gave me the courage to leave the bathroom, face the praise band, and find my seat just in time for the sermon. The pastor, hanging to the back of a stage covered in purposefully tattered fabric streamers and patio party lights (mood lighting?), wore stonewashed denim, a sweater that wouldn't be out of place on a Goodwill rack, a thick beard, and sneakers just dirty enough to prove he wasn't your mama's minister. His talk centered on the evils of racism, which I would have applauded had it been more logical. On the one hand, he was saying we shouldn't be racist, but on the other hand, he suggested we should invite Muslims to dinner so we could convert them to Christianity. I considered how this might go over with my favorite taxi driver who always listened to Muslim prayers in his cab. "Hey, I know you really like Allah and all, but would you like some mashed potatoes with a main course of Christ?" Choking on the bitter message, I wrote sarcastically in my notes: "Not racism... religiousism!"

From an altar decorated with burlap, the pastor offered the communion elements—blood from a 1970s stoneware goblet that wouldn't be unwelcome on my grandmother's dining table, and a fresh-baked body wrapped in a cotton table runner.

A girl skipped through the communion line wearing sparkly tights and pink, sequined shoes. She happily tore the bread and dipped it in the juice, smile twinkling, and I wrote a short message to her in my journal—*I hope you never try to squeeze your feet back into those tiny shoes, only to discover that you can't click your heels and be home.*

"Peace be with you," intoned the pastor in a closing that seemed a peculiar nod to liturgy in a service otherwise devoid of it. As the congregation echoed, "And also with you," I thought: *If only peace were that simple.*

I recessed down the aisle miserably, sure the past hours hadn't brought me any closer to the peaceful woman I hoped to be. *I'm sorry,* I mentally apologized to my future self, feeling like I'd let her down. *I'm doing the best I can to get to you.*

When the bracing cold of the parking lot whipped about my face, I could swear she whispered back: *Be kind to yourself today; you are doing the hard work of creating tomorrow.*

I'd thought meditation training would be all Buddha laughs and angel kisses, but it felt more like Buddha was cackling in the corner as angels smacked me around. I woke up at 4:45 a.m. most weekdays, cursed myself and my alarm clock, and trudged into freezing weather to wipe the snow and ice from my windshield. The Sickness fought me at every step; sometimes I felt like a recovering alcoholic holding fast to my resolve for just one…minute…more. Most days I showed up at boot camp and let the Torturer beat up my body before meditation training beat up my mind, but sometimes I skipped exercise and went straight to St. Lydia.

I showed up at the Urban Monk's sanctuary door an angry, freezing, sick, wet mess only to turn into an angry, freezing, wet, sick, *non-meditating* mess. I sat on a hard wooden pew that was digging into my butt and back already, even though I'd only been there for three minutes, and closed my eyes—which were acting like those cartoons with roll-up window shades instead of eyelids, and attempted to quiet my mind—which would not be quiet, not even for a half-second. I spent fifteen minutes or so wondering how this outer pain was helping me find inner peace, then fifteen minutes thinking that I had no idea why I was sitting here anyway with my poppy-opened eyes and achy butt and sleeping sickness. Almost without warning, peace descended for twenty seconds, drowning out everything else…and then disappeared as quickly as it came, leaving me hopeful and disappointed in equal measure.

For the balance of the hour—or more, depending on the Monk's mood—I sat inside my own head, which was possibly the scariest place on the planet. This was no post-yoga shavasana relaxation, where you're welcome to fall asleep on your mat in fetal position; this was war. I came face to face with my every internal demon, undone to-do list item, and doubt. At the beginning of this journey, I was on the floor of my closet terrified to peek over the edge of my spiritual injuries because I was afraid of what I might find there. In meditation, I wasn't just peering over the edge; I was going spelunking.

See, there's a nasty, nagging truth no one tells you about meditation for spiritual transformation: it's like running one endless, rocky lap around the inside of your skull, day after day, until you wear down a track. I had a hell of a lot of laps to go, one long second of silence at a time.

After a few weeks I said to the Urban Monk, "I think you should know that my brain is full of those scary roller-skating monkeys from *The Return to Oz.*"

He smiled. "Acknowledge the scary monkeys. Acknowledge, then let go. Let them skate away."

"But my mind won't slow down enough to acknowledge them!" I exclaimed in frustration. "It's like I shut my eyes and I'm suddenly driving full-speed on the Autobahn!"

"If you're going a hundred miles an hour, you don't immediately stop. You slow down. You slow down some more, and only *then* can you brake and come to a complete stop. Be patient: you're learning to slow down the car."

"But why don't I *feel* like I'm slowing down?"

"We do not seek a feeling in meditation; we seek redemption of our minds and union with our Creator."

"Yeah—about that union thing. How can I get that?"

"Patience you must have, my young padawan." (Just kidding. He actually said: "Practice.")

I would return home just as Trent was leaving for school, and we'd have a conversation that went like this:

"No offense, babe, but you don't look very good."

"Hmph. Don't pretend that you aren't impressed that I'm going to church every morning when a few months ago I couldn't go to church at all."

"Is this what going to church every morning is supposed to look like?" he asked skeptically.

"Hell if I know."

Then we would kiss goodbye, and I would fall asleep on the couch, fully clothed—shoes and all, until I had to wake up for meetings. Sometimes Trent would come home from school and find me still collapsed there, snuggled up with Oxley, too exhausted to pretend. I was like a hibernating bear; often he would poke me to make sure I was still breathing. Trent called me Sleeping Beauty; I called it a Sleeping Nightmare.

So what kept me going back, day after day?

In part, it was because I knew I had to be awake anyway for my prepaid boot camp. But mostly it was the Urban Monk himself, who consistently showed me what living peace looked like and encouraged me to keep moving toward it.

He never turned anyone away, never thought twice about losing sleep or missing appointments to help neighborhood families. He cooked and cleaned up three meals a day for the homeless, helped the kids with their homework, and answered the door all through the night. He drove a rickety van that limped along a route from food pantries to free clinics to the ER, shelters and back, several times a day or week, depending on the season. "I'm the only transportation for about twenty families," he would apologize if he missed meditation training, as if my spiritual development was as vital as the health of his flock. When I asked why teaching me to meditate was important when there was so much other work to be done, he pointed to my head and said: "This is the most important work in the world. Every battle we fight is won or lost in our minds."

One morning, I confessed that in light of his work, my Thirty by Thirty project seemed a selfish pursuit. The Urban Monk looked at me as if I had grown three heads. "We must all work out our own salvation. We must each walk our own path. You are walking your path courageously."

Courageously? I thought, *Clearly this guy doesn't know me.*

"The first miracle is self-healing," the Urban Monk said. "That it is God's miracle does not make it any less ours. Never discount your participation in the miraculous. You are brave, Reba, even if you don't believe it. You have the courage to come here every day and face yourself to find truth."

I considered this. My daily pilgrimage to St. Lydia was something I clutched with both hands: my own imperfect, clumsy recovery program. *Courage.*

Courage is just dreams with shoes on.

Fumbling through my days, I felt small changes that were large in aggregate. In the same way that my jeans seemed suddenly loose around the waist after a few weeks of morning boot camp, spiritual recovery came by degrees. I noticed I no longer recoiled at the word "God." I could write the words "Lord" and "pastor" and "church" in my journal. It's not that the sting wasn't still there; it was. But it felt further away, like my time with the Urban Monk had insulated me.

One freezing morning, I reached for the heater and accidentally flipped on the radio. Mark Schultz's "I Am" was playing again, just like on the first day of my meditation training. Déjà-forward overtook me, and somehow I knew to turn it up instead of off. Words stampeded through my mind so quickly I scarcely had time to grab a pen.

What if, when God said I AM, we misunderstood? What if God simply said I AM to all of humanity, but that wasn't good enough? Maybe we wanted more, needed more, more than I AM. Perhaps we needed a predicate nominative, a fill-in-the-blank ad-lib, an In Whom To Place Our Faith. A mighty I AM "_____": summarized with words that we could understand, an image we could see. Something we could draw lines around and call our own.

And what if, after we consumed the "_____" with our utterances, we still needed more? Did we add to I AM? Did we follow all the nouns with verbs, round out phrases with adjectives? Did we complete all the parts of speech that never existed? Did we create sentences wrapped into paragraphs that filled up pages and flowed into sacred texts? Did we cry out with words that formed religions…whole cultures of grammatical dissent?

 What if the only phrase, the only origin of the world, was a quietly whispered I AM? The affirmation of Divine Existence, of all Creation, of God, us, the whole Universe…the whole Godiverse. The simplest statement of Being, the first noun and verb we learn in any language. What if all God really said was…I AM?

I believe in I AM.

I clicked the pen and looked at my words, aghast. The Christian radio was still playing; my fingers were still freezing, but the evidence was right under my nose: the meditation was working. I couldn't get to St. Lydia fast enough.

"You're not going to believe what just happened," I said, breathless. I told the Urban Monk the story and read him the journal entry.

"You speak truth," he said with a tremor of feeling. His smile lit up the sanctuary.

The harsh hours of meditation had changed me by gentle intervals. And even though I still couldn't find my breath correctly or clear my mind thoroughly, I knew that as I logged hours inside my head, the track I forged there was getting smoother.

See, there's this lovely, tugging truth no one tells you about meditation for spiritual transformation: sometimes, when you're running through the rocks inside your head, you sense rays of light on the horizon that promise perpetual sunrise if you can just…keep…going.

16

Promises

"This year I'm not only ready for Christmas Eve; I'm ambushing it like a Nativity Ninja," I told Trent on the way to his parents' house for the holidays. "Your family's Christmas Eve curse isn't getting me this year, no sir. If I'm spending my entire twenty-ninth year experiencing various religions, I will be in attendance on the most-churched day of the year."

In the previous four holiday seasons, our clan had made it to a Christmas Eve service only once—not that I'd been disappointed about this fact. Our absence was not for my mother-in-law's lack of trying. Circumstances like lack of available seats or bad timing had always conspired against Becky. We'd spent several Christmas Eves driving around looking for a church that would have us, but alas, there was no room in the pew.

"Even my contingencies have contingencies this year!" I proudly showed my husband the arrows I'd drawn from secondary options to tertiary plans. "Just promise me we'll make it to church tonight."

"Why do I need to promise? It looks like you're ready for everything,"

Everything except what happened.

"Becky?" I called nervously to my mother-in-law from the bathroom. She entered wearing a Jingle Bells apron. If she was surprised that I was not wearing any pants, she didn't show it. Even though I dearly love my mother-in-law, showing her my naked backside is not high on my list of holiday bonding activities. Still, in need of a second opinion, I bent over and pulled down my underwear to show her my rear.

"Is it just me, or do these hives look a little dangerous?"

She examined the lower half of my body, which looked like I'd been attacked by killer red slime in a 1980s horror film, except the slime was still growing: even as we watched, conjoined, welted bumps crept slowly up my body.

"It certainly looks painful." I could hear concern in her voice. "Does your throat feel tight?"

I swallowed. "A little."

"Let's take you next door. Our neighbor's son is a doctor."

Five minutes later I was half-naked in the back hall of the neighbor's Christmas celebration, showing my nether regions to a stranger while the sounds of Christmas played merrily in the next room. Children were laughing. Chestnuts were roasting. My throat was closing. Or, at least that's what the visiting doctor thought *might* be happening.

"Can't really tell without my tools," he announced, peering down my throat with a flashlight and a Popsicle stick. "But I advise you to get to the nearest doctor."

(Doctor? Wasn't *he* a doctor? I do not expose myself to neighbors' visiting sons just for fun! It turned out he wasn't licensed for Ohio practice.) The doctor went back to his kids and their presents; Becky and I went home in a panic.

"I need you to drive me to the ER," I told Trent in Becky's kitchen. He groaned and put the Yuletide Ale he was about to open back in the fridge.

"You're both overreacting," he said. "It's just some red spots. You've had hives every day for months." Trent is so calm that I'm not even sure he considers death an emergency. Becky handed him the keys, leaving no room for discussion.

"I have huge hives," I explained at the Urgent Care check-in. "My breath feels squished, like I'm trying to breathe through a straw." Rarely have I seen a nurse move so quickly. Urgent Care is usually like Wait-Five-Hours-Care, but this lady had me in a room, naked but for a paper gown, and two other nurses examining me faster than you can hum "Away in a Manger."

One nurse fetched a doctor, who examined me with lightning speed. He pointed accusingly at Trent. "Driving is faster than the ambulance. Take your wife to the Emergency Room. *Now!*" Trent's eyes widened and the color drained from his face. The staff bundled us out the door without even asking my name. They must have wanted to avoid a scandal. Holiday deaths are notoriously bad for business.

Five minutes into the drive I began choke-breathing in the passenger seat and Trent's version of panic hit—which is to say, he broke the speed limit.

"I love you," I squeaked.

"I love you, too," he said, accelerating.

"Focus on your breathing. In and out," the Urban Monk had instructed in meditation training when I became frustrated that I couldn't concentrate my attention. Well. My breath certainly had my full attention in the car on Christmas Eve. (Perhaps Throat Closing Meditation could become a new craze. *100% Guaranteed to wipe your mind of every extraneous worry!*)

I wondered how many more people find God on the way to the Emergency Room than in church. If I could have spoken, I might have told Trent that churches angling for converts should set up a little Salvation Stand on the way into the hospital, where you could be splashed with holy water on demand. When we arrived at the hospital, for example, I would have accepted a splashing of Holy Boiling Oil if it meant I could breathe.

The ER staff pumped me full of adrenaline and Benadryl and steroids, but it could have been liquefied Twinkies for all I cared. Suddenly I breathed pounds upon pounds of delicious air:

"In and out. In and out. In and out," soothed the nurse.

My mind went completely blank but for the beautiful, beautiful air. My own powerful, healing breath filled me so completely there was no room for thought, and it was just as peaceful as the Urban Monk had always said it would be.

Doctors couldn't tell me what I'd reacted to on Christmas Eve, or why the reaction had been so severe. But I was so accustomed to not having medical answers that I simply shrugged my shoulders, stashed an Epi-Pen in my purse for emergency use, and didn't worry about it. A one-time ER experience was much easier to dismiss than the perpetual Sickness, and besides, I had more important things on my mind: I needed to get back to my project, my meditation training, and the boot camp. For a Thirty by Thirty jumpstart, I clicked the "Request a Free Bible Study" link on the Jehovah's Witness website.

When my doorbell rang in the early evening the very next night, I was surprised to find a beaming young couple on my doorstep.

"Hello! We're Mary and John Prince, with the Jehovah's Witnesses!" said a couple in unison.

"Hello," I replied, wishing I had real clothes instead of fuzzy purple slippers and frog pajamas since they were dressed in their Sunday best. "I submitted my request less than twenty-four hours ago. You work fast!"

I felt obligated to ask them inside since I had invited them (sort of). I offered beverages, which they declined. Maybe this was rule #1 at the School of Door-Knockers Missionary Training Academy: Do not accept beverages of unknown origins.

Mary and John sat together, on the opposite couch, and it felt like that moment on a date when you know you're going to get naked, but you're not sure who is going to make the first move. They smiled, and I considered that I couldn't have chosen a more gorgeous couple for my first spiritual threesome; from their ebony skin to glowing smiles, the couple was a study in beauty, and they seemed eager to make lots of little Jehovah's Witness converts together.

Mr. Prince plunged right in: "Tell us about your spiritual background!"

Explaining my project should have made it clear I wasn't a candidate for conversion, but they looked at each other knowingly, seeming to telegraph with their eyes, *You've got this one, babe!* before Mrs. Prince asked me an opening question.

"If you did believe we had the truth, then would you be willing to convert?"

Tsk-tsk, trying to sell a saleswoman, I thought.

Unfortunately for the Princes, I was not a yes-woman. I evaded her question with a statement. "Your question makes the assumption that I believe there is only one truth."

This stopped them, but only briefly; Mr. Prince made a fast recovery. (Perhaps a battery of difficult statements was included in Missionary Sales 201?)

"I'm not trying to be difficult," I apologized. "I've just been through a lot, religion-wise. I do believe in truth, but I don't believe one religion has it."

Both Mr. and Mrs. Prince nodded sympathetically, as if they had arrived to comfort me. Pity hid behind their smiles.

"Poor, confused girl," I imagined Mr. Prince telling Mrs. Prince at the dinner table later that evening.

"I know," Mrs. Prince would sigh, passing the mashed potatoes. "Thirty religions? Imagine the confusion!"

I did not take kindly to being pitied for seeking, but I recognized I was likely projecting my insecurities. Affording them the benefit of the doubt, I asked about their position on hell. Mr. Prince explained that what Jesus *actually* taught about hell was that it didn't exist. I enjoyed this reasoning until he casually dropped the fact that God destroys wicked souls.

He filled the next half-hour with so much memorized scripture and conviction that I cheered him on internally—*You go, Mr. Prince! Rah-rah-sis-boom-bah!*—in spite of some of his odder statements such as, "Satan was evicted from heaven in 1914," said so matter-of-factly that it seemed a historical fact, like the Revolutionary War or the invention of pantyhose.

Mr. Prince didn't need me as his cheerleader, though, because Mrs. Prince looked as though she might joyfully jump his bones right after he finished discussing the Bible's original Greek text for this-and-that verse.

They tackled my questions in tandem, scatting through the Scriptures like a dynamic jazz duo. I began to feel a bit dizzy.

"Do you realize you're looking at the whole world through a lens of your religion?" I asked.

Mr. Prince cleared his throat. "I don't see it that way."

"What if you're wrong about your beliefs?"

"Then I'm wrong," he said in the manner of a martyr telling the Inquisitor to light the flames, "and I'm a better person for being wrong."

Mrs. Prince nodded her head in agreement, and I saw they had a point. He couldn't get in much trouble with a Bible in one hand and his wife's knee in the other.

I drove to Mr. and Mrs. Prince's Kingdom Hall the following Sunday morning and was surprised to realize I'd passed it a hundred times without noticing. I pondered how often we fail to see what's right in front of us because we aren't looking.

But for the sign advertising it as "Kingdom Hall," the building looked like it could be an office; it was concrete with glass doors. Mrs. Prince waited for me inside. She looked beautiful: her outfit, jewelry, and nails were perfectly matched, and all around her were men and women dressed to the nines. It reminded me a little of the Baptists—sadly, without the hats.

I'd done well to change out of my frog pajamas.

Mrs. Prince introduced me around. "This is my mother...and my grandmother...and my cousins." Three generations of lovely African American women hugged me in welcome, but Mrs. Prince's grandmother took a particular interest in me. She looked up intently through her spectacles as I spoke, her presence stately despite her cane.

"I, too, conducted a spiritual search when I was your age," she informed me, taking my hand. "I found Jehovah at the end of it."

"And here we all are," laughed one of the cousins.

They are so kind, I thought. *Of course Mrs. Prince is a Jehovah's Witness. What else could she be?*

"If you earnestly seek the truth and study for yourself," added Grandma, "you're sure to find it. I remember how moved I was when I found Jehovah for the first time." She closed her eyes in remembrance. "I knew in my heart this was the truth."

The unspoken end of her statement was that if I searched hard enough, I, too, would find Jehovah's truth. Throughout the service—which was held in a simple, large room with padded chairs, a stage, and a pulpit—I was troubled by this question: *Why do so many people believe that if I seek the truth with an open mind, I'll end up thinking exactly as they do?*

It wasn't that I didn't want to be a Jehovah's Witness; they were very nice people. I could imagine a pleasant future of spiritual adoption and potluck suppers with this kindly family, where we would eat seven-layer salad and laugh at my days of Thirty by Thirty seeking. But I knew I didn't ever want to think about spirituality within a self-sustaining system again. Life isn't a multiple-choice game show, with Regis Philbin demanding, "Is that your *final* answer?"

After the service's conclusion, the Prince family surrounded me once again for a round of warm goodbyes. Mary's grandmother tugged my coat and gestured for me to lean down so my face was close to her own.

"Do all the seeking you need to, dear. But when you talk about your journey, make sure you tell everyone that you found truth here."

I thought of the kindness her family had shown me, her daughter and son-in-law's tireless commitment to Jehovah, and the depth of their dedication. They knocked on doors several evenings a week, after working full-time jobs during the day. At every door they risked rejection and ridicule. Had I ever been that committed to anything so selfless?

"I'll do that." I said, covering her hand with mine. "I promise."

17

Miracles

The following week, my cell phone rang.

"Reba Riley?"

"Speaking."

"I'm a recruiter for a position at Orange Tiger Industries."

My heart beat faster. I knew this company well; it was Fortune 500. Back before we'd relocated, I used to confide in Trent that I would change teams if Orange Tiger ever called.

"We'd like to interview you for a territory sales position that just became open. Are you available for a phone interview tomorrow, and—provided that goes well—could you fly to Houston next Tuesday?"

I had to sit down.

"Yes," I said, trying to not sound like a teenage girl in the front row of a concert. "I can make that work."

I flew to three different cities in as many weeks for interviews. How the Sickness allowed me to do this without falling asleep on the wrong plane and waking up in Albuquerque is a mystery. Drooling in window seats, I dreamed about how this new job would change my life. A promised land of blissful employment beckoned to me from my possible future, promising a small geographic territory, customers and products I already knew, and a company car with brand-new tires. No more backwoods West Virginia with lumberyard owners who kept their scary dogs and scarier hunting rifles in the stock room and suggested with lascivious winks that if the snow got too bad, I could just, "Stay the night at my house, Honeybun." No more sleeping at rest stops. No more lubricated nails, *ever*.

"Sick or not sick, you are the best person for this position," I told myself in my compact mirror in bathroom stalls. I visualized the dusty sales awards hanging in my home office, all won while my mystery illness strangled me behind the scenes. "You can do this. You can *rock* this."

I got the job.

"Excellent!" exclaimed the Urban Monk when I told him the good news. "External circumstances are realigning to reflect your internal change."

"How is changing jobs a spiritual event?" I asked, perplexed. In my mind, a dichotomy existed between my mornings with the monk and what I did to pay the bills.

He laughed. "Everything is a spiritual event. Did you think you would undertake a yearlong spiritual journey and find things unchanged?"

"I imagined changes, but…," my voice trailed off as I considered what I'd hoped this year would bring: spiritual healing and—maybe—physical healing (if I could find the right diagnosis). "I guess I never thought life would change like this. It kind of feels like a miracle—just not the one I was looking for."

"Continue on this path and everything will change," he foretold. "Miracles will swirl around you."

The Urban Monk talked a lot about miracles. He often challenged me to think about the relativity of time and space, to consider that perception does not equal reality. "Miracles are not only possible," he said one day, "they are happening around us continually. We need only open our eyes to see them."

On one particularly bad day for the Sickness, when I had felt the weight of my mystery illness in every word, I'd answered his miracle-talk too sharply, "I could use a miracle healing any time now, Father. Yesterday, preferably."

He had not corrected my tone; he simply lifted his hand in a "stop" motion and gazed above my head for several minutes. It was eerie; I could almost feel his energy field expand right into mine. I finally understood why people sometimes fall down in Pentecostal churches: had I been standing up, I might have fallen over.

With his hand up, he closed his eyes and spoke: "Just because we do not feel it immediately does not mean we have not been healed. Time is an illusion; your healing already exists."

As much as I wanted to believe his words that day, I brushed them off. They didn't make me feel better; they didn't keep me from missing a few days of meditation training due to the Sickness. But something about this everyday work miracle—the one I wasn't looking for—made me wonder.

"Maybe there are miracles in my future," I conceded to the Monk after we discussed how the job change had come about. "I think maybe I will be healed one day."

"Don't think you will. *Know* you will."

"I *know* I will," I echoed. I disbelieved the words, but the act of saying them aloud seemed a good place to begin. Church bells rang out the hour. We'd spent our whole morning talking instead of training. "I'm so sorry we're not praying or meditating right now, Father. I know that's why I'm here."

"This *is* prayer. This *is* meditation," the Urban Monk gently corrected. "Make your life a prayer. Live your meditation."

Although I wasn't quite sure what it meant to "live" my meditation, I did notice I wasn't struggling as hard in my morning regimen. At boot camp, I found my muscles responding as if the miles were shorter and the weights lighter. In meditation, my mind didn't always fight me, and minutes blurred into hours faster.

One morning I sat across from the monk, bobbing atop the meditative water as I had for months when—suddenly—I slipped under the surface tension, as easily as I used to dive into the pool as a kid. It felt like I was floating underwater on my back, breathing through a snorkel, and looking at everything from a different, still viewpoint. I breathed in and out, in and out, without thinking about it. I wasn't conscious or unconscious, I simply *was*. I was part of the Godiverse, and I was the Godiverse. If I had any specific awareness, it was that I was floating in the current of energy I'd always felt from the Urban Monk and others, the same energy that often tingled my scalp.

Though I didn't make the connection in the moment, the peaceful weightlessness recalled scuba diving with my Dad, and not only because of the breath. Because of the reconciliation.

After my parents' divorce, Dad and I stopped speaking for the better part of my early twenties. We were simply too hurt to engage until we made a last-ditch effort to restore our relationship: we went on a scuba vacation. Two wounded, angry family members spending seven days together in a situation where they could easily suffocate one another was probably a terrible idea, but there we were anyway—toes over on the edge of a bobbing boat, each wearing a hundred pounds of diving gear as we jumped in the ocean.

After flailing on the surface to get our bearings, we descended into a different, underwater world. A world where there was no space for our hurt, and no words existed for our anger. We floated far beneath the surface when Dad saw something and waved for my attention.

He pointed to a pod of dolphins playing under streaming shafts of sunlight. *This is so beautiful, daughter,* said his gesture. *I didn't want you to miss it.* My breath deep and metered, I waved back, aware of a joy that stretched far beyond the sea. Even a pod of swimming dolphins could not compare to the beauty of becoming weightless in an instant.

I passed thirty minutes in buoyant meditation before my mind bubbled up to the surface of consciousness, popping up to discover warm Energy washing over my scalp.

So this is what all the fuss is about.

I blinked a few times to reorient myself.

"Welcome back," said the Monk quietly. "I take it you didn't hear the police sirens?"

"No," I answered, astounded. "I heard nothing at all."

Even though the Urban Monk didn't actually speak like Yoda, I started posting Yoda-esque snippets of our conversations on Facebook.

Monk: You have to learn to surrender.

Me: I'll try to surrender.

Monk: Don't try, do.

Me: I'll try to do.

Monk: Let God do.

Then one day a private message popped up from Joanna, a girl I'd gone to Christian high school with. *Hey, I know it's been a long time, but we need to talk.*

A long time? It had been ten years, and we weren't best friends to begin with. While I puzzled over the message, Joanna added: *It's about the Urban Monk. There are some things you need to know.* Even in print, her tone sounded ominous. My heart palpitated, beating an unsteady echo. *My job interfaces with the monk's neighborhood association,* Joanna wrote. *The rest I want to tell you in person.*

A terrified tingle spread through my body, as if I'd awakened in the night to the sound of an intruder's footsteps.

I barely slept, but it wasn't the monk's potential misdeeds that made me sweat through my pajamas. Cold fear informed me of just how closely I'd tied my spiritual journey to the Urban Monk. I'd let the guide become the path.

"What if he's a criminal or worse?" I asked Trent on my way out the door the next morning, knowing that even if Joanna's news turned positive— the Urban Monk had once won the lottery and given away all his winnings to the poor!—the blow had been dealt. I'd realized my mistake, and could no longer look at the Urban Monk the same way.

"I guess you'll have to find yourself another monk." Trent joked.

I didn't laugh.

"I don't know quite how to tell you this," Joanna treaded carefully, pouring us both tea. All the way over on the drive to her house, my heart had rapped a staccato warning: *Please don't let him be a bad person.* "The Monk is not who you think he is. He claims to be an archbishop, but no one is beneath him. He…he was *kicked out* of the Eastern Orthodox Church."

I felt relieved. "That makes me like him more."

I searched my mind: had the Monk ever directly claimed to be an archbishop in the Eastern Orthodox Church? No. But he had attested that he'd taken his vows there and omitted any mention of a schism. His laugh about Post-Traumatic Church Syndrome suddenly made more sense.

"Do you know why he was kicked out?" I quizzed.

"No one is sure," Joanna said, fidgeting with her napkin. "I'm so sorry to have to be the one to tell you. I thought you should know the truth before you get too involved."

Too involved? It's a little late for that.

"Please don't misunderstand me," Joanna continued. "I like the monk. He's always been very kind to me, and he does a lot of good for the homeless here." She appeared to struggle for a balanced explanation. "I just saw all your Facebook posts and it seemed like you were buying into everything he said and, well, I didn't want you to get hurt…again."

From our messaged conversation, I knew her short pause before "again" contained her own decade of spiritual struggle. As the daughter of missionaries to Africa, Joanna also suffered from a case of PTCS and was still trying to reconcile the God of her childhood with her adult identity.

"Didn't you ever wonder why he's the only monk in his monastery?"

I shook my head. "I just thought it was because people were afraid of the bad neighborhood."

She rolled her eyes. "Most of those stories are old."

I thought back to the Urban Monk's stories: every day it was a new situation he had turned around. I sipped my tea too fast. *Scalding.*

Joanna continued, "It's not as bad as he makes it seem. There's more grant money flowing here than anywhere else in Ohio."

"If there's so much money, why doesn't he have enough?" I challenged.

Joanna sighed. "He's…very bad with money."

I almost jumped out of the chair. "Is he stealing?"

In all my time with the monk, he'd never asked for money; I'd even heard him speak against tithing. (Coming from a background where tithing was about as optional as death or taxes, his perspective refreshed me.) Then again, he didn't have to hint around: the need was so obvious it could choke you. I'd been sending St. Lydia checks monthly.

"No, no; nothing like theft. He just doesn't keep accurate logs. He's been cut off from neighborhood revitalization funding because of it."

I felt reassured but swallowed hard on the next question. "Is that why he doesn't have any help in the kitchen?"

"Well, that…and he runs volunteers off," she explained. "Everything has to be his way or the highway. And if he disagrees about how things are being done in the neighborhood, he'll just storm out of meetings."

"Is that all?" I asked, tongue burning. "If not, please just tell me. It's better to get it over with."

Joanna sighed again. "Not quite. I couldn't find anything to back up his history."

"Do you mean all the stories he told about making a lot of money in business and studying in India are a lie?"

"I don't think they're outright *lies*," she winced at the word, "but when I asked him for specifics, he got super defensive and wouldn't answer my questions." I thought back to when I'd asked the Monk what his name was before he took his vows. "Oh, I don't reveal *that*," he'd said, almost offended. "The old me is gone." At the time, I'd considered the answer highly spiritual, but now it made me wonder.

I fell silent for a minute, tallying up his purported sins. I trusted Joanna because of our shared past and because she had nothing to gain by sharing this information with me, but her words didn't fit with my experience. Mentally, it felt like I was trying to solve a wooden puzzle designed to fit North America with pieces shaped like other continents.

When I finally stumbled from Joanna's house a few hours later, I bit a lip until I could get into the car. The news wasn't *that* bad: he wasn't a criminal or even a man with an outrageous past. He was just…a regular guy. A human being with flaws and cracks. He wasn't a sage, a prophet, or the Buddha reincarnate. I'd been holding onto an illusion of the Urban Monk instead of an actual person. I'd set myself up for failure by putting a leader on a pedestal. What was I *thinking*?

I'm like the girl who runs straight from a bad relationship to the first willing guy she meets, I thought. *The Urban Monk was my spiritual rebound. I need to take a step back, gather my thoughts, take time for me.* I groaned aloud when I realized that if I added *It's not you; it's me* and *We need to see other* ~~people~~ *religions* to the list, I'd have a full-fledged break-up on my hands.

I drifted mentally all day, unsure of what to do. I felt disillusioned, like when I found out the money under my pillow wasn't left by the tooth fairy. Should I give up the Urban Monk altogether? Should I keep studying with him?

I mulled over my questions while walking Oxley late that evening. Preoccupied by the freezing wind whipping my face, I almost didn't hear a ragtag group of homeless people yell at me as they crossed the street.

"Hey, Miss, can we pet your dog?" a man called.

"Sure," I replied, trotting Oxley over. Mr. Toothless had asked the question. He bent down to rub Oxley's ears.

"Where are you guys headed?" I shivered, hoping they'd say a shelter.

Mr. Toothless smiled wryly, making a face at Ox: "Shelters all packed up. We're headed to the bridge."

I thought of the Urban Monk's warm sanctuary with folded blankets on the pews for nights like this. "You know, the Mission Kitchen might have a spot for you."

"Oh, the Father up a ways?!" exclaimed Ms. Ponytail. "We know him. He saved Peter's life!" She gestured to a third guy carrying a beat-up guitar case.

"Got stabbed in the stomach," Peter explained, lifting double sweatshirts to show me his scar. "Father'd never met me, but it was a miracle that he found me on the street and drove me to the Emergency Room. He stayed with me all night, and brought me food once I could eat again. Say, I wrote him a song—want to hear it?"

Peter pulled out an old guitar and strummed the worst, most beautiful song I'd ever heard. "Father sav-ed me/ He sav-ed me/ He sav-ed me from dying/dying on the street/It was a miracle, miracle…"

Ms. Ponytail picked up Oxley and hummed along, dancing a little in time. Mr. Toothless joined in out of key. I swayed there under the stars, dumbfounded by the answers to my questions—standing right in front of me, dancing and singing on the sidewalk, and echoing in my own heart to the tune of their song.

It's not about what the Urban Monk is or isn't; it's about who he is when someone needs him.

For Peter and me, the Urban Monk had been exactly what was needed when it was needed, but I couldn't stay with the Urban Monk forever.

Joanna's words had shaken me out of the comfort zone I'd created at St. Lydia. Watching the small group sway under the stars, I knew with certainty that it was time for me to move on. There is a time to heal and a time to hustle. It was time to hustle.

I called the Urban Monk the next day. I wish I could say I explained myself, but I didn't. I was strong enough to recognize my mistake and remedy it, but not yet strong enough to confront someone who had done so much for me. "I'd like to change our sessions to once a week in the evening," I said, without offering further explanation.

"Certainly. But if you ever need me, you know where to find me."

I do. You'll be where you always have been, just in front of the altar, leading the way to God—however imperfectly.

He said: "You have worked hard, Reba. I'm proud of you."

But I heard: "The Force is strong with this one."

I stared in disbelief at the Aletheia church sign with a sense of certainty that the Godiverse was messing with me for the fun of it. I'd just discovered that my morning boot camp had been inexplicably moved to Aletheia's warehouse-sanctuary. Now I'd be visiting the church I never wanted to see again. *Every morning.* In the place my former selves had closed in around me, forcing me to the bathroom, I'd now be at the mercy of the boot camp Torturer. I could almost see God standing off-screen, waiting for me to do something reality TV–worthy, like graffiti the sign or run my car into the building.

The cosmic joke couldn't have come at a worse time; settling into my new job had triggered the Sickness. Even at the early hour I knew this would be a Lost Day. I'd felt lead collecting in my blood when I dragged myself into St. Lydia for meditation the evening before, and the Energy that buzzed around my head then didn't slow the onset of the episode. Today, sitting in the parking lot, my limbs were weighted down. I recognized that no matter what I did—run the laps or not, lay down or not—nothing would stop what was coming. In three to six hours, I would be sleeping like the dead. How long I would be down—a day, a week— was anybody's guess. But down I would go, and from the feel of things, I would be crashing hard. People with migraines talk about halos as a sign of coming pain, but with the Sickness I felt the opposite of sharp light; I felt a blurry darkness, heavy with physical weight, pooling in my limbs.

I was angry, so angry: at the Godiverse for engineering the ridiculous situation at Aletheia, and at my body for consistently failing me. I slammed my car door, stomped through the snow, and threw open the church door, as if I could defy the Sickness just by showing up for the stupid workout.

My joints ached and my head pounded as I ran my body ragged in the church boot camp, completing the required exercises. My body filled with exhaustion so quickly that I could cry, and any success I'd had with meditation seemed like a far-off dream that had slipped like silk through my fingers and fallen into black waters, sinking deeper every minute.

I ran the sanctuary corridor, down and back, weaving around chairs set out for the church faithful as my mind yelled ugly things at my body, things I wouldn't say to my worst enemy. *You are weak. You are lazy. And this Sickness? It's all in your head! You are a complete failure, and someday soon everyone is going to see you for what you really are: a crazy person, unfit for daily life. I hate you.*

I moved faster, but I couldn't outrun the Sickness or the thoughts. The only thing I could do was put one foot in front of the other. So I fixed my gaze on the altar, then the church's rear doors, then the altar, then the doors. I ran slightly unsteadily, my tennis shoes pounding the sanctuary floor.

Then my eyes caught on a table I hadn't noticed before. It was a simple display: a photo of a little girl, a daughter in this church, a blonde pixie with bright eyes and leukemia. Next to the photo was an explanation of her illness, followed by a list of what her family needed: prayer, casseroles, babysitting, and donations for medical bills. I lapped the table a few times, and the gravity of this family's plight shut up my mind, if only for a few minutes. The third time I passed the table, I noticed the sign-up sheet. It was overflowing with names written in the margins and on scraps and napkins, names shouting one thing so loudly I could almost hear it: *"We love you. We will support you. We will bear this burden with you. We will lift you on our shoulders and take care of you, so you can take care of your baby."*

My sneakers stopped; I tripped over my laces; I fell to the ground in surprise before this table-turned-altar. I didn't hear the whistle of the boot camp sergeant, or see him start to walk toward me to find out if I was hurt. I simply stared in wonder at the face of this little one for whom the congregation cried, this baby girl lifted up by the prayers and alms of her people of faith. There was no Christ child here, just a simple typed sign, yet the glory of the Lord shone round about. An entire temple—even the entire Vatican—could collapse under the weight of this faith, this display of God's people helping each other; but here it was, in this warehouse converted to a church I did not like.

Here it was: Faith, held up by three plastic legs.

Had I been able to think, I would have given God a hard time. "So this is where you would have me find faith? On a dirty warehouse floor? With the smells of stale coffee and sweat mingling in the air? Yeah, this is a *great* story." But I couldn't think, because it all happened too fast. One minute I was thinking about how horrible I felt, trying not to fall behind the group; and the next I was having a transcendent moment where All Became Clear. It was like a car accident I didn't see coming until—*WHAM!*—I was the victim of a hit-and-run perpetrated by the Almighty.

There on my knees, I found Faith.

I saw that Faith wasn't in the strength of an institution; it wasn't about the institution at all. It was about this clipboard full of grace. It was about Mrs. Kelley signing up to clean this little girl's house while her mother sat by her hospital bed. It was about Mr. Smith cashing part of his paycheck to contribute to medical bills. It was about Miss Betty, who stayed up the past four nights in a row praying for healing.

Faith lived beyond these walls, knocking them down with the force of a thousand oceans, with every person, everywhere, who chose to carry a neighbor's burden in the name of something greater. Someone Greater. But Faith also lived here, even where I felt unwelcome; it lived here, where the sermons grated my edges and the style of worship annoyed me.

Faith lived here on this little table, doing sprints of love around me, lapping me more quickly than an Olympian.

Faith: the essence of community hoped for, the evidence of love unseen.

I found Faith on my knees, but not in prayer. I found it in a church, but not during a service. I stumbled over the miracle because it had been right there all the time, waiting for me to notice.

18

Shaking

"This sandwich is so good it should have its own religion," I said on date night.

"Agreed," Trent replied, biting into his own gourmet grilled cheese. "But would it count as one of the thirty? Church of the Big Cheese sounds like a place you would like."

I was making a face that said, "Don't push your luck if you plan to get lucky," when we saw the troop of young men file in the restaurant's front doors two-by-two, like cute pairs of Noah's ark animals in matching suits. I didn't need the Book of Mormon to know these twenty clean-cut guys were missionaries for The Church of Jesus Christ of Latter-day Saints (LDS); they were wearing nametags. I elbowed Trent and pointed.

"Stop staring," Trent whispered.

"I'm just trying to figure out how to approach without looking like I'm hitting on them."

"You're going to hit on another guy when I bought your dinner?"

"I bought *your* dinner, pal," I reminded him.

On our way out, I slipped the missionary at the end of the table a napkin with my cell phone number and said, "Please have someone call me." (In retrospect, I failed miserably. It definitely looked like I was hitting on him.) I may not be the only gal to ever have picked up twenty missionaries, but I bet I'm the only one to have done it in sweatpants, with a to-go box of grilled cheese and husband in tow.

The missionaries must have been salivating more over my potential salvation than their dinner, because there was a voice mail waiting on my cell when we got back to the car. "This is Elder Deck," went the message, "Please call me back to set a time up for us to get together."

"Wow, these guys are a well-organized militia of world-savers!" I said to Trent.

I called Elder Deck back right away. We set two times: Friday to meet with the missionaries and Sunday to attend services near OSU's campus. I asked him if anyone had ever volunteered their cell phone number.

"Well," he answered, "I've *heard* of things like this happening, but they've never happened to me...or any missionary I actually know."

Aha! I was *so going* to become a Mormon missionary urban legend! I felt certain the story of "The girl and her cell phone number" might circulate evermore among the sweet, suited missionary-mafia. Perhaps it would even grow from the truth to full-on lore. *I heard she found the truth right then and there... I heard she begged for The Book of Mormon on her knees! I heard she disappeared right in front of them... She was an angel sent from heaven to test their knowledge!*

Well, maybe not the angel part. But it's not every day a gal gets to become an urban legend.

I met my pair of assigned missionaries at the local meetinghouse for their ward (congregation), which was located right off Ohio State's campus. They wore matching white dress shirts, black ties, and serious yet friendly expressions as they waited for me by the entrance.

"I'm Elder Deck," said the shorter of the two, as he opened the door for me. He was a handsome, well-built fellow with dark hair and a wide smile.

"And I'm Elder Bedford," said the taller one. I'm not sure whether it was his thin frame or innocent eyes with blonde lashes, but he seemed very young.

We sat in the meetinghouse foyer, which was set up much like a living room. I sat on a long couch, and the Elders faced me from two armchairs and I learned a little about their missions. They each *volunteered* to do a two-year mission, during which they would give up TV, Internet, e-mail (except once a week to family only), radio, music, reading (except the Bible and selected LDS texts), seeing their friends, dating, and thinking about dating. This was in addition to having already given up or never partaken in: sex, drugs, porn, coffee, masturbation, and cigarettes, among other things. They chose to surrender control of where or with whom they would live, knowing they would not see their families for twenty-four months.

In slight awe of their dedication, I asked how they did it.

"Simple," Elder Deck smiled. "Our service to God means more than anything."

"How does it feel when other Christians say you aren't saved, or claim you are part of a cult?" I asked.

"It hits me right here," Elder Bedford answered, slamming a fist to his chest. "It really hurts. I love the Savior. I believe in God the Father and the Holy Spirit. How can people say that?"

The Elders did most of the talking during our conversation, and their countenances shone with spiritual fervor. I knew this look well; I used to wear it myself before the Breaking, back when I had all the answers. When he talked about Jesus, Elder Deck's passion became more pronounced. He believed so hard that he almost shimmered, *Twilight*-vampire style. It was the kind of light Mrs. Easton reminded me about, the glow I wondered if I could ever have back.

Talking with them reminded me so much of myself at eighteen that I choked up. Elder Deck was positively on fire about the truth of the Book of Mormon; his dark features were animated by a faith he would never think of as blind. Then again, I wouldn't have called my faith blind either when I was his age.

You can't know what blind faith is until you see what it isn't.

"The LDS church is all I have ever known," he admitted.

I hoped the day would never come that he would question his identity as an elder. I wanted to put him in a glass box so he could always glow, so he would never have to lie in bed in the night and realize he gave up two years of his life for something he could no longer believe in. I didn't want him to ever lose the faith that made up his life, because I didn't want him to have to wake up with total emptiness like I did.

Did.

Did I just speak of emptiness in past tense?

For my Sunday visit with the elders' congregation, I raided the back of my closet.

"Well, hello," I said to a conservative navy suit I hadn't worn since my Focus on the Family days, back when I was ten pounds and a spiritual lifetime lighter.

I knew it would still fit, but only with control-top pantyhose. While shaking my booty into the hose, I tripped over Oxley and landed on the floor with my legs in the air. Since only half of me fell into the hosiery, I wriggled around on the floor trying to stuff in the other half. Then I heard Trent open the bedroom door.

"Look away! Look away!" I cried. "Some things are simply too shameful for a husband to witness!"

Things like shoplifting on the way to church, for example. I didn't realize I was ferrying stolen goods onto LDS property until Elder Deck was introducing me to the bishop.

"It's so nice to meet you!" I enthused, removing my gloves to shake hands. Stuffing the gloves into my coat pocket, I found a granola bar—an item I'd forgotten to pay for at the gas station. (For a girl who once turned herself in for stealing a red-hot from a teacher's candy dish, a contraband granola bar seemed akin to bank robbery.)

I did not confess, though. I had my urban legend status to safeguard.

"This is the girl doing the religions project," Elder Bedford said to a group of missionaries. They all nodded knowingly, which made me feel as if I had been the subject of prior discussion. I imagined myself on a list of conversion prospects like the sales prospects lists I make for my Monday morning conference calls; perhaps my name had even been drawn on a brainstorming sheet in a missionary conference room. How exciting!

Elder Bedford and I were late joining Elder Deck for the start of the service; the singing had already commenced. As I slid into my seat, Elder Deck whispered excitedly, "This is such a great song!"

It was number 196, "Jesus, Once of Humble Birth." While we sang, I studied the lyrics, thinking how sorely disappointed anti-Mormon Christians might be at the orthodox-sounding verses:

Jesus, once of humble birth,
Now in glory comes to earth.
Once he suffered grief and pain;
Now he comes on earth to reign.

Scripture study, hymns, prayer, and the taking of the sacrament (communion): everything was so unremarkably normal in comparison to a Protestant service. One exception was that the sacrament featured water instead of wine or grape juice. This made me think of Catholic holy water, except this was for drinking, and I considered that if I were to partake in communion ever again I'd still prefer wine to water, if only for the holy tingle on the tongue.

I'd been taught as a child to regard the LDS church as a cult, the same word we used for sects that brainwashed members into living in compounds and committing mass suicide. As I looked around at the rows of shiny, singing people, it was hard to compute how this crowd ever fell in that category.

It was the first Sunday of the month, which, I was told, meant everyone was fasting. *It's a good thing I didn't chow down on my stolen granola bar in the lobby!* Fast Sunday also meant that instead of having assigned speakers, there would be "testimony time"—basically open mic night, except in the morning and without any bad poetry.

Though this ranked as my first Mormon testimony meeting, I had logged scads of hours in similar services. In my experience, it always became an adult version of story time—with pews instead of carpet squares and God stories instead of stuffed animals. There was always the over-sharer; the one who said, "Um, um, um…," instead of speaking; and the one who talked an inappropriately long amount of time about an unsuitable topic. Depending on the age of the congregation, an embarrassing medical condition or gruesome surgical maneuver might be explored.

"Brothers and sisters, the time is now yours to bear your testimonies," the LDS leader announced. An awkward silence ensued. I could almost hear everyone's heart beating questions like, "Is that indigestion or the Holy Spirit telling me to go forward?"

A brave soul trooped to the microphone, daring to go first. He began with, "I know the Church is true, the Book of Mormon is the Word of God, and Joseph Smith is God's prophet," and continued into a lovely story of God's provision for tuition money. With the ice broken, a line formed and one person after another bore testimony, all beginning with the first guy's proclamation and ending with, "I say these things in the name of Jesus Christ, amen."

Many spoke of reading the Book of Mormon, asking the Holy Spirit to "bear witness of the book's truth," and feeling that truth in their hearts. I recognized the feeling they described. It's the same feeling you get when the power goes out, and you think the battery might be out of flashlights, but…aha! Then it flashes on, illuminating everything.

That was a feeling I had missed for a long time before starting Project Thirty by Thirty. *But since meeting the Urban Monk, it had started happening all the time*—a tiny, everyday miracle. A miracle I wanted to share.

I have to testify.

Where did *that* thought come from? I squinted at the elders, like one of them might have planted it.

I felt a familiar draw to the microphone, then a question. *Wait, am I even* allowed *to testify? Being non-Mormon and all?*

I leaned over to ask Elder Bedford. His eyes got big as saucers, and he consulted with the missionary on his left, who consulted with the eldest elder on his left. They all looked back at me, nodding their assent quickly as if to say, "We can't stop you, but we are not responsible!"

I got up on quivering legs, wondering even as I did—*What am I doing?* I felt the elders' collective eyes on me, begging me not to embarrass them. As I made the long walk to the line for the microphone, I gave thanks for control-top pantyhose; they were so tight my knees couldn't knock.

I was up: mouth two inches from the mic; hand wrapped around its clammy base—or was it just my hands that were clammy? I stared at a hundred freshly scrubbed believers and thought: *I am so going to be the person who just says, "Um…"*

"I'm not a member of this church," I felt compelled to say—as if everyone didn't already know. This congregation—a young adult ward near OSU—was like the Mormon singles version of the neighborhood bar; if I had belonged, everyone would already know my name.

"So, um, I hope it's okay that I'm up here, um, talking," I looked at the Bishop in charge for verification, and he nodded his puzzled permission. "I…I've been through, well, an awful lot really with God, and with the church, too much to talk about here. But I just wanted to tell you…" *What did I want to tell them? What did I want to tell myself?*

"God will meet you wherever you are or aren't. I used to think my doubts and questions were what kept me from God, but now I know that they brought me closer. Sometimes the greatest miracle happens when you are willing to say, 'I don't believe. Help me.'" I cleared my throat. "And I wanted to say to all the missionaries, especially Elders Bedford and Deck, your devotion is an inspiration."

Elder Bedford gave me a thumbs-up as the room erupted in applause. Or at least that's how I remember it. My friend Jana, a wise Mormon, later informed me that congregants don't typically clap in church, which made me wonder if the sound had only echoed internally, as when you finish a tough workout and mentally hear the *Rocky* theme song. Heart still pounding, I scooted back in my row.

Elder Bedford offered a discreet high-five. As I slapped his hand, I took a startled breath: with a few shaky steps up the LDS aisle, I'd reclaimed the right to have a story, and to tell it. I'd testified. Out loud. In a church.

Elder Deck whispered, "That was very brave!"

Maybe it was. Or maybe it was just one more step to freedom. With a little help from the Elders, another piece of my spiritual history had been redeemed.

Take that, *Post-Traumatic Church Syndrome.*

"Oh, Rebecca," my mother's voice broke. I could hear the strain in her tone, like a violin string pulled too tight.

I'd just finished updating her about the latest Sickness attack. A few days after my visit to the Mormons, my fingers had stopped working mid-brush stroke, as if going on strike against a good hair day. Trembling had overtaken my body, and knocking knees forced me to collapse on the toilet—the lid of which was blessedly closed. (Losing control of one's body is one thing, but to then plunge unexpectedly into the commode? *Ugh.*)

I was used to the Sickness's muscle cramps that struck at inopportune moments like mascara application, resulting in great, black streaks across my face—but these full-body earthquakes, muscle spasms on the Richter scale, shocked me. They struck willy-nilly now, almost every hour, and caused me to do things like spill gasoline and perform unexpected pirouettes. Had these acts been captured on video, I would be YouTube famous. With the shakes came hives, joint pain, and the oh-too-familiar, soul-crushing fatigue. Except I couldn't sleep, because I would wake up shaking like an overloaded washing machine. My doctor thought I was just suffering from severe anxiety and gave me enough tranquillizers to relax a tense rhinoceros. When the episodes finally subsided after five days, I looked even more haggard than I felt.

"I just wish I could take your place," Mom exhaled. "When your child is in trouble and you can't do anything, it's the most helpless feeling in the world. You only have two choices: fall to pieces or fall on grace. You know I've been praying for you around the clock," she continued in the tone a surgeon might use during major surgery.

"I know…thank you." This wasn't euphemism. I could envision her lips moving silently as she cooked and cleaned: my mother, God's favorite housekeeper.

"What you don't know is I've been praying for more than your illness. I've been praying for your heart—that you would have the spiritual breakthrough you've been searching for. Especially after you felt let down by your monk."

"It's not that *he* let me down. I let myself down."

"After all the progress you've made, I don't want you to give up now."

"I'm not giving up," I promised, thinking of the NPR producer's card on the refrigerator door, "even if I have to shake all the way to my thirtieth birthday. Hey, maybe I'll try to cross the Quakers off next—that way, in case I start trembling in church, no one will notice!"

We both laughed, but my Mom's laugh sounded stiff. She paused, a mannerism I recognized as the preface to a loving sermon. I steeled myself.

"Remember after Christmas when you asked me to find the recording from Word Alive Church, the one where Mark Radcliff gave the prophecy over your life? The one we talked about in Chicago?"

I nodded as if she could see me. I'd asked her to find the recording because I'd told the Urban Monk about the experience. "Perhaps you should revisit that moment," he'd advised. "Messages from God come in many forms."

"I remember," I said to Mom.

"I was feeling pretty encouraged because it seemed like you were making a move toward God by asking me to find the recording, but I was freaking out because I had no idea where it was. After Christmas I tore apart the house looking for it, but it was nowhere to be found. I said to God, 'I trust You to help me find this important word for Rebecca in Your time,' and let it go. Well, while you were going through this shaking episode, I was praying for you while dusting that photograph of Grandpa in the hallway and the frame *fell off the wall.* I mean, it just went *Boom,* straight to the ground."

"Okay…" Every hair on my body felt electric. That frame held a photograph of my mother's father, he of the "Persevere" dream. *Eerie.*

"And you know how I never have any nails?" We both snickered—my mother is not handy around the house. "To rehang the picture I had to look in the kitchen junk drawer for nails, so I was rummaging elbow-deep in junk when I feel the edge of a cassette case. I pulled it out, and it was the prophecy!"

"You're kidding," I said, even though I knew she wasn't.

"Nope. That's exactly how it happened. I immediately went to listen to it and—you aren't going to believe this because I almost didn't—right in the middle of the whole thing the prophet said, 'Do not be afraid to be outside the understanding of the church, for I am calling you inside, inside Me.' I realized I'd forgotten that God doesn't have to guide you the way I think He should. Here I've been praying for you all this time but forgetting that God has His own plans. I may not understand it, and I may not even fully accept it, but God has you on your own path for a reason. I can't control your Sickness or your project; but I don't have to. God is bigger than my questions."

"Wow." I counted myself eminently fortunate that my mother is the type to fall on grace instead of fall to pieces, but I was still shocked. "So you're not afraid I'm going to run off with a guru anymore?"

"Sure I am, a little. But even if you do, I trust God will be with you."

"Mom? Remember how you said, 'God never gives you a Word like that unless you're going to need it'? Maybe it wasn't just me who was going to need it."

"I think I need it more than you!" said my Mom, her voice much lighter. "God gave us both that Word way before the problems even started because He knows the beginning from the end, and nothing is too big for Him. He always has and always will have you right in the palm of His hand, even if I don't understand how. I'm going to copy the tape onto CD and put it in the mail."

"Reba!" my neighbor Andre flagged me down. "Hey," he said as I approached, "USPS accidentally delivered this to us." He proffered an envelope, which I took. "Where are you headed this fine Sunday morning?"

"Church," I smiled. "Quaker service."

"Aren't Quakers like Pilgrims or Amish or something?"

"I only know three things about Quakers," I held up my fingers. "One: I love Quaker Oats. Two: they used to shake or tremble during their services, hence the name. Three: I used to play with a set of historic Quaker paper dolls." (I know not how the prim Quaker cutouts made their way to my toy box, but I much enjoyed changing the Quaker ladies' aprons and bonnets. True, the dolls were not the Barbie brand I might have preferred, but they projected a certain drab appeal after I covered them in gold glitter.) Andre raised his brows.

"Long story," I said, "and I have to get going. See ya!"

In my car, I opened the package. A CD was inside, with an accompanying note: *I love you! I hope this helps your journey! XOXO—Mom*

I pushed the recording into the CD player as I backed out of the driveway. I cannot say why I thought delving into my spiritual history while navigating downtown Columbus was a good idea, but the recording, circa 1995, surrounded me with static before I heard the voice of Mark Radcliff, the traveling minister—or prophet—depending on who you're asking.

"Is there a Becky here tonight?" he said through my car's speakers.

His sentence had been phrased as a question, but there was no question in his tone. He'd known I was present, and that God had a message for me. And even though I'd never gone by Becky, I knew he meant me; seconds before he spoke, my hands had started shaking and the Energy—which I'd then called the Holy Spirit—had swooshed around me with almost physical vibration. It wasn't quite the earthquakes the Sickness had subjected me to lately, but it was a shaking nonetheless.

Mark's voice paused. "No, it's Rebecca. Is there a Rebecca here tonight?"

I'd stood on shaky limbs. *In this entire crowd, how am I the only Rebecca or Becky?* I remember thinking. *There were three Rebeccas just in my small seventh-grade class!*

"Hello there…hi!" he'd said this to me, then turned to the congregation: "Extend your hands to her."

Hundreds of people had reached toward me, in silent yet electric agreement, their hearts prayerful and gazes expectant. The feeling had pulled against me magnetically, as if the crowd could enfold me with love. And they did love me, I had known. Not only were my parents part of this congregation; the room had held hundreds of people who regarded me as a lamb to be protected and praised, a princess in Jesus' kingdom. Whatever was about to happen to me would also happen to them because we were a *family*.

At the memory of this, my hands began to tremble around the steering wheel, just as they had in 1995—well before I could drive. I tried to attribute the trembling to the Sickness or to PTCS, but it felt so different: where the full-body earthquakes and PTCS symptoms pressed on me externally, this trembling felt as if something inside me quaked for release. Something big. Something I wasn't ready for. I flicked the off button on the stereo.

I maneuvered into a parking spot at the Quaker Meeting House, which almost directly faced the house I'd lived in for several years at Ohio State. I'd systematically rejected God in that house. I'd spat at the ceiling above my loft bed many times: "Leave me alone! I don't want your calling; I am done with you and your church. I don't want to hear from you ever again."

I'd driven into the veritable Bermuda Triangle of my spiritual life with a prophetic CD in my stereo. I was sitting in the middle of my past with my foretold future just one click-of-play away. I thought, *The Godiverse really went out of her way on this one.* And suddenly *I knew*.

Just like I knew before I knew that Mark Radcliff was going to call my name in 1995, I felt the shift in 2011. The Godiverse was about to give me a second chance to accept my first calling.

My finger hovered, but I couldn't press play on the CD—not yet.

This is partially because I was raised to believe the call of God was unavoidable, like answering the Soviet Union/United States red phone hotline in the '60s. (In case you were wondering: God, in this analogy, is the communist on the other end of the line.) I lived most of my childhood in fear that God would call me to be a nun in Africa. The fact that my church lacked nuns did not quell this fear. If God called you to wear a black habit in 120-degree weather, you would do so with a joyful spirit, lest you be nuked to smithereens.

But I was confused: why would the God I'd just been getting to know, the I Am, call me from the red phone of the God I grew up with? Couldn't he just send another prophet or something—preferably one of a different religion who wasn't tainted with PTCS?

I wasn't ready to press play because I knew that once I did, there would be no turning back.

I turned off the car. I had a service to get to.

"Are you new here?" blinked a middle-aged woman near the back door of the Meeting House. Wearing a tweed jacket, slacks, and a hairstyle from the early 1990s, she looked like an off-duty professor.

Strictly speaking, my answer could have been no; Trent's fraternity house sat across the street, and we'd often sneaked away to kiss under the cover of the Quaker church's bushes. (A strategy that, incidentally, did not work. If I could only count the times his fraternity brothers whistled at us from the patio.)

I assumed her question referred to the church and not stolen kisses, so I nodded a quick yes.

"That's terrific!" She ushered me through the door. "What brings you to us this morning?"

Lady, that's a loaded question. I smiled. "Curiosity, I suppose."

"How very *interesting*," she said with a faux-British lilt. "I'm Barb. Come, you must meet everyone!"

Barb swept me through the Meeting House, which was, well, a converted house; half of its downstairs had been renovated to create a meeting space, and the upstairs rooms furnished space for "children and multi-generational worship." She introduced me to a cast of characters I would have never expected given my Quaker paper-doll history: Orville, a twenty-something gay man who was serving as minister of the day ("Every Quaker is a minister; we have no lay persons"); Jaden, an enthusiastic Pagan/Quaker who carried Catholic, Buddhist, and Pagan rosaries in her purse ("We're very 'live and let live'"); Donald, a rocket scientist ("I'm a professor in my spare time"); and Nathan, president of the Ohio State Interfaith Association ("We don't care if you're a Christian or an atheist; all are welcome here").

I joked with a few of them about Quaker Oats and pilgrim hats, and confessed I had expected a more straight-laced crowd.

"We get that all the time," laughed Barb. "The funny thing is, we're about as liberal a congregation as you can be. We're all about justice, peace, and equality, and believe the Inner Light of God is in each person."

For the service, we settled into concentric rows of chairs that faced each other in two half-moon shapes, similar to theater in the round. For the Quakers, even the arrangement of the chairs contributed to the idea of equality.

Orville began with the instructions to sit quietly, relax, and wait on guidance. "We gather in silence to submit to the Divine Presence which is accessible to all. Sometimes speaking arises out of the silence; sometimes no words are spoken. If a still, small voice is calling, listen to the Inner Light that is the Divine Presence in our midst."

Well. If I had hoped the Quakers would distract me from my eventful morning, I had come to the wrong place. *Still, small voice? Try the static, loud voice of a prophet from your past.*

Everything went quiet. If show-and-tell was the motto of most church services, the Quaker motto was wait-and-see. I closed my eyes, glad that even though I was only meeting with the Urban Monk weekly, my near-daily, personal meditation practice had eased me into the stillness of group meditation. I slipped under the silence until a member of the congregation spoke. I sneaked a peek to see if he was quaking—due diligence!—but he sat prayerfully: eyes closed, hands clasped.

"The Divine Light is in all of Us; we are all part of the I AM, all part of the Universe's vibrating energy. Sink into the Light within and embody all that is."

I faced windows with thin, white curtains, and as the congregant spoke, sun broke from behind the clouds and light streamed in over all of us, as if we really could sink into the Light.

I sat. I waited. I listened.

There is only Light, whispered a still, small voice.

I'd misunderstood what was about to happen in the car. Pressing play wasn't a second chance at my first calling; it was my first chance at a second life.

I acted polite post-service, but I couldn't wait to get back to my car, where I pressed play.

"You are called to be a healer," said the prophet. "You are called to lead by example."

Called. The word would have bristled only a few months ago because it was so entwined with PTCS, but no longer. *Only Light, fractured into a thousand pieces.* I smiled. The choice wasn't between the calling of my childhood and the calling of my future, between the God of my youth or I Am. It wasn't letting go of one to embrace the other; I had to let go of the idea that I had to choose.

"Do you accept this calling?"

You don't have to choose religion to choose God...or good.

"Do you accept?" Static followed Mark Radcliff's question on the CD.

I looked at the car speakers, and my hands trembled as they had long ago, when my faith was still blind and my heart unbroken. This time, though, they shook because my eyes were wide open, and I knew I would never be the same.

"Yes," I said. "I accept."

Part 4
Come and See

19

Fasting

"I'm thinking about fasting for thirty days," I told Trent over dinner one Friday night. "I feel like that's what the Godiverse is telling me to do."

He put down his fork. "Um, God's *talking* to you now?"

I shrugged. "God's been talking to me my whole life; you know that. I just stopped listening for about a decade."

"I always thought you were being metaphorical."

"Nope."

"*Thirty* days? Is that even safe? Shouldn't you consult a doctor or something?"

I rolled my eyes. After approximately two hundred doctor visits, tens of thousands of dollars, and most recently the lack of answers about my chronic hives and shaking episodes, I washed my hands of the medical profession altogether—at least for the time being.*

"Religious and health-conscious people have been fasting for centuries. As long as I keep up my caloric intake with liquids I'll be fine. My plan is to drink juice and protein shakes only—no food and no booze, but definitely not starvation."

Trent resumed eating, chewing on my idea and his broccoli as we continued our dinner in silence.

I didn't blame him for being skeptical. The idea of the thirty-day fast had come on like an illness with a long incubation period. Even though I'd been considering the plan for weeks, it still felt bizarre, like something Lady Gaga might do as a publicity stunt. Spiritual seeker I was. Spiritual stuntwoman I was not.

---

* Legal disclaimer from the desk of my husband the attorney: I am not a doctor and my personal experience does not constitute medical advice. (Besides, do you really want to skip eating for a month? Didn't think so.)

The first time the Godiverse floated the idea, Oxley and I were feasting on Beggin' Strips and cheesy doodles, respectively.

"What do you want more than you want food?" The question arrived internally, via the same post that had delivered my project. *That's an easy list,* I answered mentally while throwing Oxley a treat and stuffing a cheesy doodle in my mouth.

I want to see God. I want to be healthy.

"Fast."

The prospect of fasting seduced me with all the allure of a colonoscopy, but somehow I refused. I thought: *Very funny. I don't even like to skip breakfast.*

This is how I knew the communication wasn't from my psyche: I had negative-zero desire to fast. The longest I'd ever fasted in my Christian heyday was three days, a time I recalled with the pleasure usually reserved for having a toenail ripped from my body. Still, I toyed with the idea of a thirty-day fast in the margins of my life—on the same page as the list of "Things to Do When I Win the Lottery."

Apparently this microscopic chink in my armor was all the Godiverse required to start working on me in earnest. I opened Facebook to stories about fasting. I received random e-mails about juice cleanses and intermittent fasting for health reasons. I flipped on the TV to ministers calling for fasting and prayer. And every time I ate anything, I thought: *I want God more than I want this meal. I want to be healthy more than I want this pizza.* (This wasn't strictly true when I was kissing a deep-dish pepperoni, but close enough.)

And every time the Sickness forced me into bed, I violently desired to rid my body of disease. If there was even a tiny chance that fasting could help me, I was willing to try.

As furiously as I wanted to get well, I desired the Light even more. After accepting my calling—which was a lot like putting my hand into the Divine's—I yearned to know the Godiverse, even though I was unsure what that even looked like in this new world of spirituality. Between my body's weakness and my soul's hunger, I was desperate, period.

Desperation is powerful motivation.

I fell into the Google research hole, and my search history read like something out of *Austerity Weekly*: fasting, how to fast safely, long-term fast, juicing, balanced liquid nutrition, intermittent fasting, mystical fast. I checked out library books. I e-mailed people who had completed fasts of a month or longer. One fasting veteran said: "I can't guarantee your life will change, but I can guarantee *you* will change."

I was still seeing the Urban Monk a few times a month for meditation practice. I knew he had undertaken more than his fair share of fasting, being a monk and all, so I consulted him about the prospect. "Thirty days is too long," he said, shaking his head.

"Jesus fasted for forty."

"Are you Jesus?"

I laughed. "Clearly not. Jesus lacked abundant access to shelf-stable juice and protein powder."

I knew there was no guarantee that a fast would help the Sickness, and I didn't believe fasting curried spiritual favor, as though God were a gumball machine and I could insert fasting to receive health or enlightenment. But everything I read indicated that fasting isn't something you do to change God's mind; it's something you do to change your own.

People undertake fasting for some of the same reasons they scale mountains, run marathons, attend silent retreats, enter the boxing ring, compete on *Survivor*, or skydive. They want to do something extraordinary to feel fully alive, to mark time into "before" and "after." They want to dig deep and find out what they're really made of. They want to know that they have given everything in pursuit of a dream. They hope to be transformed.

I hoped to be transformed.

The idea of a thirty-day fast pulled at me with every pang of hunger and fatigue—approximately three hundred times a day—until I was worn down enough to put my commitment out to the Godiverse. I wrote in my journal: *"I want to Come and See for myself, so I'll start the fast next Sunday. But I demand some serious help, and Trent has to be on board."*

As he stood up to clear his place, Trent didn't know that his reaction would tip the scale one way or the other. I felt like telling him would break the rules. Half of me hoped he would say I was wacko and try to force feed me some mocha gelato (not that it would take much force), but the other half—the half in tune with the Godiverse—wanted his support.

Trent rinsed his plate and turned to face me. "Thirty-day fast, fine. But if God tells you to kill me and Oxley, could you at least give us a running start?"

"Sure," I laughed, simultaneously relieved and terrified. The fast was on. I was going to do this crazy thing.

Sometimes divine help comes quietly and in an organized manner, like a casserole left on the doorstep. In the case of my fast, divine help arrived in a more violent fashion. (Let this be a cautionary tale to all who demand help from the Godiverse. Consider yourselves warned.)

Around 11:45 on the Saturday night before the Sunday I was scheduled to begin my fast, horrific stomach cramps alerted me to an urgent bathroom need. Doubled over, I ran in the direction of the nearest toilet.

I did not make it in time.

(I should pause here to note that I have not soiled my pants since the tender age of Pampers and pacifiers, and I am not keen to announce my sphincter's failure to the world. My mother has always maintained that one's bathroom *business*—whether coming up or going down or, in this case, both—should remain a private matter. Under normal circumstances I would agree, but a savage virus randomly attacking on the eve of a thirty-day fast is not a normal circumstance. Hence my oversharing.

I threw up twice in fifteen minutes and attempted to clean myself and my yoga pants in the shower. Naked and wet, I curled up in the fetal position on the cold bathroom floor. *I won't be able to eat for days,* I thought, lunging for the toilet again.

I'm still not sure where I stand on a theology that would allow for divine diarrhea—it seems a tad Old Testament plague-y for me—but the timing was very suspicious. Just to be safe, I plan to add an addendum to any future demands for heavenly help: "Body fragile. Please handle with care." Or better yet, not make demands in the first place.

The next few days found me in bed except for emergency trips to the toilet. It was easy to pray, even if my prayers were mostly, "Help me make it to the bathroom!" Trent joked that God had clearly decided to help me with my fast, because I couldn't tolerate the thought of solid food. On the second day of The Plague, which was also Valentine's Day, my husband wondered aloud whether he should buy me flowers or Depends.

Somehow this was less than helpful.

When I finally recovered enough that solid food sounded appealing again (and the Arby's that Trent brought home for himself smelled magically delicious), the fasting took on a new level of challenge: hunger kept me awake at night. I'd gone from one extreme to the other. In the daytime, the fast made me petulant. When I met clients for lunch, I cited my recent stomach virus as the reason for ordering only cranberry juice. Watching as the guys slopped down burgers and beer, I hated them. I hated the entire eating world. I was so hungry, in fact, that I even hated Oxley for eating his dog food. I wondered if the fast was squeezing hatred out of me, as a sauna extracted sweat.

Late one night, Andre started cooking one floor down while I was trying to sleep. *The nerve of that guy, making dinner!* I considered calling the police to report a scent disturbance. I flopped around in the bed like a dying fish, prompting Trent to grumble, "Just because you aren't eating doesn't mean I don't need to sleep." Hunger pangs woke me up again at 2 a.m. and didn't let me go back to sleep. I wrapped myself in Snuggies (plural) and triple socks because I was freezing—a side effect of fasting I didn't know about before I began. And, by the way, here are some other side effects I had read about but failed to fully appreciate until I was famished:

- Stinkiness: Between dragon breath and cringe-worthy BO, I was keeping Scope and men's-strength Degree in the money.
- Dizziness: A Tilt-a-Whirl ride had nothing on me. I administered field sobriety tests to myself before driving and failed more than one, even though I hadn't had a sip of alcohol.
- Forgetfulness: Now, what was I going to say about that?
- Irritability: I didn't want to talk about it, okay? Leave me alone!

By 3 a.m., I was clawing the walls of the living room. I wanted bread so badly that I hallucinated the smell of toast. I tried to meditate, but ended up watching infomercials instead. If my fingers hadn't been too tired to dial 1-800 numbers, I'd have ordered a whole new me for express delivery. With silky hair, a perfectly rounded Brazilian bottom and clear skin, I'd be sure to sleep perfectly on my NASA-engineered pillow.

This was going to be impossible.

Early one Sunday, I entered the closest movie theater to attend a church that billed its weekend services as "experiences." When the chipper greeter offered me earplugs "just in case the sound is too loud for you!" I wondered just what kind of experience I would be having. Answer: A loud one.

The theater was dark, lit only by exit signs, blue spotlights on the live worship team, and song lyrics playing on the big screen. The set-up reminded me of the time I took my little sisters to an 'NSYNC concert: the five guys leading worship were all very young and too-cool-for-school, so it wasn't much of a stretch to imagine them launching into a synchronized dance when the beat changed. There is a limit to how much boy-band one woman can endure on an empty stomach. At the half-hour mark I was rolling my eyes at the "religi-tainment."

But, no. I caught myself. *I refuse to be uncharitable simply because this church/movie theater isn't my cup of tea.* I remembered my experience on the floor at boot camp of Aletheia and reframed the movie theater congregation as individuals coming together to put their love for God and each other in action.

In my mind, I heard the soft voice of my first yoga instructor, Anne. "Breathe. Accept what is today, as it is today. Don't strain. Relax into the pose. When we soften the body, we bend the will." So I accepted this church for what it was today, as it was today. I relaxed into the darkness, the music, and the experience. I considered that fasting might be another mechanism to bend the body in order to flex the soul.

I took a deep breath out, exhaling all my judgment and expectation; I took a breath in, inhaling…the scent of buttered popcorn. This was, after all, a church that met in a movie theater. *What was I thinking?*

Anyone who says you aren't hungry after nine days of fasting is a liar. I'd say I hit a wall, but it was more a reverse-pitch climbing cave, where if you fall, you drop straight down into a river gorge. I wanted to eat like an addict wanted to score, so I dialed-a-monk, thinking surely the Urban Monk would understand. The monk didn't answer his phone, so I assumed it had been turned off and drove over to St. Lydia. I had an urgent, burning desire to get inside a church—something I never thought I'd say—where the space was sacred and very, very far removed from Trent cooking fajitas.

St. Lydia was shuttered and locked. So I tried another church (closed) then another (closed), until my steeple-chasing wore me out. I slumped in the car, praying, "Please give me the strength." Then I waited to see what would happen, expecting something mystical. Instead, a bird pooped on my windshield.

During the fast I avoided almost everyone I wasn't required to talk to and everything I wasn't required to do for my job or my project. I chose to be secretive because I knew everyone would ask me questions or doubt my motives. Scarcely anyone knew how sick I was, so they wouldn't understand my desperation on the physical front, and the spiritual yearning—well, that wasn't a breeze to explain either. I could hear the number one question, the one I'd have asked myself if I hadn't already known the answer: "You aren't doing this to lose weight, are you?"

Of course I was! This was all about weight…spiritual weight. I wanted to shed every ounce of spiritual poundage I'd been dragging around for a decade; I wanted a complete makeover.

I wanted to be so spiritually thin that I disappeared into Infinite Love.

I may not have disappeared into Infinite Love, but good things were beginning to happen. I felt more aware, more connected, more alive.

At a lunch meeting, I noticed a family in the restaurant join hands and bow their heads to pray before eating. I'd done this at every meal for almost twenty years, and the sight of people praying aloud in restaurants had turned my stomach a little since The Breaking. But on this day, I watched them give thanks without judgment.

Give thanks. I thought I knew what it meant. I thought I was thankful for the abundance in my life. But as I watched the child squirm and the father pray, my stomach churned with emptiness. *I've never truly been thankful for food, because I've never before known hunger.* It was a good thing my client hadn't returned from the restroom, because my eyes filled with tears. *So many go hungry around the world, and I've eaten my whole life without giving thanks.* I fiddled with the fork at my left and knew I would never pick up an eating utensil again without being deeply, incredibly, thankful. *Perhaps this is another function of fasting? Physical lack reveals spiritual deficiency.* Part of me still shouted many times a day that I should quit the fast, but the volume was declining.

And the very next day, something tangible shifted: a new tranquility descended. The quiet struck me first: a vast muffledness surrounded me, pervading my consciousness. The part of me that was shouting that I should quit fell completely silent. It's like fasting added deep, piled carpet around me, and the steps of everyone who came near were less agitated. I hardly even wanted to write for fear the scratching of the pen would be too loud. I just wanted to wrap myself in the experience; I feared that sharing it, even with ink, might dilute it. *Maybe this silence is a harbinger of the clarity that mystics speak of?*

The routine of my life certainly changed. I never realized the rhythm that eating and drinking lend to life. My days and weeks lacked the punctuation marks of meals, so they blurred together like a run-on sentence. I used to rely on breakfast to tell my body that it was time to work and on happy hour to signal the start of the weekend. Now I had to create stand-ins for these signals. I meditated or went for reflective walks at mealtimes, and spent Friday nights in gentle yoga classes—a different kind of happy hour—where I stretched the week away.

The Sickness seemed to be receding; in spite of not eating, I had more waking energy than in the past few years. Though I lacked any earth-shattering mystical moments, every day empty of food filled me with the benefits of meditation and silence. I was still hungry, but I used the hunger instead of letting it use me. With every pang, I alternately gave thanks or prayed. Of course I prayed for my own physical healing, but my prayers extended far beyond my own needs—I prayed for my family, my friends, strangers on the street, and the world at large. Where I used to think of prayer as a straight line up from my mouth to God's ear, I now experienced it as circular, surrounding me and rippling out to the Godiverse.

Because I knew my best friend Erin was going through a tough time, I found myself praying for her all the time—so often, in fact, that I added a third item to my permanent fasting list: *1. I want to see God. 2. I want to be healthy. 3. I want Erin to meet her future husband.*

Even though I didn't believe fasting added weight to heavenly lobbying—the Godiverse isn't a politician pandering for contributions—I figured it couldn't hurt. Even when I was too tired to actively pray, my body prayed for me. I became more in tune with the Infinite, like my spirit was being recalibrated to a higher radio frequency. It felt like I'd spent my whole life listening to a fuzzy AM station on a broken set, and the past days had repaired it. I was connected to every person, animal, experience, and—even though I've never been the earth-hugging type—every tree. I plugged into the Energy that animated everything. Emotions were stronger; colors appeared brighter; scents smelled more intense. (This last transformation was not a positive when I changed my niece's diaper.)

I also experienced vivid dreams. In one, a banquet was laid before me with every food I craved and have ever loved. I smelled Grandma's macaroni and the Melting Pot's chocolate fondue and Panera's freshly-baked asiago bagels spread with cream cheese. There was no one around; I was free to dig in.

But instead of picking up a spoon, I pushed away from the table and turned my back on the meal.

"No," I said in the dream, "I am after something so much better."

When I woke up I realized I had crossed a threshold. My subconscious was aboard, guarding me even as I slept.

20
Deeper

I knocked loudly at the House of Krishna Consciousness. Jagannatha Dasa, the priest, who had invited me via e-mail for "chanting and feasting this Thursday," answered. I blinked once because he looked so different than what I'd expected: a swarthy, middle-aged Indian fellow with a protruding belly. Instead he was a white, *white* guy—nearly albino— whom I would card for cigarettes. He was also completely bald, except for a long braid sprouting directly from the top of his head, cheerleader-style. I could market this hairdo as the Reverse Friar Tuck: ancient Protestant monk flies from west to east and gets inside-out hair in the process.

"Welcome, Reba," he declared formally, performing a little bow with his hands together. "Do come in."

I entered and removed my shoes. Twenty or so barefoot devotees gathered in a living room empty of furniture, decorated with Eastern paintings of deities (incarnations of Krishna?). Two prominent statues bookended the room. Decorated with garlands, they seemed to observe the devotees in amused silence—a pair of jolly golden justices. I imagined one looking at me and telepathically communicating to the other, "Who invited the gal with the smelly feet?" and the other replying, "She looks hungry. I hope she doesn't try to eat our flowers."

Jagannatha Dasa swept in, a rush of white robe, and invited everyone to sit cross-legged on the floor. I noticed three students slouching nearby, notebooks lazily in hand. Their collective expression read, "I'd so rather be at Dollar Beer Night." I spied a Comparative Religions 101 syllabus; their attendance was clearly an assignment. Seeing them gave me a twinge of fear: I hoped I never came across as a grumpy tourist. *Tourist is as tourist does,* I heard, my psyche accented by Forrest Gump. I put away my own notebook to honor the experience.

Jagannatha Dasa explained that we would engage in a chanting meditation for half an hour. "Karma is a big part of what we believe," he stated, looking pointedly at the students who were mentally picking their noses. "You'll get out of this evening what you put in."

We chanted the *Maha Mantra* ("Great Mantra"), a sixteen-word sequence: Hare Krishna Hare Krishna Krishna Krishna Hare Hare Hare Rama Hare Rama Rama Rama Hare Hare—over and over, until the syllables became slippery, the verbal parallel to color blindness: you knew there was a difference between the words, but it was invisible. I became entrenched in the communal effort, as when saying a tongue-twister ten times fast and forgetting other words exist. As the chant rose and fell with the voices of the congregants, my emotions followed the tide. I was joyful, clapping along in time with the chant, then sober and pensive. Within the chant, I had no baggage, just experience. It felt fundamental: voices and simple words only, as if we had reduced spirituality by Pareto's Law and been left with only the good stuff.

As our words flowed out, meditation flowed in. The chant was a ventilation system for my spirit; the Krishna Consciousness, harmony with All That Is, breathed for me. *In and out* I rose with the words; *up and down* I flowed with the song. I closed my eyes to intensify the feeling. Karma was at work: the energy I put into this song was great, but the energy I received was greater still.

The chant concluded abruptly, or maybe it just felt abrupt because I had gotten so into it. A petite blonde girl moved forward, her voice lilting softly, a halo around us all. "Compassion for others begins with compassion for yourself. To love and forgive others, we must first love and forgive ourselves."

The devotees nodded in quiet agreement; I shifted uncomfortably. Self-forgiveness and compassion were not my primary virtues. I was much better at self-flagellation, especially when it came to the Sickness. I thought through the years of the things I had done to my body in the name of the Sickness. I'd poked, prodded, exercised, dieted, gained and lost weight, undergone exploratory medical procedures, taken all manner of drugs and supplements, and cursed my situation. Since the first day it began failing, I had treated my body mercilessly.

Jagannatha Dasa's voice filled the room. I was surprised to hear him begin to tell the story of Jesus and the rich young ruler who couldn't let go of his wealth. "The rich man couldn't make room for love in his mind," he said.

I imagined that if the young ruler was as bogged down with gold as I was with hatred for my sick body, it would indeed be impossible.

"We change the world by changing ourselves," Jagannatha Dasa urged. "What is keeping you from fully accepting love? Leave your unforgiveness of self here tonight." His words drifted over the room, an invitation, an opportunity: the Hare Krishna version of an altar call.

The chant started again, swelling around me; I hugged my legs to my chest and touched my face to my knees. I thought of my body, how it had served me in spite of my disdain, and how it had suffered through this fast on my behalf. I realized this was why I was here tonight; to take the one step I could toward healing.

"I forgive you," I said silently to my body and the Sickness.

For the first time since it began failing me, I observed my body with love and compassion. I pictured what I would tell a friend suffering my symptoms: *Be gentle. Treat yourself well. Don't worry; the important things will get done. Look at what you've accomplished despite being sick! I accept you and love you just as you are. You are beautiful. You will get well.*

And, finally, finally, I said these things to myself.

Then I began the chant again, joining my voice with the chorus. I let my resentment float away on the words of the Great Mantra, because true healing always begins with forgiveness.

21

Wind

Although the Sickness had partially diminished during my fast—and my bitterness toward it had definitely ebbed, thanks to the Hare Krishnas and forgiveness—I was still spending much of my time in bed except for work.

During the third week of my fast, Don, my boss of fewer than two months, sent me this e-mail: "I'm coming to town to travel with you next week." If my career were a basketball game, this was a foul—no whistle blown.

In field sales, the Boss Coming To Town is an event that requires lots of scheduling, refining, and confirming. In an office, you get 230 days a year to wow superiors; sales reps might get two or three. His e-mail meant that I had days to do weeks of preparation, all with zero food in my belly. Also, we would be sharing six meals—three with customers.

I told myself things would work out. (Self-delusion can be a charming companion.)

I was working on my plans when the phone rang. "Reba," Erin said, her voice full of excitement. "You aren't going to believe it! I was walking out of Mass and tripped on the sidewalk. A guy helped me up. His name is Nick, and we're going out next week."

My scalp tingled. I thought of all the prayers in my journal for Erin. *This is the guy.*

"Oh, don't worry," I smiled. "I believe it."

I prepared for my boss's visit on warp speed, ignoring the fatigue pulling at my limbs and the fact that I was running, literally, on empty.

I congratulated myself on getting all the meetings, meals, and plans scheduled, confirmed, and reconfirmed.

And then I heard the wind.

You know the story of the three little pigs, two of whom had their homes blown in? Well, the Big Bad Wolf had nothing on this storm. Hurricane-force gales huffed and puffed and blew shingles off every other roof in central Ohio. Several counties declared states of emergency, and—this being the construction industry where a disaster equals contractor gold—all eight of my appointments cancelled, leaving me with no presentations for my boss.

I called a last-minute meeting with my senior co-worker, Sharon, a fifty-something African American Baptist woman who is equal parts Mother Teresa and Jaws. She loves her family, her church, and her Jesus (but not in that order), and I have personally witnessed her put out-of-line men in their place with one queenly glance. She knew only a little about my project because the first time I mentioned going to a Buddhist meditation center she said, "It's good to explore, but you have to be careful not to be led astray." Sharon was not on the short list of people I wanted to tell about my fast.

"My plans have all fallen apart," I said quietly to Sharon, staring into my teacup while we strategized at a local restaurant. "How am I going to get through tomorrow and the next day?"

She launched into an award-winning professional pep talk, but I stopped her midway. "Sharon," I began, feeling every inch of the emotional, physical, and spiritual costs of fasting, "in addition to the windstorm problems, I'm also fasting. How am I going to tell Don that I'm fasting? I can't just *not* eat six meals in a row without explanation. He—and our customers—will think I'm anorexic."

"Excuse me," Sharon responded, "did you say *fasting?*"

"Yes," I replied, so quietly I practically whispered. "This is day twenty-three of a thirty-day fast. He'll be here for days twenty-four and twenty-five."

She looked a little stunned, like I'd announced the Easter Bunny and I were expecting a child together. I crossed my toes in hopes that she'd understand that there was no way I could quit now, even if Don thought I was off my rocker. I didn't know what my boss's religion was, but I could almost guarantee that it didn't include month-long elective fasts that had to be explained to customers at lunch.

"Thirty days? You've already done twenty-three?" she squinted at me. "Well, honey, you can't go quitting now. You must persevere!"

At the word, I collapsed onto the restaurant table in sobs, my pride officially on vacation with no cell service.

Sharon sat up straighter and, through my tears, I saw her expression change from that of a concerned professional to a cross between a tiger mother and a preacher. She leaned three-quarters of the way over the table, grabbed both my hands, looked directly in my eyes and said, "You will persevere! God will get you through this; He hasn't brought you this far for nothing, and He hasn't brought me here by accident. Now, we gonna pray." And pray she did, in full view of the restaurant wait staff, her words a rush of air more powerful than the hurricane-force winds. I was crumpled but slightly awestruck; aside from my parents, I didn't know anyone who would pray for me like that. I mean, Sharon *brought it,* all of it—the burdens of the job and my journey and my fast—and threw it down in front of the throne of her God, as if she fully expected Jesus to pick it all up. When she finished, we just kind of looked at each other like, "Whoa."

Sharon and I walked out of the restaurant, and my phone started ringing with voicemails. Three of the cancelled appointments had called to reschedule.

"Sharon," I said, "Sometimes I think God just likes to show off."

Trent looked surprised when I was humming in the morning, as peaceful as one of the painted saints on the Urban Monk's wall. "What's up with you?" he asked. "Aren't you stressed out about your boss?"

I thought about it for a second. "I actually feel very calm, like everything is going to work out."

It did. Contractors showed up to my presentations; I sailed through meetings and managed to look too busy to eat during buffet lunches. When Don and I attended our final client dinner, the scents briefly overwhelmed my reason—*this is my brain on fasting.* I briefly considered barreling into the kitchen at full speed and demanding they serve me every dish on the menu, twice. But, no, this would be a bad idea. First, I'd probably get fired when I turned in the expense report. Second, it was day *twenty-five.* I couldn't quit now; I didn't even want to quit. Except for my stomach, which was rebellion incarnate; it detached from my spiritual quest and spun triple-axels in my midsection.

Welcome, friends, to The Final Temptation of Reba Riley.

The nine men we dined with ordered adult beverages (*Oh wine, how I love thee! How I miss thee! How I long for thy sweet embrace!*) and so many appetizers that the table actually slanted a bit when they were delivered.

It groaned, or maybe I did. There was one blessing amidst the Final Temptation; the guys were oblivious to the fact that I wasn't eating. (Maybe because they were too busy licking melted butter from their fingertips?)

If the Big Bad Windstorm was a test, this was a freakin' exam. I mean, these men were eating more food than twenty pregnant women—family-style steak and lobster and chicken and garlic mashed potatoes and, oh my *God*, fried cheese? It wasn't just my mouth that was watering now; my entire body salivated—except my fingers, which were white and icy because even my blood conspired with my rebellious stomach.

I excused myself, ostensibly to the ladies room, but actually to flee the restaurant and call the Urban Monk for moral support. Hiding out in my car, I filled him in on the Final Temptation.

"Sometimes God must break us down to break us through," he said.

I considered this; it seemed true, or maybe I just hoped it was true because I'd had so many breakdowns that I wanted them all to mean something.

He continued, "All your loss is actually gain. This is the meaning of fasting. Your meditation practice and your mantra will help you see."

"But I didn't have time to meditate today," I reasoned, "and I *still* don't have a mantra."

"The mantra will come when the time is right. May God take charge of your schedule and give you the time you need to practice meditation. Remember: you can meditate with open eyes, too."

I tried to follow this advice back in the restaurant, where I ordered hot tea by the pot and tried desperately to keep my mind off the table and on the conversation. Usually I loved these guys, but at that moment? I wanted to shove the blunt end of my unused fork in one of their eyes.

Inevitably, my buddy Shaun, salesman extraordinaire and fantastically nice guy, leaned over. "Hey. Why are you drinking so much tea instead of eating?"

"I'm...fasting?" I heard myself squeak the question instead of a statement, as though my subconscious wasn't sure I would survive this meal.

"Fasting, why?" three guys asked in stereo, and the table went silent. I couldn't answer the question. I refused to bring up religion at work. Before I could stammer a response, Shaun rescued me. "Oh yeah, isn't it Lent right now?" and the conversation moved on.

After dinner, I found myself with an unexpected break while Don took a call. I heard the Urban Monk's voice in my mind ("May God take charge of your schedule...") and realized this stolen moment could be my meditation time. I sat alone in my car, breathing deeply for a few minutes, letting the activity carry away the day's chatter. All was quiet for a time, until a parade of words manifested in my mind—fully formed and strung like beads on a necklace: *Jesús-Rama-Krishna-Christo-Abba-Allah-lleluia-Jesús-Rama-Krishna-Christo-Abba-Allah-lleluia.*

I recognized the phrase instantly; it was my mantra, sure as if it had been made to measure and hung around my neck as a gift. It tasted sweet on my lips—and sweeter in my heart as I understood I was uttering these few names of God, not to the exclusion of any deity, but to symbolize an all-inclusive meditation on the God of all forms and no forms.

Jesús-Rama-Krishna-Christo-Abba-Allah-lleluia.

I mouthed the mantra, eyes still open, awed by Mystery. My mantra had dropped into my lap at the most unexpected time. I'd been looking for it everywhere it wasn't: outside my regular life, in religious books, in the mind of the Monk.

But my mantra was always inside my untidy life, hidden amidst all my daily cares. All I'd had to do to find it was sit down, be at rest within the mess, and listen.

Trent clasped my hand as we sat into a wooden pew at Indianola Presbyterian, the church where we married. The old stone sanctuary was dimmed in deference to the Friday evening Taizé service, a French style of worship characterized by meditative prayer, singing, and silence. Taizé attracted me because "silence" was in the description. Silence and fasting seemed well-matched dance partners in the search for the Divine. (I'm still not sure if they were mutually beneficial or if I was just afraid to open my mouth lest I gobble up the nearest edible item.)

The only light came from the last slanting rays of sunset through two stories of stained glass. The usually sparse altar was decorated with painted icons, more reminiscent of European cathedrals than Midwestern Presbyterian churches. Fewer than twenty congregants scattered about the pews, but the physical space between us didn't dilute the collective purpose of reverent stillness. Perhaps it is this stillness that is missing from some modern worship; the Bible verse, "Be still and know that I am God," seems to require stilling as a prerequisite to knowing.

Stillness resided everywhere in the Taizé tradition: in the space between the cantor's reading of the verses of Psalm 23, in the notes the flautist and pianist played as we sang. Or maybe I just noted the stillness because, during my fast, I had become still.

Even the musicians were off to one side in half-darkness so as to remove any distraction. For a few beautiful, quiet moments, the world was only candles, silence, and slow songs of contemplation.

The Reverend, Pastor Skip, gave words of instruction from behind the congregation:

"We will now have a time for silent meditation."

Usually I might have worried about what Trent thought of the service, but even that worry stilled. I slipped into the meditation easily, and time passed quickly. Everything inside and around me was sandwiched in a delicious buffer of silence.

The musicians led us in the song *Kyrie Eleison* ("Lord, have mercy"). With closed eyes, I realized I had completely redefined the word "mercy." I used to view a request for mercy as a petition from a place of weakness, as though it meant humanity was less-than, worm-like, begging God not to squish us on the bottom of His Holy Sneaker. But now I believed mercy wasn't less-than and needy, but greater-than together; it wasn't a plea for rescue, but an addition of strength for the journey. When I thought of mercy now, I pictured this sanctuary as it had been during our wedding. We chose to call upon all who loved us to come alongside our marriage, requesting their support in advance. We asked, "Will you support and honor these holy vows with all that is within you?" to which they stood in solidarity and promised they would.

So I sang a long, slow, *"Kyrie Eleison…* Lord have mercy," and imagined the whole of the Godiverse standing to surround me, helping me complete this fast, this journey, this life.

Pastor Skip invited everyone forward to light an individual candle from the Christ candle on the altar. The sun had set, so the only lights were those held by the congregants. This was the holy hush of a candlelit Christmas Eve service, but on a random Friday. When we all had our candles, he read a verse from 2 Corinthians 5: "Behold, everything old has passed away; see, everything has become new!"

In the stillness, my heart expanded with gratitude. I repeated the words of the verse aloud with the tiny congregation, because I knew they were true.

22

Disco

I grabbed a light jacket to walk to the library. The sky over me winked blue; birds chirped; tiny green leaves grew on bare branches. As I tromped down a wooded path in the park, I thought of my father. From the time I was old enough to walk, he would take me on a nature tour of our backyard to look for signs of spring. Holding his big hand, I would point out tiny buds on our willow tree, and he would show me where our flowers were going to bloom. "Even though we can't see it yet," he explained, kneeling to my level and patting the earth, "things are changing down there. Soon you'll wake up and everything will be different."

I sniffed the air and couldn't stop a smile. This was a scent I remembered: fresh earth, melted snow, and hope.

Though conscious that I was less than forty-eight hours from the finish line, food was the farthest thing from my mind. Walking Oxley, I floated along the sidewalk in a spirit-haze (which is a little like a hangover, except awesome) listening to *Boston*, one of my regular Pandora internet radio stations.

Like an alert from the emergency broadcast system, the song "I Can Only Imagine" by Mercy Me broke through the station. I can't explain how, but this song—one I sang in a hundred school chapel services and church meetings—thrummed loudly in my ear buds. The ballad is about heaven and being close to God, two things I had thought were lost to me. In exactly the way a song can conjure your first love and first heartbreak, this song had the power to open the floodgates of being in love with the God of my youth, and then being heartbroken.

Nine months ago, I would have cringed at the first notes, shut off the radio, and punched anyone near me. But on this day I stopped mid-step. Speechless with wonder, I dropped to the nearest bench.

My eyes were open and my senses intact: I could still see Oxley straining to chase a rabbit; I could still feel a slight breeze on my face. Everything was there, yet the physical reality seemed hazy compared to the sharp focus of my soul. This song that once represented my pain had been transformed. It crested with an overwhelming wave of beauty, a beauty that transcended the chords, the instruments, the vocalists.

The beauty of the song's *intention*: the intention to reach out to our Creator, touch Something Greater than we are, and jump in faith, believing we will reach the other side. It was the songwriter's intention; it was my intention.

Our words and methods were different, but our hearts were the same.

In that moment, with a barking puppy to my left, cars whizzing past on my right, the sounds of the city near and yet removed, I was immersed in beauty. Though no water was involved, that neglected urban corner—with its cracked sidewalk and weeds pushing through the concrete—became my baptismal font.

The song, formerly poison to my spirit, washed my whole being—over, under, and through—in a swirling bath. With wave after wave it cleansed my understanding. As I used the chorus to reach out to the Godiverse, I reclaimed everything that was lost to me. I looked past the words and the action to the heart, knowing that it wasn't just the song that could never hurt me again; nothing related to my old spiritual life could hurt me again. When the last notes faded, the negative power of religious ritual dissolved with them, replaced, at long last, by peace. Josh's peace, the Urban Monk's peace.

My peace.

"I'm here for the Tranquility Meditation? Sorry I'm running behind," I murmured to an older woman as I slipped off my shoes. She was stationed by the entrance to the Buddhist Center's main shrine room, sitting guard on the stairs, observing me with mirthful eyes.

She patted my arm. "You can never be too early or too late, dear. Everything happens right on time."

I found a cushion and surveyed the people—about forty of them, varied in race and age. All were seated, solemn and quiet, on purple floor cushions. The only sound was deep breathing. I twisted my wedding ring as I settled cross-legged on my own cushion, closed my eyes, and thought how much had changed since my first visit, when Mr. Hotness had easily eclipsed the Buddhist Center in my mind.

I tried to sink my body into the cushion and my mind into the infinite, but the cushion was too hard and my mind too soft—full of memories from this journey and my fast. Wriggling in discomfort and chiding my mind for playing recess, I peeked at the Indian guy one cushion over and felt pity that he was stuck next to restless me. *Ehipassiko,* I reminded myself, breathing deeply and focusing my mind. *I am here to come and see.* To further calm myself, I mentally recited lines from the poem "Impermeable Peace" by Ajahn Ocean, a Zen nun:

> Look upon me in the light
> and you will clearly see your own reflection.

Part of me was still seeking the touchy-feely, ooey-gooey, "aha moment" that mystics report; after all, "I want to see God" was the first item on my fasting list a month ago. But as I reflected on all the ways the Godiverse had met me in my fast, I decided peace was enough. Still, my muscles contended in discomfort, and the thirty minutes passed slowly. I felt the Sickness in my joints; though the pain had lessened during the fast, it had not disappeared. Floor meditation only made it worse, so I gratefully rose when the bell rang to signal ten minutes of walking meditation.

As we circumnavigated the perimeter of the room in silence, I contemplated the paintings of great Buddhist lamas on the walls. *Did you ever fast?* I asked one. *Have you seen God?* I inquired of another. They remained tight-lipped and wise, sentries modeling inner tranquility.

Not looking forward to more time on the floor, I stifled a sigh as the bell rang for our second thirty minutes of meditation. Fidgeting through muscle cramps, I grasped my mantra tightly as a string of prayer beads. Then I issued an invitation: *Only Light of the Godiverse, come forth from eternity to meet me here.*

Nothing.

I breathed, trying to relax into the experience…or nonexperience, as it were. And just as I exhaled, completely letting go of expectation, a tsunami of energy rushed in through the top of my head. My being filled with light. I glowed with it, pulsed with it, dissolved into it. The light expanded until I was weightless and weighted, whirling and still, together and alone. I wasn't even confused by the opposites, because neither turmoil nor words existed in this space. There was only perfect peace.

Prisms of rainbow light danced around me, and I understood that each point of light was a soul. I saw them all over the world, kneeling before their God in one form or another, submitting their prayers and songs and beads and candles and bare feet with the same beautiful intention: to reach the Divine.

Within each point of light a scene sparkled: children danced around a fire, monks chanted stoically, men prostrated, women bowed their heads, priests made the sign of the cross, choirs swayed and clapped, groups gathered in awe of nature. Each scene became a thousand scenes, then ten thousand. The points of light constantly moved—bending, bowing, laughing, sitting, kneeling, singing, crying, and dancing—and the scenes combined, dissolved, and recombined in time with their worship. *Worship*, another word I had disliked until right then, when I understood that God was everywhere, in everyone, whether they knew it or not. We were all connected. I heard the bells and gongs and voices and chants blending together in a harmony without beginning or end. All of humanity created one joyous song heard by I AM and recognized as beautiful. Rituals that seemed so incomprehensibly different, so resolutely at odds, played together harmoniously in the pit orchestra of the Godiverse.

The points of light emanated from a round diamond with incalculable mirrored facets—a Divine Disco Ball. Without words, I understood this was a picture of God and humanity. I was seeing it because I *was* it: one little mirror, a small yet essential piece of the Whole.

Every soul was a mirror: each reflecting light and dark; each joined with others to form this beautiful picture of Truth that is too large for any one of us to understand alone. Our placements and angles—our beliefs and nonbeliefs, practices or nonpractices, histories, experiences, and personalities—were distinct, so our individual perspectives differed, but the Divine Disco Ball shimmered with commonality. We cannot experience God without each other, because God is love. If faith is love in action, God is love in action times infinity.

I understood the Disco Ball as a way to stop judging and start loving. By recognizing that each soul had its own part to play, its own perspective, its own light to reflect, I could release myself from judging the judgers. I didn't have to like them or understand them, and I didn't have to allow them in my daily life: they were simply on the other side of the Disco Ball, playing a part in the larger Truth that spins between us.

No differences existed here because no differences *can* exist at the heart of Infinite Love.

The Divine Disco Ball's innumerable diamond mirrors pulsed with light and life, and the entire Godiverse sparkled before me—a brilliant, fiery diamond, spinning in the space where separateness stops and unity begins.

From somewhere far away, a gong signaled the end of meditation. The rainbow lights dimmed, and I became conscious of the weight of my body, which felt curiously heavy. My eyes fluttered open as if waking from a dream. I'd been elsewhere for a full thirty minutes: my cheeks were stained with tears; my body was so numb from the waist down that I had to use my hands to uncross my legs.

People bustled around me, talking and clearing the room, but I just sat, awestruck and silent, until only I remained. I never wanted to move from this cushion where the Divine was still near enough to taste on my tongue and smell on my skin. Eventually, someone returned to ask if I was okay, but I was still too dazed to answer. He left me alone, probably because my glassy eyes and dazzling smile made me look as if I was (A) on drugs; (B) among the criminally insane; or (C) both A and B.

With the knowledge that what I had seen could never be undone—not by a church, not by a person, not even by my own doubt—I sat in rapture until I knew it was time to go. While stretching my arms over my head, the full exhilaration of the experience sideswiped me and I began to laugh. In exactly the manner of a slaphappy teenage girl with a backstage pass, I squealed aloud: "I just saw the Godiverse! And it looks like a Divine Disco Ball!"

I then performed a spontaneous, ecstatic dance that was 50 percent Ellen DeGeneres, 50 percent *Napoleon Dynamite*, and 100 percent terrible. But what can I say? Sometimes the most reverent thing you can do is dance.

Pulling a final, Travolta-esque pose, I suddenly remembered the Christian Spiritualist pirate who'd told me I was supposed to "dance more."

"Like a jig?" I'd asked.

"Dance the disco, baby," he'd replied. "You're going to dance the disco."

I can't be certain of this, but I think Psychic Jesus and the Great Lamas shared a smile.

Before breaking my fast, I wrote one last journal entry:

This fast was like tearing up a yard that had been overtaken by weeds. The act of forgoing food turned the soil of my heart over, and brought to light soft, moist earth that had been buried for too long. Fasting was simply an implement; other tools might have worked, but for me the fast was the right tool at the right time, tilling my heart for peace and faith.

I started this fast asking the wrong question: "What am I made of?" I'm only made of fluff and straw and a little heart. The right question is, "What happens when I come to the end of what I'm made of?" This is similar to the same question that drove explorers to the edge of the known world: "What happens when we come to the end?" They found out the end of the world doesn't exist, and so did I. Where I stop, an unfathomable Source of strength begins. Never again do I have to fear coming to the end of myself, because there is no end; there is only ever a continual, beautiful, beginning.

At sunset, Trent and I drove to the Urban Monk's church. In a formal conclusion to my fast, the Monk blessed me and said: "Now go forth and eat!"

"I have never been so hungry in my life," I joked to Trent on the way to Max & Erma's restaurant. "I know people say you should ease back into eating after a long-term fast, but those people have more self-discipline than me."

"What are you going to have first?"

"Everything on the menu…and then some."

That night, I fell asleep with a stomach full of tortilla soup and a heart full of gratitude.

I dreamed that I stepped inside the Divine Disco Ball, and Psychic Jesus— he of the Christian Spiritualist Temple and my mother's painting—was there petting his lambs. In my waking life, I would have guessed the center of the Divine Disco Ball contained metaphysical nougat: the lovechild of Snickers, raindrops on roses, and those tiny sweaters people knit for penguins caught in oil spills. (It's a real thing; Google it. You're welcome.)

But my mom's Jesus? He was the last guy I would have expected to see here.

Still, he sat patiently on a bench, as though he'd been waiting a long time. I opened my mouth to ask all my existential questions, but the room glowed warm with a rush of the aforementioned nougat, endlessly multiplied. It took my breath away.

Of course it's you, I knew in an instant. *It couldn't be anyone else.* No one else lived closer to God in my Christianish heart than Jesus, a representation of the most beautiful love: Love that would give itself up for you, for me, for all. If I were a different person, it might have been someone different. But I only am, and can ever be, me. So it was my mother's Jesus, the Psychic Jesus, the Jesus I couldn't quite reconcile, who smiled at me.

Jesus held up (tattooed!) arms in a gesture I named, "Peace, be still," and I knew why the storms had stopped when he told them to. I was still, because everything in me and around me was still. The whole Godiverse was still. My questions mattered not, because I already knew the answer to all of them:

Love is bigger than everything.

Part 5

Spring

23

Sandwiches

"**D**id you *live with* your husband before you were married?" She leaned in, looking precisely like a prim soldier taking aim.

Fifteen sets of Amish eyes watched me from beneath bonnets. The question came from Mary, a mouthy young mother of six. (Funny how I'd never thought of "mouthy" and "Amish" in the same sentence.) She said "live with" in the tone I'd use to describe stepping on a tarantula with bare feet, so I knew she was really asking if I'd *slept* with Trent pre-vows.

In a grand hurry to find something to say—anything!—I rushed into a makeshift apology. "I feel really bad about telling you this…"

Mary the Mouthy cut me off. "It's good you feel bad about it!" she approved. The older ladies—some of them older than my grandmother—clucked their agreement, commending my guilty conscience with nods.

Maybe I should have just let them all feel good about me feeling bad, but I'd had quite enough religious guilt and wasn't about to let a table full of women sex-shame me, even if they were wearing aprons.

I threw up my hands in a referee gesture. "Oh, no, no! I don't feel bad about living with my husband. I feel bad that I'm *telling* you about it."

All the air in the room disappeared into tension so icy and hard that even my clean conscience froze. I looked around the table. *This is happening. I am discussing my sex life with a table full of Amish women.*

Since the Amish weren't trying to convert anyone—the whole "no electricity" thing being a tough sell—I had actually campaigned to be interrogated about my prenuptial living arrangements. Several months prior, when I was still selling nail and power tools, I had a sales appointment with Mr. Wiebe, a strict Mennonite gentleman with extensive grey facial hair and a scowl that said, "I am *this close* to smacking you with my old-fashioned hat."

He picked up a power tool. "My wife has some Amish cousins who use guns like these. They like it 'cause it's propane, no electric."

Amish?! In my mind I was already wearing a bonnet. "Any chance your wife could introduce me to her cousins?" I asked, trying to act casual.

"You want to sell them some nail guns?" He scratched his whiskers in confusion.

"Something like that."

Poor Mr. Wiebe. I called him every other day—ostensibly to check on business. When he finally said in an exasperated tone, "Miss, you really want to sell those guns!" I broke down and told him about Project Thirty by Thirty, bracing for a dial tone.

"Why didn't you just say something? Let me just call Rachel and Eli; I'm sure they'll host you."

Well. Knock me over with a pitchfork.

"They have a phone?" I asked, incredulous.

"Not in the house—just in the cabinet shop."

Explaining my project to Cousin Eli over the din in his shop was the next hurdle.

"Rachel will call you!" he shouted, reminding me of the proverbial breakup line and a call that never comes. Between his thick Pennsylvania Dutch accent and the background noise, I couldn't tell whether I was invited or not, so I had all but given up hope when, several months later, an unrecognized number rang. In bed with the Sickness, I sent it to voicemail and forgot to listen to it until the following Saturday when Erin was visiting. I played it on speaker.

"Reba, this is Rachel, Rachel Yoder? We would like to invite you to spend the night so you do not have to drive too far on Sunday morning before church!"

"Wow," I said. "I'm not sure if I'm more surprised that an Amish woman returned my call after six months, or that she left me a voicemail, or that she invited me to be a houseguest."

"Voicemail," Erin decided for me.

Should I continue as planned, drinking skinny-girl margaritas with Erin, or should I spend the night on an Amish farm? Would it be alcohol or aprons?

My decision hinged on my fear of outhouses. Specifically, outhouses I might have to stumble to in the dark if I needed to pee in the middle of the night, with only a candle to guide my way. An unwelcome mental image of accidentally falling into the latrine hole made up my mind in favor of margaritas. I called Rachel back and made arrangements for Sunday morning.

The next morning, I headed out for the Amish world wearing one of the world's ugliest dresses, which I had procured the night before on a last-minute Goodwill run with Erin: an oversized blue cotton jumper with a complementary black cardigan that featured shoulder pads. The dress was high-necked and stretched to the ankles; overall, it promised to make any wearer resemble a beached whale. I finished off my look with flat black shoes, a bare face, and a demure bun.

"Stunning!" Trent teased when I appeared à la Amish on Sunday morning. "*All* the boys are gonna beg you to ride in their buggies."

Minutes later, Andre saw me in the driveway. "Hi…?" he cocked his head at my outfit.

"The jumper was only three dollars," I said. "But the embarrassment is priceless."

Two hours later, I pulled into the Yoders' farm. Rachel appeared in the front yard and directed me to park next to the buggy. With a strong, slim frame beneath her modest dress, and dark hair with wisps of grey tucked into her bonnet, she looked to be in her late fifties.

"Welcome," she sang out. I expected her to act like the nuns in *The Sound of Music*—proper and restrained—because I was surprised to meet an actual, nice person, with a wide grin. We shook hands and then, as if thinking better of it, hugged.

After pleasantries, she showed me around the house. Though I'd filed the archetypal Amish—a mishmash from literature and film—somewhere between the Pilgrims and *Little House on the Prairie*, Laura Ingalls would have been shocked by Rachel's modern kitchen—complete with all major appliances—and bathrooms that were nicer than mine. (No outhouses in sight!) I asked about the power obviously humming through the house.

"Kerosene," Rachel explained, gesturing through a window to a large fuel tank and generator.

"This woodwork is beautiful!" I exclaimed over walls of built-in bookshelves in the cozy living room—shelves that held only Bibles, religious books, and several encyclopedias. As if on cue, Eli entered the room.

"That would be Eli's work," Rachel said, gesturing to him.

"Welcome," said Eli, folding his large, rough hands in front of him. "We're glad to have you."

They led me to the buggy. "Don't be worried if anyone looks at you twice; we've never had an English visitor at church," Eli said.

I gulped—*No pressure or anything.*

Rachel asked questions. "Are you married? Do you have any children? When are you planning to have children? How many children do you want to have?" (Not *if* I wanted children, but when.) "We'll see about kids," I replied.

"Children are a blessing from the Lord!" she rejoiced.

Hitching up the horses, Eli chimed his agreement. "They are indeed!"

"Well…I'm not ready yet, with Trent being in school and all." I didn't say what I was really thinking: *Not being sick would be the first blessing I need.*

Rachel stopped. "You work to support your husband?" she said, eyes big as saucers.

"Most days," I replied in a light tone. *Most days when I'm not in bed.*

Black with mint-colored crushed velvet seating, the buggy was a much more posh affair than I would have expected, but also less sturdy. When Eli helped me climb in, the whole buggy dipped under my weight, springing back only when I sat down. *Thank God I don't weigh more,* I thought. *I might have capsized. I can see the headline now: "Woman crushed by spiritual quest!"*

Eli sat holding the reins; once Rachel alighted to the passenger seat he signaled the horses and we began clomp-clomping down the drive. *I'm riding in a buggy!* I thought, looking through Eli and Rachel to the brown horses' tails waving ahead.

"Can I take a picture?" I asked, "Not of you—I know you don't allow pictures—but of the horses?"

"I'm sure the horses won't mind," Rachel laughed. She and Eli leaned to either side so I could snap away. I had a few questions of my own for the couple: How many children did they have? (Nine!) Did they believe the Bible was the literal Word of God? (Yes.) And what is up with *rumspringa*, the time for Amish youth before they officially join the church and have a brief opportunity to rebel and live in the English world without condemnation, sort of like a hall pass from the Amish life?

Eli and Rachel both laughed heartily. "English people are always so curious about that!" Rachel said, turning around from the front passenger seat to face me while Eli drove steadily on. "In our community it's never been very wild, though we hear some places it is. Here it's nothing like the media reports—just kids being kids. We rarely lose a youth to the English world."

Silently, I noted her use of the word "lose," phrasing that implied death. I changed topics. "Will your family be here today?" I asked, hoping to meet all nine children.

"Oh yes," Rachel said joyfully, "you'll meet four generations this morning, including our oldest and youngest!" Eli and Rachel had grown up, met, and married in the area, and she'd borne their last child at fifty. "He's now fourteen. Perfectly healthy!" *Sixty-four?* I thought, viewing her profile. That revelation certainly blew through my earlier guess that she was in her fifties. She had fewer wrinkles than the Botoxed Real Housewives, and I wondered if it was her lifestyle, good genes, or—I looked again—happiness? She smiled at Eli as we rode along, thrilled to tell me about her children and grandchildren. Rachel and Eli were an absolute conversational delight, and by the time we pulled into a drive thirty minutes later, I felt I'd known them forever.

I saw a host of parked buggies in front of someone's home. About a hundred people milled about the lawn—men dressed in hats, vests, and trousers clumped around the horses, women holding babies and watching over the children. Rachel turned back around, looking the slightest bit uncomfortable.

"We believe in greeting one another with a holy kiss, like the New Testament instructs," Rachel said, "but please don't feel that you need to participate."

"I'm sure I'll be fine," I assured her…until I discovered that greeting one another with a holy kiss meant kissing On. The. Lips. *Hello, literal reading of The Holy Bible!*

Even if the snogging did serve the dual noble purposes of spiritual growth and making Amish friends, I just wasn't that committed, folks. Fasting for thirty days? Sure. Kissing strangers on the mouth? No, thank you.

Astonished, I watched the holy greeting. Eli greeted the men with a quick peck; Rachel greeted the women with the same. Now, before anyone gets overly excited about this development, I should pause and explain that it was about as sexy as giving your grandmother a sponge bath. The pecks were done so quickly, with such nonchalance and efficiency that you could blink and miss the whole affair.

In lieu of kissing me, everyone said, "Peace be with you," and looked like they were trying to avoid openly staring at me. Except the kids. They stood, mouths agape, looking my way like I was an alien life form. I suppose I was. "Why are *you* here?" a young boy asked, disappearing behind his mom's knees.

I just smiled and reflected on what caused me to harass poor Mr. Wiebe and make this trip, even though I suspected the exertion would put me in bed for a few days. Aside from the novelty, I wanted to know what the Amish had that makes living without the conveniences of this world worthwhile. I watched Rachel greet her family, kissing her mother, sisters, daughters, and granddaughters. *Half this room is Rachel's family,* I realized. They were all laughing about something and as Rachel stroked the cheek of a newborn grandbaby, I considered that I might see this many members of my family in one place twice a year (maybe). Rachel saw them every week, maybe even every day.

No one looked at a watch wondering when the service would start; no one was distracted by the ringing of a phone; none of the teenagers texted in a corner. I had left my cell in my car and felt lighter without it, almost like I was on vacation. I worked so hard to "live in the present" and "make time for the important things"; for them, the important things were a way of life. I felt I was witnessing absolute engagement: with God, love, and family, values we "English" say are important even while we pass them by in search of something else. I knew I was romanticizing their lifestyle; these women had worries I knew nothing of and faced challenges I would never see. But still, as I watched Rachel's sister help their mother up so she could hold her great-grandbaby, I realized that while I had many things the Amish lacked, I also lacked many things they took for granted.

I hung back, afraid to disrupt the family party, until a teenager with Down Syndrome flounced over. She stepped around Rachel to hug me.

"I'm Esther," she whispered, leaning her head in and holding fast to my arm. "I'm so happy you are here!"

"I'm Reba," I whispered back. "Can I tell you a secret?" Esther nodded enthusiastically. "You're my favorite person I've met today." She squeezed my arm. If everyone else in the room had shunned me, Esther's exuberance alone would have made me feel welcome. And when she hugged me again, I felt the press of an otherworldly kiss, the holiest of holy greetings.

The meeting place, a plain outbuilding away from a main house that usually served as the host family's place of business, had been cleared to make room for the 120-member Amish community. The room was filled with long, backless benches in two sections—right side for the men and boys, left for the women and girls—people filtered into their assigned places, oriented by family status. Youngsters and singles sat in the front, married and the elderly in the back. Rachel guided me to a middle bench and sat next to me.

"Do I have time to grab some water before the service?" I asked.

"Go right ahead," she smiled, pointing to a table at the back. Next to a large punch bowl full of water was a ladle and exactly one cup. *Hmm: choose your own adventure—stay thirsty or cozy up to germs?* I decided to take a drink.

I slid back into my seat just in time for the Bishop to greet the people…in German. The closest I had ever come to speaking German was Oktoberfest, so I tried to listen with my heart instead of my ears. Then the hymns started, and I listened with my whole body. For nearly an hour, melody wrapped around me, reverberating in four-part harmony as a multitude of voices stretched and shaped the vowels.

If Rachel had called me six months ago, I thought with my eyes closed, soaking in the music, *I would have hated this.* Now, the sheer beauty raised gooseflesh on my arms, and I didn't care that my backside hurt from slouching on the hard bench. Next to me, Rachel's wee granddaughter had fallen asleep over her lap. I smiled. *My peace is as deep as your sleep, little one.*

The sermon began; I understood nothing save the little Rachel translated for me. The lay minister preached from John 15:5, reminding me of a song I used to sing in Sunday school: "He is the vine and we are the branches, / His banner over me is love." Sometimes the men took turns speaking or reading Scripture, and I could catch a word here or there. It didn't matter: every few minutes Esther turned around and waved at me, smiling like she'd been waiting her whole life for me to visit and sit behind her. Or maybe I'd been waiting my whole life to sit behind her.

Two hours into the speaking, I shifted uncomfortably. *Why didn't I consider my small bladder before drinking half the punch bowl?* I excused myself to the outhouse, and was thrilled to find a Porta-Pottie. The ground beneath it sloped, making it rickety. When I stepped inside, the Porta-Pottie rocked so much that I imagined another headline about my demise: "Woman Buried in Spiritual S***!" I braced my hands on the walls, which put me in the uncomfortable position of looking straight down the hole, the contents of which offered proof positive that the Amish were real people, too.

After the service, the gathering took on the celebratory feel of a quiet, well-organized party. "It's time for fellowship and food!" Rachel explained, pulling me toward the back as the men rearranged the seating and the women bustled to prepare lunch.

"They're so fast!" I said to Rachel, watching the action.

"Lots of practice," she said, patting my shoulder before going to join the women. I offered to help, but in the manner of hostesses the world over, she refused.

It wasn't long before Rachel came up behind me bearing a huge platter of food. Children and their mothers clamored for seats, excited to eat. I was excited too, imagining the gravy-covered extravaganza of homemade chicken and noodles served at Amish restaurants, so when Rachel put down the platter with sandwich fixings I was perplexed. Sandwiches? I thought. I became even more confused as the mothers started making them; they piled two homemade slices of bread with peanut butter, jelly, thickly-sliced ham, cheese, condiments, and pickles. It was every sandwich I'd ever eaten smooshed into one.

Rachel saw my expression. "This isn't just any peanut butter," she said, as if that explained everything. "It's a homemade mix of peanut butter, marshmallow cream, maple syrup, and sugar."

I decided it was wisest to eat the peanut butter, jelly, meat, cheese, marshmallow cream, and maple syrup sandwich without comment, but once I took my first tentative bite I couldn't help myself. "Oh my Go—Oh my goodness, this is the best thing I've ever tasted! It might be the best sandwich in the history of the world." It was the perfect juxtaposition of salty and yum.

"You've never had one before?" asked a girl with a lisp. She looked as confused as I'd been a minute earlier. Mouth full, I shook my head.

"The children look forward to this all week," said her mother. "It is their favorite! We have it every Sunday and at events: weddings, funerals— it is easy to prepare for a crowd."

I practically drooled while making my second plate. "It's so good I'm forgetting all my manners!" I exclaimed to Esther with my mouth full and two elbows on the table.

"Want some of mine?" she offered.

I winked. "Maybe when I finish this one."

After lunch, I visited with the Amish women for hours without a sense of time passing…well, except when Mary the Mouthy plopped down to interrogate me about my sex life. That felt like three hours, until I started to laugh. Mary the Mouthy followed my lead, and soon the whole table was giggling. I'm sure they were laughing a little at me, but at least I was laughing with them, too. Once they got over my prenuptial sins, they treated me like a minor celebrity, asking about my house, hobbies, family, job, and project. I could barely get a question in edgewise.

"What don't the English know about you that you wish they did?" I finally asked in a mixed-age group.

"That we like to laugh and have fun!" one mother shouted. "We're not serious all the time!"

When Rachel signaled it was time to leave, I felt a little sad. Even though I was tired, I wasn't ready to leave this kind and gentle circle. I hugged at least twenty people on my way out. The last few pulled me over to the freezer, Mary and Esther among them.

"This is for you to take home to your husband," our hostess smiled beatifically.

"What is it?" I asked, peeling the lid from a frozen container. "The special peanut butter!" I squealed.

"Now you can make our sandwich for Trent," Rachel said.

"And you can remember us when you eat it," chimed Mary, "and come back again soon."

I can't say I've teared up over peanut butter before or since, but on that day, their kindness overwhelmed me.

When we arrived back at the Yoder farm, Rachel and Eli invited me to sit on their porch and tell them about the adventures I'd had with Thirty by Thirty. Rachel and I rocked slowly on the swing, and Eli sat opposite us, fetching iced tea and snacks as the hours wore into late afternoon. At first I held back, thinking they would be judgmental, but Rachel and Eli shocked me with their openness. Sometimes we just sat in companionable silence, rocking away the minutes. "The English think we give up so much," Rachel said quietly, "but really we gain so much. What we do not have frees us to concentrate on our many blessings: family, community, faith, and work."

The rest was so absolute that I couldn't help but be reminded of my fast, and I wanted to sit on the porch forever with Rachel and Eli. But I could tell they were growing tired, so I stood to leave.

"Wait," said Rachel. "Before you go, you have to tell me two things. After your journey, what is your faith now? And what do you think about God?"

I paused. No one had asked me these two huge questions, at least not since I finished my fast. "Maybe I'd better sit back down. Those aren't easy to answer." I thought for a minute, then spoke—hesitantly at first, but gaining steam as I went.

"I think my faith is a lot like your Sunday sandwich. To outsiders, it's a sandwich with an identity crisis, but to your family it's a mishmash of deliciousness. I've taken a lot of faiths and jammed them together in a way that may look confusing to others but makes perfect sense to me." My new faith embodied opposing forces, but felt mysteriously in balance. "As for God, well…I think God is a lot like a disco ball."

They stared at me blankly, as though I'd spoken Klingon.

"Wait," I said, reality dawning. "Do either of you know what a disco ball is?"

They shook their heads.

Laughing internally at my epic fail, I doubled back. "I think God is like a round diamond with millions of facets. You have a facet; I have a facet; everyone has a facet. God spins in the space between us, reflecting the light in each of our perspectives."

"I think a diamond is such a beautiful way to explain God," Rachel said, hugging me tightly goodbye. "But what's even more beautiful is how your face shines when you talk about it, like you're lit up from within."

My face: shimmering with belief. Thankful tears gathered in my eyes.

Rachel pressed a *Give Us This Day Our Daily Bread* community cookbook into my hands, inscribed with her address.

"So you can cook for your husband," she said.

"And my children?" I added. Something about the day made me believe I would be well one day.

Rachel beamed, her face luminous in the fading sun. "And your children."

24
Peacock

"How are you planning to commemorate the completion of your project in a few months?" asked the Urban Monk after one of our evening meditation sessions.

"I'd like to plan an event where I invite representatives from all the places I've been this year and maybe do a ceremony of some kind."

"An interfaith rally?"

"A cross between an interfaith rally and a baptism…except not a baptism. Something symbolic of my journey."

"Have you thought about using rocks?"

Strangely (or maybe not so strangely considering how things had been going), I had considered rocks. "How do you always read my mind?" He smiled. "Yes, I was thinking maybe I could get a slab of bedrock to represent my Christianish past, and thirty smaller, unique rocks to represent what I've added to my faith from each place I've been this year. During the ceremony, each representative could carry a rock to the front, say a few words about faith, and drop it on the bedrock."

He stroked his beard. "An altar of sorts."

I smiled. "Just one thing; you have to officiate."

He nodded. "We'll do a prayer and invite Jesus and Allah and Buddha and Krishna…and they'll all come to honor your journey."

I thought he was poking fun at me until I realized he was dead serious. It was settled before I left the chapel: we would do a rock ceremony; the monk would officiate; I would find the rocks. The obvious question—*Where the heck am I going to find a bedrock?*—entered my mind.

"Godiverse," I said. "I'm countin' on you for the bedrock."

Trent and I were packing for a weeklong ski trip with my in-laws when I received my fifth blanket rejection e-mail from a Native American tribe.

"No one wants me," I informed him. "How am I going to find a medicine man if no one will even talk to me?"

"Maybe you'll meet one in Colorado," he said.

I shoved my ski helmet into the suitcase. "Doubtful."

"You never know."

It didn't seem like Trent's words were going to come true during the first few days of the trip, which I spent mostly in bed while everyone else went skiing. But the words came back to me several days later when, buoyed by a temporary abatement of the Sickness, I felt well enough to go souvenir shopping.

I passed a store in the Mountain Mall and felt the Energy buzz. I walked forward and it faded; I about-faced and it started up again, a cosmic game of Marco Polo.

I'll bite, I thought, turning into a store that had rocks everywhere I turned: nothing but rocks. An old guy reclined on a stool in the back, reading a magazine. I tried to act casual, an act that lasted forty seconds, until he looked up and smiled. I, Reba the Tactful, blurted, "Are you a Medicine Man?"

He boomed out a hearty laugh full of streams and mountains. "I dabble," he said. "What can I do for you?" His name was River, just River. With skin like tanned hide, white hair, and a stout, almost square frame, his intense face transformed into a valley of happiness when he smiled. "I'm not a shaman," he apologized, "but I do teach guided animal totem meditation."

Okay, I steeled myself. *This is where he shakes me down for money.* Instead, he puttered behind the counter.

"I know it's around here somewhere... Aha!" He blew dust off the cover of an old book. "Let me make a photocopy." He headed to the back room and returned with stapled pages and a CD. "Read this, listen to this, and come back tomorrow to tell me what happens."

I recruited Becky for River's meditation, because, really, isn't it every mother-in-law's dream to bond with her son's wife by meditating together in the dark basement of a ski lodge? We read the back of the CD and photocopy together.

"'Shamanic drumming and sacred music will help you find your Animal Totem,'" Becky read. She looked up. "What's an Animal Totem?"

I Googled it. "Looks like it's a power animal. Do you remember that scene in *Fight Club*, where the guy's power animal is a penguin?" She nodded. I dimmed the lights and we lay on the floor. Though trying hard to stay solemn, we burst out laughing. I knew I should be taking this more seriously; how often do old men in rock shops give out CDs like candy? (Answer: Not nearly often enough.)

"Okay," I looked at Becky. "Get ready to quiet your mind."

"Breathe Deeeeeply and Exxxhaaaaale," said a dangerously hypnotic voice, all fluffy clouds and waving feathers. If the owner of this voice told me to "Driiiink the Kooool-Aiiide," I would consider it.

The shamanic drums beat out *Boom-BOOM, Boom-BOOM,* growing ever louder as the voice guided us through a series of visualized caves, oceans, and waterfalls. By the time we reached our destination, "A bright clearing deeeep in the foooreeeest," I was asleep—or something like asleep; with meditation it can be hard to tell.

In my dream, or whatever, I entered a clearing. I was barefoot, feeling the dew on the emerald grass. I heard the wind rustle the trees gently. And then I saw it: my strong power animal, my Spirit Totem, my...bird that can't fly?

My power animal was a *peacock*?

I didn't even like peacocks. They struck me as vainglorious roosters.

The peacock studied me, and before my eyes its plumage grew until it was much larger than me. Then things got weird. (If you're thinking, "Reba...things were already a little weird!" I'm right there with ya.)

A man walked out from behind the feathers; his identifying feature was silver-white hair that fell to his waist. He leveled his wise brown eyes, looking into mine. And then *Poof!* he disappeared.

Ba-ba-boom-boom!—I woke to the sound of drums.

My mother-in-law was already rubbing her eyes, so I asked her what she saw. "A buffalo," she breathed. "It was very majestic. What about you?"

"A peacock," I sighed, annoyed that exercise hadn't worked.

"At least it's..." Becky searched for the upside. "Pretty?"

The next day, I trooped back to River, CD and photocopy in hand.

"What happened?" he inquired, leaning forward on his stool.

I told him the short version, ending with one hand on my hip. "What kind of person gets a peacock as a power animal? Did I do something wrong?"

"Animal Totem," he corrected, reaching for another old book and donning his glasses. "Ah yes, the peacock," he read. "Those with peacock as a totem are powerful healers."

At the word "healer," my mouth went dry with disbelief.

"Because the peacock sheds its feathers only to grow more beautiful plumage, it has become a symbol for rebirth and renewal," River continued. "Shamanic cultures use peacock feathers in healing rituals, and many religions feature peacock imagery around deities… In Christianity, the peacock symbolizes the resurrection of Christ… The 'eyes' on the peacock's feathers represent a strong energetic connection, the ability to see beyond the physical world…" Pausing to look up at me, River laughed at my astonishment. "Just wait until you hear this next part: 'The peacock is considered by many to be the physical manifestation of the mythical phoenix, rising from the ashes of its grave.'"

With every sentence, my eyes got wider. "A phoenix?" I sputtered, knowing that even if I searched for a thousand years, I would never find a better image of spiritual healing than this peacock-phoenix, *my* peacock: set on fire, burned up…and reborn from the wreckage.

Life, resurrected from flames.

An image arose, emblazoned like a tattoo on my mind: vibrant feathers emerging from blackness; beautiful plumage materializing out of grey ashes. Strength born of fire.

My *Peacock Rising*.

River smirked at my stunned expression. "Not bad for a bird you claim 'can't fly', is it?"

My mind brimmed with questions, but only one tumbled quickly out, as though it couldn't wait one second longer.

"Do you happen to have a bedrock in here?" I asked. If he was as surprised by the subject change as I was, it didn't show.

"I do," he answered, walking behind the counter. "But it's not for sale." He retrieved the bedrock from a low cabinet and told me the story. "My son and I were hiking ten years ago when we found this rock covered in cobwebs. I noticed it had an unusual shape so I dusted it off." He placed the rock on the counter and I saw what he meant. It resembled an arrowhead with grey with white markings throughout. Large and flat, a bowl-like shape had been worn down in its center by dripping water. It was apparent from the depth of the indentation that this was one old bedrock.

"And see these black ashes here?" I nodded. "These were already in there. I showed it to my Chief friend—don't get too excited, he's in Wyoming now—and he thought it had been used in spiritual ceremonies."

"So it's not for sale," I verified, already knowing: *This is my rock*. I told River about my project, the Urban Monk, and the Rock Ceremony we'd planned.

"Take the rock," he said. "It was obviously meant for you all along."

I convinced him to let me pay for it, or at least buy some of the other rocks I would need for my ceremony. We spent a pleasant half-hour picking out thirty rocks and crystals in varying shapes and a rainbow of colors, and he sold me the whole lot, bedrock included, for twenty dollars.

"Good luck," River said as I left. "I hope you find everything you're looking for."

I looked at the bedrock balanced in my arms and back at him. "I'm well on my way."

"How's your project going?" asked Trent's Aunt Mindy the following week over home manicures with the girls in the family.

"Not well. I think my Native American visit is cursed. I found an online advertisement for an urban drum circle, but no one showed up while I was waiting except for a catawampus guy who mistook me for a hooker—even though I was wearing a trench coat. Then it started to rain and I got drenched!"

"That's too bad," sympathized Grandma Joan, blowing on her OPI Rosy Future-colored nails. Aunt Mindy applied a second coat of Red My Fortune Cookie to my fingernails. "What are you going to do now?"

"I have no idea," I shook my head. "I've asked every tribe I could find within driving distance, and I'm not getting any response from my e-mail to the drum circle guy, Chief Hoopwatcher, a.k.a Iggy Garcia."

"Did you say Chief *Iggy Garcia*?" Mindy asked, missing my pinky. "We know him! He coached Will's soccer team. Do you want his cell phone number?"

"YES!" After so many months spent trying to find a shaman, could it be that easy? I spilled an open bottle of sparkle pink polish in my excitement. Cousin Emma, whose lacquer was already dry, came to the rescue with paper towels.

"Emma," I said, "How fast can you dial?"

And just like that, Chief Iggy Hoopwatcher Garcia—Suburban Shaman, Shahaptian Guide Medicine Man, and Natural Healer of Good Intention in the Native American Church of Nemenhah—invited me to *Itsipi*.

If the Godiverse hadn't given me such a clear thumbs up about Chief Hoopwatcher, I would have chickened out when I Googled "Itsipi sweat ceremony" the night before the gathering. (Helpful hint: this is a one-way ticket to hyperventilation. Googling anything scarier than a stubbed toe after midnight always results in a terminal diagnosis.)

"People have *died* in sweat ceremonies," I informed Trent on the morning of Itsipi while loading my gear in the car: a blanket for sitting, several gallons of water for drinking, clothes that could be ruined by mud, and a towel for patting dry. "Granted, the people who died were in the desert and hadn't had food or water in a couple of days…"

In my head, I knew the chances of my personal demise were slim—about equal to the chance of a Canadian invasion—but in my heart it was like our friends to the north were already armed with hockey sticks and crossing the border. Hide your women and children!

To participate in the sweat ceremony, I would have to crawl into a tiny, hot, crowded hut and, in doing so, face several fears at once.

1. Claustrophobia: On my honeymoon, I passed out in the airplane bathroom. A flight attendant had to force her way through the door so the plane could land. I refused to get on the next flight until my brand-new husband plied me with booze and the promise of a Caribbean beach.
2. Severe heat: Two hundred degrees Fahrenheit is for slow-cooking pork chops, not roasting Rebas.
3. Crowds: My idea of hell is a flash mob.
4. Strangers: Half-naked ones, sitting close to me in the dark.
5. The unknown: I had no idea what awaited me during Itsipi. (Possibly death, according to Google.)

Just add in snakes and spiders, and I'd have almost all my fears covered. *Oh wait, Itsipi is outside. There might be snakes or spiders—eek!*

My husband was unsympathetic. "You're not going to *die*." He studied the item in my hands. "Wait, why are you packing up pieces of Andre's Christmas tree?"

I pushed the logs into the trunk. "I'm supposed to bring wood for the ceremony, but—surprise!—grocery stores don't carry firewood in the spring." Andre's Christmas tree, parts of which had been languishing in our shared yard since January, was the next-best option.

"I'm also supposed to bring an offering and a covered dish," I sighed. "But I don't know what constitutes an offering, and I was too tired to make a casserole." I held up some cash and pointed to a platter of chips and dip.

He stared at me doubtfully. "You're going to bring the Chief a Christmas tree, Hint of Lime Tostitos, and some cheese dip?"

I realized this was almost worse than my *Salade d'Shame*, but I'd had enough Sickness self-doubt. Store-bought nacho cheese was the best I could do, so store-bought nacho cheese I would offer to God.

"The Godiverse works in mysterious ways," I told Trent. "Who knows what It can do with Hint of Lime Tostitos?"

Promptly at noon, I pulled into Chief Hoopwatcher's driveway, a winding gravel path that led to a brick ranch on a few acres of wooded land. In a clearing beyond the house, I glimpsed the wooden skeleton of what I assumed was the Itsipi. I gulped. If I was slightly terrified to pile into a tiny space with strangers only be plunged into darkness and possibly fatal heat before surveying the structure, which was approximately the size and shape of the model igloo in my fourth-grade classroom, I could definitely feel the claustrophobia pressing in now.

I have to crawl into that thing. My pulse raced and my blood pressure skyrocketed. A lot of things in Project Thirty by Thirty had been emotionally scary, but aside from the drive home from the Hindu temple, I'd never been afraid for my physical safety.

Still frightened, I grabbed my gear and marched myself around the corner of the house before I lost courage.

And the first thing I saw around that corner? The very first thing?

A miniature disco ball, reflecting all the colors of the blazing sunlight.

The baby disco ball sat on a blanket, surrounded by the things you might expect to see at a tribal ceremony: feathers, rocks, tribal jewelry, and a ceremonial pipe.

Chief Hoopwatcher looked up from where he knelt in the grass near the blanket.

"Hello," he greeted, his tanned, practiced hands arranging the items just so. Joy showed in the lines around his wide-set cocoa-colored eyes. Wearing casual clothing, a dark goatee and a grin, he looked infinitely approachable, but his beaded leather necklaces and woven poncho lent an air of spiritual authority. He reminded me of a wrestler: compact yet powerful, serene but strong. I'd want to share a pitcher of beer with this guy, but I also wouldn't want to mess with him.

"I'm Reba," I offered. "Mindy's niece?"

"I thought that's who you might be." He extended his hand and I put down my bags to shake it. "Welcome to the Condor Eagle chapter of the Nemenhah."

"You have no idea how glad I am to finally be here." I gave him the CliffsNotes version of my project and the Divine Disco Ball. It was a lot to squeeze into five minutes, but we had some major *déjà forward* going on. He caught up fast.

Chief Hoopwatcher looked down at his small disco ball thoughtfully. "A friend gave this to me," he said, palming it. "He meant it to remind me of dancing, because dancing is part of my medicine." He spun it around on his finger. "You should have it now." He tossed it my way.

I caught it. "Are you sure?" I sputtered. "It seems like a meaningful gift."

"The things that bless the altars of our lives are meant to be shared. We are only caretakers. Your journey inspires me, so today I give the disco ball to you. Someday you will pass it on."

I gripped it with both hands. "I find it hard to believe that I'll ever want to part with it."

"One day you will," he smiled. "But for now use it to start your own Bundle." He gestured to the collection of items grouped on the blanket, and I divined that a Bundle meant a collection of sacred items.

"I already have something for my Bundle," I produced my bedrock from one of the bags and related the story of its origin.

"Cool," he grinned. "Very cool."

I felt someone pass behind me. The Chief stopped him. "Tony, come meet my new friend. Reba, this is Tony 'Silver Bear.' He is also a medicine man, a powerful healer."

Two shamans for the price of one, I thought, turning around.

For a moment, I wondered if I was experiencing a mental break. From his silver-white hair to his wise brown eyes, Silver Bear the Healer was the same man who had appeared in my peacock dream in Colorado.

"I know you!" I shrieked.

He did not know me, but to his credit, Silver Bear gave me a look that implied I should continue instead of the one I probably deserved, which was more along the lines of, "Step off, crazy lady."

I tried to settle down, as to not scare my new friends. *Ahem.* "Silver Bear, I don't know any other way to tell you this; I dreamed about you three weeks ago. Except…" I studied his silver locks. "You had longer hair. Your hair was all the way down to your waist."

"I just got a haircut," Silver Bear said. "Three weeks ago my hair *did* reach to my waist."

Silver Bear and Chief Hoopwatcher exchanged a knowing look.

"Welcome, my sister," said the Chief, placing a hand on my shoulder.

Members of the Native American Church of Nemenhah had already arrived. Some arranged blankets in a circle in the grass clearing; others milled about chatting or helping the Chief. A few did yoga poses nearer to the woods. Joining the crowd, I set up my red blanket and placed my bedrock and disco ball on top of it.

It was the kind of day I wish for in the middle of Ohio winters: air fragrant with recent rain, but not a cloud in sight; sapphire sky framing many shades of newly budded green. Sunshine streamed down extravagantly, warming my arms and feet. I stretched out on my back, crossed my arms behind my head, and breathed it all in. Looking up, I was conscious of being in nature, the greatest cathedral of all.

The smell of burning sage filled my nostrils, prompting me to sit up and look around. Wearing an outfit that looked like a karate suit, a bottle-redhead waved a fragrant, smoking stick, the source of the scent. She approached.

"I'm Joanne," she said, her voice placid as a still lake. "Would you like to be smudged?" Imagining myself as a smudge of mascara, I must have looked unsure. "It's a purification ritual," she explained. "Meant to clear you of any negative energy and make way for healing."

Healing? I thought of the Sickness. *Heck, for healing I'll smoke the stuff, bathe in it, and bake it into wholesome cranberry muffins.*

"Smudge away," I answered, perhaps a little too enthusiastically. I stood up; she waved the smudging stick around me, leaving a feathery Reba-shaped smoke trail around me.

For me the smoke acted like truth serum. I started babbling on about my claustrophobia and concern about the safety of Itsipi.

Joanne squinted at me. "Were you Googling recently, by any chance?"

"Yep," I confessed.

She laid a gentle hand on my arm. "Poor thing, you were probably terrified!" Uh-huh. Her voice took on an authoritative tone. "Chief Hoopwatcher is highly trained, certified, and ordained. Safety is our top priority. If you feel uncomfortable at all, just wave at me and I'll get you outta there." She made a gesture like pulling someone off the stage. "We don't want you do anything that doesn't feel right for you today."

Just hearing I was allowed to be uncomfortable made me more comfortable. "Thanks so much," I smiled.

Even though no one told us to sit down and be quiet, everyone eventually felt the pull to reverence and drifted to our respective blankets, waiting for the ceremony to begin.

The Chief sat on his blanket, Sacred Bundle before him. "Itsipi is where we gather to pray and purify ourselves. We gather to make way for healing, reconciliation, forgiveness, insights. The Itsipi is built with willows according to sacred geometry rules. Together we will cover the wooden structure with blankets and tarps, representing the Womb of Mother Earth, where we may enter to be reborn through the spirit of the four elements.

"The Condor Eagle chapter of the Nemenhah operates under the principle of Spiritual Adoption, meaning we welcome well-intentioned people of any race, ethnicity, color, gender, culture, or religious belief. We accept all traditions to join our circle and call on *Wyakin*—God, the Source, the Divine, the Universe. Together, we will smoke the ceremonial pipe to purify ourselves and create space for healing. First we share our intentions."

Everyone in the circle stated their names and reasons for gathering. Experiencing the Divine and walking a spiritual path were the common themes. When it was my turn, I offered my truest truth: "I'm here for healing."

Chief Hoopwatcher lit the ceremonial pipe and passed it around. When it came to me, I followed his instructions: acknowledging the four directions, I lifted the pipe high to Father Sky and down to Mother Earth. I recognized *Wyakin*, set my intention to honor the Sacred Breath of life, and raised the pipe to my lips.

When all had partaken, Chief Hoopwatcher led us to Itsipi. In silence, we covered the skeleton of willows with layers of blankets and tarps, a team exercise that reminded me of building a campsite. Work completed, we gathered around the bonfire pit where Andre's Christmas tree burned, helping to bake the rocks that would heat our ceremony. Stones glowed red and orange within the blaze.

"We dance around the fire to shake up our egos," said Chief Hoopwatcher. "We begin by letting go of all that no longer serves us."

Several members grabbed drums, and the Chief started a chant as we began dancing around the flames. If an exuberant wedding conga line got as serious as surgery, this procession would be the result. People of all shapes, sizes, ages, and races wriggled and shook, equal parts reverence and joy. Energy crackled in the fire and between us, the exuberance reminiscent of a pep rally right before the Big Game.

And then, we stopped. Except for the pops and snaps of the fire and the sounds of nature, all was silent.

"We enter Itsipi on all fours, showing humility. We go in backwards to represent returning to the womb." Chief Hoopwatcher said, demonstrating how to perform the entry.

The members disappeared one by one, a clown car in reverse. Except for the Chief, I was almost last in line—giving me plenty of freak-out time. But, whether it was the disco ball, the Chief, or Joanne, I was actually okay. I felt like I was pointing my skis straight down the mountain. If I wanted to move forward I had to let go.

I took a deep breath and crouched in the dirt. Nodding to the doorkeeper that I was as ready as I'd ever be, I crawled backwards into the darkness.

My eyes adjusted quickly. Facing a central pit dug in the dirt, the group of twenty sat in two rings around the perimeter. Crowded was an understatement: My head brushed the top of the Itsipi as I crawled in between Silver Bear and a young guy. "Michael," he whispered as I squeezed in next to him. I rubbed shoulders and knees with Michael and Silver Bear, but to my surprise, their closeness felt like the good kind of crowded—brothers supporting me instead of people who might trample me in a stampede. Maybe all my dread had been for nothing. Then again, it wasn't very hot yet.

Chief Hoopwatcher entered. "Welcome to all my relations!" he whooped.

Using a set of antlers to handle the glowing rocks, the doorkeeper delivered them directly from the bonfire. Chief Hoopwatcher used a second set of antlers to pile the glowing stones in the central pit. As each addition ratcheted up the heat, we shouted, "Welcome, grandfathers!"

Within minutes sweat slicked my arms, making them a Slip 'n' Slide against Tony and Michael's limbs. Chief Hoopwatcher splashed the stones seven times. Steam sizzled around us.

"It's good to be here!" he yelled.

"It's good to be here!" the crowd roared back. If dancing around the fire was a pep rally, this was the cry of an army on the move.

"In the sweat, we face ourselves and meet *Wyakin,*" lifted the Chief. "We face the parts of ourselves we have closed off."

If I had ever closed off my sweat glands, they were now working overtime.

"In Itsipi we will visit all four doors: west, north, east and south," explained the Chief. "The doors correspond to the seasons. This is the west door, the autumn, where we give thanks and seek counsel from our ancestors."

I imagined the collective wisdom of my ancestors coalescing in the heat, which was quickly becoming thick, dense as water.

The Chief began a simple song of thanksgiving, and we joined him on the second round:

Ogou helo
Nemenhah-hemene helo
Meninshtena helo
Solistena helo

I closed my eyes against the heat, and the song made my mind silent.

The Chief led us through the west door, alternating between singing, chanting, and silence. Over the course of thirty minutes the heat grew more intense until it became an entity hanging over us. The hot air stung my skin, filled my lungs, engulfed me. My sweat turned the dirt beneath me to mud, until any movement was slippery. Sometimes it was the welcome pain of a tough workout, boot camp for the soul; but mostly I felt like a hunk of meat in a slow cooker.

What am I doing here? I wondered at a break between doors, when the members crawled out to rehydrate and ingest sea salts. I stretched out on the ground, grass tickling my toes. The answer came swiftly from somewhere else: *I am offering up everything that does not serve me to be sizzled away like water on the rocks.*

I groaned inwardly. Mysticism is so much easier when you're not lying on the ground covered in hot mud.

Silver Bear noticed my struggle and knelt beside me. "If you're too hot, suck mud," he said, handing me some frozen watermelon. (Food of the gods!) "Root yourself to the earth. Put your face down in the dirt where it's coolest, and breathe."

When he walked away, I solemnly removed my Furnace '02 t-shirt and Miller Lite sweatband. They were fine as reminders of where I'd been, but I didn't need them where I was going.

Even stripped down to a sports bar and shorts, the Itsipi heat was searing. I wasn't sure I could continue through the final session, so I followed Silver Bear's advice: I bent over my knees and put my face down and "sucked mud," my mouth so close to the dirt that I could lick the earth.

And then it hit me. *I am every person who has ever sat in the forest or the mountains or the desert or the Arctic and called on Something More.*

"This is the east door, the spring door, the 'sees far' door," Chief Hoopwatcher said. "This is also the hottest door." When he added water to the rocks, I tasted the burn.

"It's good to be here!" we chanted, and I felt the Great Spirit swell into my words, into my very being. Created by our connection to the ground and each other, the words transformed to liturgy of the highest order. Covered in sweat and muck, I had never felt so pure. Mother Earth was beneath me, Father Sky above; the ancestors were all around, silently cheering us on. *Persevere*, I could almost hear them chant, my grandfather among them.

This was the euphoria of fasting, minus the thirty-day lag time.

The heat was excruciating, yet somehow secondary. The last time I experienced something like this, I was small enough to swim in a baby pool, and my cousins decided to make it into a whirlpool. The eight of us swam in one direction in shallow water, breathless with effort as we moved the water, simultaneously contributing to and being carried by the collective force. In the sweat ceremony, twenty-three of us moved as one, sending Energy swirling as we swayed together.

A hush descended like someone had ordered silence. Chief Hoopwatcher's voice rose powerfully as he told the story of an acorn. "Through the rain and sun of every season, the seed grows from humble beginnings in the ground, until it breaks through the canopy into the sky. An eagle lands on the highest branch. You are the tree; you are the eagle. What do you see?"

Eyes closed, face in the mud, I looked within to see without. I saw that I was not an eagle. I was a peacock with a 360-degree view of the forest. The heat had driven my mind to siesta, so I didn't fight it.

I looked to the south: miles of green trees. *Summer.*

I looked to the west: leaves blazed red and orange, fiery in splendor. *Autumn.*

I looked to the north: ice-covered, barren branches. *Winter.*

I looked to the east: new life burst through the forest. *Spring.*

"Look inside yourself for the wisdom that comes from beyond," Chief Hoopwatcher said from somewhere far away. "In Itsipi, you will see a vision of the future."

I opened my eyes just a sliver and gazed into the blazing rocks, my vision fading in and out of focus.

Before my eyes, leaves fell, snow melted, icicles cracked, buds formed; everything changed. My peacock, the bird that I had thought couldn't fly, lifted off, gliding in a slow circle through the seasons. The images faded with a soft *swish-swish* of my peacock's feathers, leaving behind only the burn of the heat and the sweet taste of hope.

Hope was enough.

I told Chief Hoopwatcher about my peacock vision over our potluck supper, after offering him my Hint of Lime Tostitos.

"You said peacocks can't fly," he replied, "but you're forgetting something."

"What?" I asked, dipping into the store-bought nacho cheese.

"A peacock can fly just as far as it needs to go."

25

Swing

I sat in my car across the street, staring at my old house: the one place I needed to visit that wasn't on my list. Even though I knew the swing my Dad and I hung together would be long gone, I strained to see the porch through the trees, as if by looking I could make it reappear. I had dreamed about our swing more than once; always in my dreams I stole it back.

The last time I'd seen the house, I was nineteen and doubled over in the kind of pain that twists memories out of shape. I'd pressed my face against my friend David's passenger window as he drove us slowly away; I'd held my fingers flat to the window, as though by reaching I could unhinge our swing, proof that my family once was.

Shaking off the memory, I walked toward the front door, smoothing my skirt and hoping I looked presentable enough to be invited in. I noticed how tall the trees had become, how overgrown the bushes were, how unkempt the yard. The house's blue paint was peeling.

As I knocked, I realized two things: the concrete was cracked beneath my feet, and I had no idea what to say. I couldn't exactly lead with the truth: *Hello, I'm here to make peace with my past.*

I heard one set of little feet running to the door and calls of "Mo-oom! There's a stranger at the door!"

A middle-aged woman opened the door, surrounded by her three young daughters. They were so like my sisters that I was speechless for a moment. The mother looked at me as if expecting a sales pitch.

My words tumbled out fast and quiet, each statement a question. "Hello? I'm so sorry to bother you, but I used to live here?"

She looked confused and I felt desperate, wishing I had a picture to prove my identity. I thought fast. "I grew up here? Me and my two sisters?

Our handprints and footprints are drawn in marker in the garage? Next to our names?"

She visibly relaxed, and the girls jumped up and down clapping, "We started doing that too! We trace our hands and feet too!"

"Which sister are you?" asked the oldest. I felt a storm behind my eyes.

"I'm Rebecca," I squeaked, giving the name that would be on the wall. "I was wondering, if sometime I could, um, maybe come in and see the house?"

The mother paused, considering. "We're having the whole downstairs renovated next week, so maybe you could come by after that."

I imagined my childhood home renovated past recognition but maintained a plastic smile. Taking out a business card, I said, "Well, okay, just call or e-mail me?" She promised she would, but her tone implied she wouldn't. The girls waved goodbye and slammed the door shut.

Don'tcryDon'tcryDon'tcry, I told myself, until I saw it hanging on the far side of the porch: cracked from weather and covered in spider webs, half the seat broken off, and tilted all the way to the ground, our family's swing was alive—just barely. I didn't care how bad it looked; it was still there. I had to have it.

"You did *what?*" Trent asked a second time.

"At least I didn't steal it," I retorted, defending myself. (Nocturnal kleptomania I might have considered, but not daytime theft.) "I just sent them a letter asking if I could buy the swing."

My husband, who has been known to eat raw meat instead of inconveniencing the wait staff, was understandably scandalized, but he rallied. "You may be the weirdest person in the world, but you're my weirdest person."

After dinner I sat down to meditate, but my phone beeped with an e-mail. I reached to silence it, but noticed the subject and stopped.

Re: Your old house

I got to thinking that maybe you would like to walk thru the house the way you remember it before we redo the downstairs? If you do, just give me a few hours notice…and about the swing, it broke last summer, and we are planning on getting a new one. I loved that swing, but it is yours free if you want it.

—Annie

This time I knocked with more confidence, probably because Trent was holding my other hand.

In my mind, the house was empty and desolate, unchanged since the day I left, but in reality it was filled with life, and not just human life. When Annie let us in I saw that her family had wildlife—as in birds. Twenty-three flying, flapping, singing birds in every color.

I had to stop myself from laughing. My old house, the place I'd thought would be a tomb, was now an aviary without trees. Fearing bird poop in the hair was a small price to pay.

Through the playroom windows overlooking the backyard, I saw the stump of my favorite tree. Lightning had struck that tree during the worst of our family's troubles; as though even the sky knew what was coming. The last time I'd seen it, the tree was strewn across the yard, split wide, open to the elements. In the fallen tree's place stood a swing set. And on top of the stump sat pots of flowers blooming bright as the spring day.

The littlest girl saw me looking and asked, "You like our backyard?"

"Yes," I said, turning around from the window to face her. "I love it."

"Come see our room!" she pulled me. Soon we were standing in my old room. Though I knew in my head this was where I had spent thousands of nights, I hardly recognized it. I looked to the place where I knelt in prayer every night, and grew teary for the first time since we entered the house—but I wasn't sad.

I imagined a younger me, kneeling in prayer beside the bed, and silently I thanked her for being so open to God. I whispered to her in my mind, feeling her so vividly that I could almost reach out and stroke her hair. *Without you, I wouldn't be here. So stay the path, little one. It will lead you home.*

Next door, I found the yellow bathroom was yellow no longer. The place I'd remembered during my Scientology audit now existed only in my memory; it, too, was shiny and new.

"We renovated it last year," explained Annie.

I could sense our time was coming to a close, so I asked, "Where's the swing?"

Annie walked us through the garage to pick it up. I was unprepared for the emotion that squeezed me, hard and fast, when I saw the marks on the garage wall. Our names—*Mary, Marcia, Rebecca*—were written next to growth charts. Outlines of our hands were traced next to the charts, growing progressively higher in crayon and pen and marker with dates in the center.

I lifted my hand to the wall, reaching back in time to the last day I was home. I put my hand inside the lines—a perfect match, proof I was that girl a decade ago, and that I wasn't her anymore.

Annie looked on. "I thought about painting over those," she said, "but I could never bring myself to do it. I guess I'm just sentimental like that." Her voice was choked with emotion as she watched me. "I sure am glad I didn't."

Fifteen minutes later, we had said our goodbyes and loaded the swing in the car.

"Happy to have your swing back?" Trent asked as we drove away.

"I am," I said, turning to look at it. "But I already have everything I thought it would give me back."

26

Forgiveness

"**I**'m meeting a real, live mystic today!" I exclaimed to Trent over breakfast.

He raised his brows. "Aren't *you* a real, live mystic—you know, since you saw God?"

"One Divine Disco Ball does not a mystic make. I think I'm more on the mystical track, like climbing the corporate ladder to heaven."

"Just so long as you don't slip; I can't break your fall from that height."

I made a goofy face. "That's good to know."

"So, who is this mystic you're meeting?"

"Rabbi Bondi at the Kabbalah Centre," I enthused. It had taken four months just to get an appointment, so I was thrilled the day had finally arrived. I imagined our meeting would be the mystical version of a sleepover: we'd become insta-BFFs by swapping stories about our Divine Encounters. I'd tell him about the Disco Ball, and he'd unlock the mysteries of the Godiverse with ancient wisdom. Together we would study Kabbalah's ancient text, the Zohar, and braid each other's hair.

"Kabbalah…isn't that the trendy religion? The one all those Hollywood people are into?"

I counted them off. "It's not quite as trendy as Scientology, but Madonna, Britney Spears, and Mick Jagger are supposedly Kabbalists."

Alluring and mysterious, Kabbalah intrigued me. If religions were people, I imagined Kabbalah as a veiled belly dancer with an exotic name, beckoning me with an enigmatic finger, at once summoning and pushing away. Even after a month of steady Googling and library research, I couldn't figure out precisely what Kabbalah was: Religion? Way of life? Guide to understanding the Torah? Ancient technology for understanding life? All of the above? I was at once bewitched by the promise of Kabbalah and failing her multiple-choice exam.

"Hey, didn't your stepmom go to high school with Madonna in Michigan? Maybe she could hook you up with a celebri-Rabbi."

I tried to imagine my Dad's sweet Christian wife Edie making a call to Madonna on my behalf. "She did. But I think this rabbi will be just fine."

Oh, how wrong I was.

Feeling more prepared for this visit than any of my others, I swished into the Kabbalah Centre with one notebook, two books on Kabbalah, and a list of questions that filled two pages. *I'm really getting the hang of this Thirty by Thirty thing*, I congratulated myself while waiting for the rabbi. Thirty minutes after our appointment was scheduled to begin, his secretary acknowledged me for the first time.

"The rabbi will see you now," she said, her expression implying I was making the acquaintance of the Pope.

I excused the wait, thinking: *Hey, he's a busy guy! He's got a Kabbalah Center to run!*

I excused his aloof greeting, thinking: *Maybe rabbis just don't look women in the eyes?*

I excused the fact that he alternated speaking to me with yelling to his secretary, checking e-mail, and typing, thinking: *This is one bad case of ADD.*

Trying to capture his attention, I outlined my project. I wasn't even sure he was listening until I asked a question.

"What would be the best way to experience Kabbalah?"

Rabbi Bondi peered over his spectacles at me, his manner less that of a spiritual teacher and more like an angry high school principal. "You can no more experience Kabbalah than you can paint your face black and experience being black!" he roared from behind his heavy oak desk, thumping a hand on a stack of books for emphasis.

The books quaked along with my resolve to keep my cool. The rabbi's thunderous answer offended on so many levels that I couldn't even process his words.

"And this 'journey' of yours sounds shallow, transient, and unable to offer any insight of lasting value. I'd be surprised if you learned anything from being a 'religious tourist.'"

He spat the words with such authority and disdain that I shrank into my chair, a kid accused of smoking dope behind a dumpster. The mental freefall was dizzying: I needed a drink of water; I needed to get out of there. I recognized this feeling: spiritual shame. Part of me wanted to stomp over the rabbi's plush carpeting and knock every self-important book from his overstuffed shelves. But, no; destroying a rabbi's office wouldn't exactly showcase maturity.

Instead, I pursed my lips so tightly I thought they might bleed. *How can he fail to see that places in my heart that were ripped inside-out have been repaired visit by visit, stitch by stitch? That the Godiverse used the needle of my project to sew me up, making me better than new?*

I attempted to interject the story of my thirty-day fast. I thought the whole month-without-food thing might showcase the depth of my commitment.

Wait...what do I have to prove? My internal question stung even more than the rabbi's accusations. *It is not my job to convince this man, or anyone for that matter, of anything. My only job is to walk my path.*

I imagined this rabbi occupying a space on the other side of the Divine Disco Ball, serving a purpose greater than I could fathom. He could reach people I couldn't, in ways I couldn't.

I smiled genuinely, mentally forgiving the angry rabbi and blessing him for giving me the gift of disillusionment. Not everyone I met would understand or appreciate my journey, and that was okay. There stretched a great freedom in acknowledging this fact.

But that didn't mean I had to stay. "Excuse me, sir," I said. "I appreciate your time, but I need to leave now."

To his credit, the rabbi walked over and offered me a book about Kabbalah. "Keep learning," he said gruffly, making me wonder if he thought I'd learned something after all.

Taking the book, I leveled my gaze with his. "I will," I promised.

Two weeks later, I strolled past a two-story brick loft a block from our house, stopping to admire its glass façade that rounded towards the street corner. The space—by turns a gallery and photo studio—was always filled with paintings or photographs illuminated by the natural light that streamed in from dawn to dusk.

Looking through the windows, I was surprised to see bare walls this time. A small sign hung on the door, the only clue to what had changed. "Stone Village Church," it stated, with a phone number.

*Stone Village...Stone Village...*the name meant something, but I couldn't place it for a second. Then I remembered: people wearing "Stone Village Church" t-shirts had marched in the Gay Pride parade right behind King Avenue Methodist. Suddenly, inexplicably, I felt compelled to go to this church. Right then. Yesterday if possible. Not for the project, but for me. Even though I knew next to nothing about this place, I sensed it could be somewhere I might belong.

Belong. A sudden yearning for community disoriented me, as when hanging upside down and coming up too quickly. Joining a faith community wasn't even on my radar; Project Thirty by Thirty was about healing and believing, not belonging. I was totally fine with playing the field of religion; I didn't need to settle down. My plan was to flit gently among lots of faiths, sprinkling around goodwill like Tinkerbelle's magic dust.

But I knew better than to ignore this magnetic pull, so I dialed the number on the sign—anticipating what, exactly? These people could be snake handlers for all I knew.

I heard three rings: "You've reached Pastor John. Please leave a message."

I felt disappointed no one had answered, but spit out: "This is Reba Riley. Please call me back! Just as soon as you get this! I'll be waiting to hear from you!"

When Pastor John got the message, he thought I sounded like the Energizer bunny on crack. "I really wasn't sure if I should call you back," he told me much later, laughing. "We weren't even a congregation; I was barely a pastor, and we'd never had a service. Plus, you sounded a little crazy."

Whether prompted by God or duty, John did call me back that afternoon while the Sickness had forced me into a six-hour "nap." He left a message.

"Reba? This is Pastor John from Stone Village. We're not officially open yet, but we're having a 'practice service' tonight at five for everyone who has helped get the church off the ground. You're more than welcome to join us."

I fell back asleep until 4:50, struggled out of bed, threw on clothes and—joints aching—walked the hundred paces to church.

John stood just outside the door, waiting in welcome. With a marathon runner's build and a smile that lit up his whole face, he looked around my age. "You must be Reba. Welcome!"

I took a seat in one of the two rows of folding chairs arranged in a half-moon around the altar—a minimalist metal table bearing a simple cross. Looking around, I realized the table fit the overall feel of the space; these walls were empty by design, a blank canvas for a young church to grow into.

Warm-up notes from the three-instrument band—keyboard, guitar, and drum—echoed from the polished concrete floor, ricocheting off a yellow metal staircase and back to the two-story rounded window walls.

Though I didn't know it then, every person there except me had been working toward this day for two years, and the congregation of fifteen rustled with collective anticipation as they found their seats.

"I'd ask if it's your first time here," said my neighbor to the left, "but it's everyone's first time. I'm Easton." A handsome fellow in his twenties, he sported dark hair, a beard, and a smile that suggested he laughed easily. We shook hands and chatted, finding common ground from the moment I mentioned Post-Traumatic Church Syndrome.

"I really can't believe I'm sitting here," he marveled, brown eyes sparkling. "I never thought I'd belong to a church again."

"I know what you mean. I *still* don't know if Christianity wants me."

"Listen, if I can belong, you can belong. I'm gay, but I went to Nazarene Bible College. I realized I was ready to stop fighting my feelings in my junior year, but I would have been expelled, so I hid who I was until graduation."

I grimaced on his behalf. "I know, right?" he responded to the look on my face. "Anyway, until I found King Avenue Methodist…"

"King Avenue?" My ears perked up at the name of an earlier Project Thirty by Thirty visit.

"Yep, King Avenue is the parent church of Stone Village. Until I found that place, I was majorly suffering from PTCS."

We looked at each other and, recognizing one another as fellow convalescents, grasped hands for Stone Village's inaugural prayer. At the opening song, a praise ballad I knew from back when, an overwhelming feeling of rightness bowled me over. Easton and I harmonized; he had the perfect baritone to my soprano, and we sang our hearts out together in the second row. I had a flash of *déjà-forward*, knowing before knowing that I was among friends.

When the time came for communion, I knew before approaching the altar that tinges of unforgiveness lingered in my heart. Any communion chalice raised to my face would have reflected the ugly judgment I still passed on Christians, especially those of the hellfire variety.

I knew I didn't have to take communion. In my heart, Christianity's rites no longer had a corner on forgiveness, because the bread and the cup were no longer my only spiritual symbols for grace.

But on this day, *for me*, there was really no other way; communion had to be transformed to symbolize my transformation. The communion table was the final sacrament left to be redeemed.

If I could not approach the table with the same grace that had been extended to me, if I could not share this bread, representing all forgiveness, with anyone, *anyone*—Christian or not—any enlightenment I experienced would fade to darkness. If I could not share this cup freely, without malice or bitterness, my new faith was meaningless.

"All are welcome at this table," Pastor John stated. "Would those who are taking communion please stand?"

I felt time slow as he lifted the bread and the cup from the altar and went from person to person, offering the elements.

As he neared me, I rose on shaky feet.

"The body of Christ broken for you, Reba."

Solemnly, I took the bread. *To those whom I have judged, I offer acceptance; to those I have cursed, I offer blessing.*

"The blood of Christ spilled for you, Reba."

I dipped the bread in the wine. *To those who have caused me pain, I offer forgiveness. To those I have hated, I offer love.*

Blinking through tears I wiped haphazardly on my sleeve, I saw the believers surrounding me and realized I was united with them, and not only them—but *all* the believers and nonbelievers beyond these walls, every single one, by the power of forgiveness.

And love, great torrents of love, cascaded through me with impossible force.

We celebrated the first service with burritos on the patio of a local Mexican joint.

"Pass that pitcher of sangria over here," said Pastor John, raising his glass in a toast. "To Stone Village!"

"To Stone Village!" we echoed. Easton sat to my right and John to my left. I suddenly remembered the Pride parade, which felt so long ago. I'd been right: there *were* "saints who drank sangria".

I told them about my project and what it meant for me to take communion. Pastor John asked, "So, after all those religions, what did you choose?"

"That's what everyone always wants to know, and there's no easy answer," I replied.

"Why do you have to pick?" he reasoned. "Can't you just choose to be a person of faith?"

"Yes," I said, a slow smile spreading across my face. "I believe I can."

27

Stories

"Pin it right there!" instructed Sundus, gesturing over my head.

"It won't stay," moaned Shine, a new friend I'd met by contacting the Ohio State Muslim Association. "The wind is too strong!" I crouched at an awkward angle in front of them, trying to shield my head from the spring gales as she attempted to secure a *hijab* to my head.

"Hey ladies," I teased. "If Allah is for us, can the wind be against us?"

On cue, a gust lifted my would-be veil. It skittered across the Noor Mosque parking lot, a silky green ribbon amidst a sea of cars.

"Ah!" I yelped. "Chase it!" Without the hijab, I wouldn't be able to attend *Jum'ah*, rendering our trip to the mosque useless. Running after the veil, Sundus and I collided in a manner worthy of a sitcom, leaving only Shine to save the day.

"Got it!" Shine panted. She lifted the scarf up prizefighter-style—and the wind almost blew it out of her hand a second time.

"One of you hold the top of the scarf and one of you grab the bottom," I said. Success!

Shine smoothed the head covering over my shoulders. "Beautiful," she pronounced. "It really brings out your green eyes."

I checked my reflection in Shine's car window—the head covering *was* quite pretty. *There is something to be said for the veil,* I thought. From fasting, I knew that giving something up usually led to getting something else back. If I wore the hijab on a daily basis, I imagined it would free up the ridiculous amount of time I spent messing with my hair. Maybe I could work on my inner beauty instead of worrying about the grey streak I'd wrestled with since I was eighteen?

I turned around to face them. "What do you girls like about wearing the veil?"

"I started wearing the hijab my freshman year," Shine answered. "It was totally my decision. For me it represents modesty, virtue, and protection."

Since *my* college clubwear had been skimpy enough to make any modest God blush, I thought I could make a convincing case for extra clothing equaling additional virtue. (Sadly, no amount of extra clothing could have added virtue to the Reba Riley of 2004. There is no modesty to be had when offering one's navel for body shots right before riding a mechanical bull.)

"The hijab is a constant reminder of my commitment to Allah," said Sundus.

"I get that," I replied, thinking of the WWJD bracelets and promise rings I'd worn in the mid-90s, when these girls were…toddlers? I briefly wondered what I might wear to remind me of my new faith—peacock feather earrings? Disco Ball necklace? "Today I will make the hijab a constant reminder to give thanks to the Godiverse," I promised.

Their nods said this was a good plan. I did not share the first line item on my thankfulness list: *Thank you, Godiverse, that I left Reba Riley circa 2004 in 2004!*

"How does it feel on your head?" Sundus asked as we walked through the huge parking lot toward the mosque, a massive structure of stone and glass. Police directed traffic around us.

I shook my head into the wind. "It feels like an AquaNet hairspray helmet!"

We looked at each other and dissolved into giggles.

Modestly dressed people of all races streamed in through Noor's entryway. But for the pristine shoe racks lining the walls, it looked like any megachurch, complete with sign-up tables and programs and free inspirational calendars (of which I was now a proud owner).

"Shoes go over there," Sundus instructed, pointing to the racks.

I happily removed my flip-flops, noting as I did so that Christians were really missing the naked-foot boat. Being shoeless implies reverence and a certain vulnerability. You have to trust that neither God nor your fellow congregants plan to drop heavy boxes on your toes.

Sundus, Shine, and I followed a crowd of women displaying the full range of hijab around a corner. Amidst the flurry of scarves in colors ranging from rainbow to black (à la *National Geographic*), I spied a bathroom sign.

I signaled the girls to wait for me. In the stall I noticed sprayers conveniently located for the washing of one's lady parts. *Uh-oh.* I'd read about the purification required before services but forgotten to ask Sundus about it. For the life of me, I couldn't recall if the process entailed cleansing below the belt. *Better safe than sorry?* I grasped the sprayer and did my best, hoping Allah would forgive me for winging it.

Back at the sink, an old woman in head-to-toe black garb engaged in ritual washing. I hung back, giving her space to splash and whisper prayers. When she finished, I tapped her on the shoulder.

"The ritual washing...*Taharah?*" I asked, the word coming back to me just in time. "I don't know how to do it. Would you please show me?"

Yes! Yes! Yes! She nodded, all smiles, before backing right out the door, leaving me very much alone and unsure of how to proceed.

I peeked my head out. "Sundus. Shine. Help!"

Placing myself in front of the trough-like sink, I explained my dilemma.

"It's hands, mouth, nose, face, ears, hair—three times each," Sundus demonstrated sans water since they had already washed at home. She counted the rhythm out loud for me, but I just couldn't get the cadence right. Every time I missed a beat, the touchless faucet turned off, prompting me to wave around wildly before giving up and starting over. Shine kindly documented my failure, snapping photos with her iPhone.

I enjoyed the idea of full-body ritual purification, a material reminder of what we hope to accomplish by gathering together before God. Our bodies exist on a physical plane, and sometimes the only way to translate the wonder of spiritual experience is to do physical things that look a little nutty. The power and beauty of balancing in tree pose in yoga, chanting Hare Krishna, or—in my case—spilling water all over the floor of the mosque bathroom, exist within our intention. I imagined that no matter how imperfectly I performed, Allah would look down and say, "Oh, bless her heart," possibly in the drawl of a southern belle.

I prefer a God who hands out participation medals, because Lord knows I'll never make it to the Mystical Olympics. (But, if I did, I'd want my event to be figure skating.)

Even though I was only supposed to splash my hands, mouth, nose, face, ears and hair three times and my feet once, I ended up doing eight rotations. Water squished between my toes on the tile floor, but I was having such a good time that I didn't even think about foot fungus.

When I finally got the ritual right, the girls cheered and offered me a slew of paper towels to dry myself off. Reaching for the paper towels, I slipped on the wet floor and fell backwards into the trough sink. I tried to stand up and fell back down again. I started laughing so hard the girls had to forcibly haul me out of the trough. Together, we studied my soggy rear end.

"At least it only looks like you *half*-peed your pants," said Sundus.

"You might want to, um, wipe your eyes too?" Shine offered helpfully, prompting me to look in the mirror. Even with mascara dripping black streaks and eyeliner smudged beyond repair, I looked as happy as I'd ever been.

The three of us left the bathroom and ascended the mosque stairs to the women's section, a balcony enclosed by glass. As a feminist, I felt guilty for enjoying the segregation. Sure, we were up in the balcony behind glass (and what did that say about equality?), but all I could think was, *How posh! Club-level seating!*

Before taking our seats on the star-and-crescent carpet (mosques don't have seats), we performed *Tahiyyat al-Masjid*, full-body prayer calisthenics intended to greet the mosque and set our intention for the gathering. Shine and Sundus moved with the practiced fluid motion of professional divers; I looked like a tubby kid doing a cannonball. Trying to keep up through *raka'tayn*, two units of the prayer, reminded me of boot camp's exercises. At least Shine and Sundus didn't seem inclined to put me in the corner for punishment. Post-prayers, we sat on the floor with our torsos folded over our knees and our backsides resting on our heels, a position I lasted in for exactly five seconds before tipping into a sidesaddle interpretation.

The *imam* issued a call to prayer from a story below us, and I noticed the beauty of the mosque's interior. With multiple-story arches and windows, the building seemed to be made of air. Spring sunshine flooded the space, belying the wind outside. "It's stunning," I whispered to Shine. "I love all the light!"

She smiled. "*Noor* means light. It's a fitting name."

Attendance was a fluid concept; women came and went, bookending their experience with prayer cycles upon entering and leaving. In front of me, a little girl chomped on Lay's Sour Cream 'n Onion chips, smearing the grease on her mother's bright, cheetah-print scarf. The mom turned around to chat with us, but was promptly shushed by an old woman to my left. Chastised, we adults settled in for the service, but the little girl refused to be hushed. Sensing that I'd like to steal her chips, she gave me the stink-eye.

I couldn't see the imam's head very well, but I heard him clearly through the speakers. He spoke in heavily accented English punctuated by Arabic scripture. Even where I didn't understand all the words, I grasped the meaning. He spoke of grace, though he didn't call it that. He said, "There is no sin which Allah cannot forgive."

If he had swapped out "Allah" for "Jesus," this could have been a sermon in any Christian church. Hearing the same message in such a foreign place felt bizarre, as if I had stepped into a parallel universe where the food looked different but tasted just the same.

The imam told the story of a judgmental Muslim who told another person he was going to hell. But Allah was angry at the accuser, saying, "Is it your job to be the judge? I am the only judge!" Many covered heads nodded in agreement at this.

Post-service, I asked the girls a hard question. "Since I'm not Muslim, am I going to hell?"

They quieted for a moment, then Sundus leaned in. "It's not up to us," she explained, her face the picture of earnestness. "Angels sit on your shoulders recording your deeds—good deeds on the right, bad deeds on the left—and they create a book that will show your deeds at judgment day."

I thought my "bad" angel must have dulled his pencil in 2004.

"You might be granted immediate access to heaven because your intentions are pure, but a lifelong Muslim might do some hard time in hell to atone for whatever sins he's committed. It is all by the grace of Allah."

To illustrate, Shine told me a story from the Quran. "There was a wicked woman, a prostitute her whole life. Before she died she showed kindness to a thirsty dog by giving him a bowl of water, and for that simple act, she was shown mercy and invited to heaven."

"So it is about intention," I mused, reminded of the story of Jesus and the woman at the well. He knew all her sins, yet she was forgiven.

As the girls relayed a few more stories with similar morals from the Quran, I considered the importance of the stories we tell. Before Post-Traumatic Church Syndrome, I believed that religious stories must be literal fact to be valuable, a vestige of the believe-it-all-or-believe-it-none theology I'd been raised to hold. But now I saw that the specifics (Did the prostitute actually exist? Where did she live? How many guys did she sleep with, anyway?) didn't matter to the meaning behind the story, a truth that showed me a picture of God, One who sees humanity with all-encompassing grace.

Stories bypass the defensive nature of our literal minds, the nature that waves angry fists and demands concrete proof. Stories deliver a knock-out punch, sending truth right where we need it—in our vulnerable underbellies, where we are filled with doubt and fear.

With a start, I realized that for me the value of religion no longer rested in the literal; it resided in the much greater metaphorical.

It no longer had to be true to be Truth.

As the Godiverse would have it, Trent and I ended up in a taxi that evening with a Somali driver who was listening to Muslim prayers in stereo. I told him I had visited Noor Mosque that very afternoon.

He eyed me in his rearview. "You Christian?"

I took the easy way out. "Yep." A three-mile fare doesn't leave much time for explanation.

"You pray in heart?"

I nodded. "Yes, sir. I do."

"The important thing not where pray, but that pray in heart. See, you and me, we not so different. You pray, I pray. This all same."

When the receipt printed, I couldn't give him a tip large enough.

28

Blessing

If my mother knew where I was right now, I thought, *she would go all Old Testament on me: falling to the ground in sackcloth and ashes, weeping and gnashing her teeth. She might even throw a little Job in for good measure—lamenting, "My child has sinned and cursed God in her heart!" while sacrificing a burnt offering of chicken cutlets on my behalf.*

To put things in perspective, I wasn't writhing naked on strobe-lit stage, shakin' all she gave me—though that might inspire a similar maternal reaction. I was standing motionless in a grassy field, wearing a yellow Mickey Mouse rain poncho over a sweatshirt, jeans, and hiking boots. Unless she was mourning the death of my fashion sense, neither my outfit nor my action should have been a problem.

Except for one teensy fact: I was surrounded by witches.

"Have you seen my rain jacket?" I'd yelled upstairs earlier that morning.

"No. But your poncho from Disney World is in the office closet," Trent yelled back. "Are you going to church outside in *this* weather?"

I climbed the stairs to his office, avoiding a shouted conversation that might disturb Andre. "How many people do you know who would go to church if the service lasted twenty-four hours and required rain gear?"

He peered at me, unsure if this was a trick question akin to "Does this poncho make my butt look fat?" "One?" he hazarded.

"None. I'm not going to church—I'm celebrating Beltane with the pagans." He gave me a questioning look. "Beltane—a festival celebrating the end of winter and beginning of summer. In other words, I'll be celebrating spring. Remember Mayday and dancing around the maypole with ribbons in elementary school?"

He crossed his arms. "I never danced around any poles with ribbons."

I laughed, imagining a serious mini-Trent, conscientiously objecting to all things ribbon-related.

"You probably did. Anyway, the Maypole tradition comes from Beltane. There's a lot more to it than that—or so I've read. Circling fires for good luck, flowers, streamers, singing, dancing, feasting, and general merry-making—all to honor and celebrate fertility…"

That got his attention. "No fertility until I pass the bar exam."

"You're preaching to the pagan choir, babe."

He looked relieved. "Did you say twenty-four hours? Don't you have to speak at King Avenue Methodist tomorrow morning?"

I'd been attending Stone Village most Sunday evenings and had met with Pastor John a few times. After hearing my story, he'd invited me to talk to Stone Village's parent congregation.

I'd looked at Pastor John sideways. "Are you sure you want me? Last time I was at King Avenue I sat in the last row in case I needed to bolt."

"From back pew to pulpit," he'd smiled.

Back pew to pulpit indeed.

"Yes, honey. I am speaking tomorrow, and the group I'm celebrating Beltane with is camping overnight. But even I have a spiritual adventuring limit. Spending a dark and stormy night with witches and druids in the woods is it."

Trent clicked his computer mouse. "At least your Beltane research explains why Google keeps advertising books of magic spells. I was wondering about that."

Between the icky weather and getting lost on the way (darn you, Ursula the GPS),I managed to ignore my nerves until late afternoon when I drove through the state park's gates. Part of my unease was general fretting associated with meeting a group of strangers, but my fundamentalist childhood contributed too. Though I intellectually understood the Beltane activities were more likely to include dancing and laughter than dark cloaks and animal sacrifice, my mind still ran wild with all manner of Dark Rites. Every witchy image I'd ever encountered flooded my mind, from Disney's Maleficent to Stonehenge to several entirely-unsuitable-for-children books I read at age ten detailing Christian encounters with "real" witches who used their powers to throw people across the room and channel demons. (How did I obtain said books? My parents, who believed the Smurfs were too racy, had left them lurking about the house. The first rule of Spiritual Warfare: Know thy enemy.)

By the time I parked my car, the rain had stopped. Sun streamed through the clouds as I walked over a grassy hill toward the appointed meeting place. At a picnic table, a dark-haired beauty weaved an elaborate flower sculpture. A blonde girl skipped toward me, holding wildflowers.

My first thought: *This isn't scary; this is a pharmaceutical commercial. "Take our allergy pill and you too can frolic in fields with cherubic children, puppies, and kittens!"*

A small group soon crested the hill. The two men and one woman were dressed for all-weather camping, which reminded me of the storm-or-shine Beltane invitation: "It might rain and we don't care!"

January, the Wiccan High Priestess, recognized me from my Gmail photo. "Hey, Reba!" she called. In her forties and five-foot nothing, maybe shorter, she wore long brown hair, silver-rimmed glasses, and an intense expression. "Let me introduce you to the crew. This is Shade," she said, gesturing to an aging hippie man with shoulder-length grey hair, angular cheekbones, and cheeks toughened by the elements. "Shade's our High Priest."

"Heya, Reba." Shade removed a cigarette from his mouth to give me a warm handshake.

I tried to focus on his friendly smile, but his black leather jacket and gravelly voice screamed: *I am the warlock your mother warned you about!*

"And this is Merlin," January said.

I gaped. With a long white beard, flowing white hair, and cloudy, heavily lidded blue eyes, Merlin was a doppelganger for King Arthur's wizard.

"How do you do?" Merlin said formally, stomping his twisted wooden staff on the ground for emphasis.

"The rest of the gang is beyond the clearing; we're just about ready to start," January informed us. We gathered our things, and the six of us trooped past the tree line into a large field. Scattered picnic tables held backpacks and bags of food, and tents circled a bonfire pit on the far end.

January introduced me to the "gang": a college-age guy wearing a purple crushed velvet cape and a fierce set of red acrylic fingernails; a pair of guitar-strumming women I thought were mother and daughter until they started kissing; and a handful of men and women of varied ages wearing outdoorsy gear.

"We all identify with different traditions," January explained as I took in the scene. "Celtic, Pagan, Wiccan, Druidic, Hellenic. I help organize some events, but there's no central order or discipline."

"Are there any common beliefs?"

"Generally speaking? Poly- or Pantheism, the Goddess, and recognition of the Divine Presence in nature. A lot of people associate Paganism with Satanism or evil, but it's just not true. We're calling on the magic of the good to achieve good."

"The Satanism/evil connection to witches was definitely taught in my Pentecostal-ish church growing up!"

"You're Pentecostal?" She stopped cold. "My husband is Pentecostal."

"No, no—not anymore." I attempted to imagine a marriage between a Pentecostal and a Wiccan High Priestess. "Your beliefs are so different," I said helplessly. *When they fought, did he try to rebuke her in the name of Jesus while she cast a spell on him?*

"It's an interesting mix," she laughed, more relaxed. "But we've been making it work for twenty years."

"C'mon guys and ladies," called January, rounding everyone up. As the group formed a circle and joined hands near the Maypole, I couldn't help but be reminded of See You at the Pole (SYATP) Day, when on-fire-for-Jesus! kids of the 1990s would make a statement by gathering around the school flagpole to pray. I imagined sneaking up behind High School Rebecca at SYATP and whispering what she'd be doing on this day, twelve or so years hence.

I suspect she would have thought I was a demon.

"Mother Earth and Father Sky, bless our celebration…" Shade began what sounded a heck of a lot like a prayer. "The earth below us, the heavens above us, and the trees around us. This is sacred time. This is sacred space."

"May the harmony of our circle be complete," the group responded without prompting, reminding me of liturgy.

"The sun has been released from the long winter to once again rule over summer," January said. "Today we celebrate the meeting of the Divine Feminine and the Divine Masculine, the God and Goddess, in the creation of the earth. We re-enact this creation with the May Queen and May King."

January motioned for Brie, a willowy young woman with red locks, to step forward. She wore a billowing purple skirt, turquoise shoulder wrap, and peacock (!) earrings. From January's body language, I understood that Brie was to represent the Goddess in our celebration. She was joined by a shorter young guy, dressed head to toe in black.

The Goddess had the air of a student who'd been called to the front of the class to do a tough math problem, while the God struck me as the kid in the back making farting noises with his armpit.

I felt the Goddess was settling, but didn't mention it.

"We will now separate to prepare the Queen and King for their union," January continued.

We led the May Queen around the clearing, walking two-by-two in front of her so the May King couldn't see her before the appointed time. The men did the same; the groups met in a line to build suspense before parting so the King and Queen could see each other.

If anyone was spying on us, we probably looked like the world's worst-dressed bridal party.

As the lines parted, I saw the God/May King. He now wore a black eye mask, which made him look like Westley from *The Princess Bride*. He ogled the goddess, smirking behind his mask. The May Queen looked a little shy, but gamely walked forward to grasp his hand.

Shade and January led us to form a circle around the King and Queen, who danced while we clapped.

"This represents the meeting of the Divine," the guy in the purple cape leaned in to tell me. "In the old days they would be having sex instead of dancing!"

I noticed the May King getting a little touchy-feely with the Queen. He looked like he was wishing hard for the "old days."

After several minutes, people grabbed guitars and drums, and we all got busy boogying down. I don't know about you, but nothing makes me want to cut a rug of grass more than the idea of celebrating spring, the season that exchanges snowsuits for swimsuits. Having removed my Mickey Mouse poncho, I danced under a great cathedral of sky. Sweatshirt and jeans notwithstanding, the feeling recalled the first warm day of the year, when Mom would let me out the door without shoes.

Our informal dance party turned into a formal threading of the Maypole. As I grasped my pink ribbon and skipped clockwise around the pole, dipping and standing and dipping, I felt like I had recaptured the glee of childhood...until I got tangled in the ribbons being pulled counter-clockwise. January kindly extracted me and relieved me of my post. I stood back and admired the stick woven with multi-colored ribbons. Apart from being flagrantly phallic, it was a pretty great-looking tree branch that would garner many Pinterest pins.

Maypole completed, the Priest, Priestess, May Queen, and May King congregated in a line near a picnic table decorated with flowers and bearing plates of snacks and drinks. It looked like a rustic altar.

"What's going on?" I whispered to one of the guitar players.

"The Beltane Blessing," she whispered back.

I followed the group as they queued up silently. Compared to the revelry we'd just enjoyed in the grass, this was eerily reverent. Hanging back in the line, I watched as people solemnly went forward one by one.

I stared as Shade made the sign of a pentagram over each forehead exactly as a Catholic priest would make the sign of the cross. Then each person ingested the cookies and juice and received a dual blessing from the God and Goddess.

Witches Communion.

I couldn't stop myself from drawing this incorrect conclusion. I knew Pagans didn't do communion, but with a lifetime of Spiritual Warfare working against me, I was freaking the hell out anyway. This was terror hiding in my subconscious, a demon ready to jump out and say "BOO!" just when I thought I was no longer afraid of the dark. Just when I thought I'd ridded myself from hardwired religious prejudice.

Prejudice is an ugly word, I know. It comes from beliefs you don't even realize are there until you go looking for something—in my case, God. Then you start running into furniture and tripping over boxes, discovering just how much junk you actually have.

I inched forward in line, internally flailing for equilibrium. *There's nothing to be afraid of,* I lectured myself. *It's a blessing, not a sacrifice.* I tried to think of all the unfamiliar things I'd done in the course of my project and remind myself I'd always come away with something good.

I put myself on auto-pilot, plastered on a smile, and pretended I wasn't terrified. It worked as I stepped to the front of the line and walked the three paces to stand before High Priest Shade. It worked as he raised his hand to my forehead and drew the first line of the five-pointed star.

It worked until absolutely everything inside of me jumped backwards, an involuntary motion that took my body with it.

A lifetime of symbolism cannot be undone with a minute-long pep talk, no matter how well-intentioned. To me, pentagrams meant demons, death, and All That Is Evil. They had serious negative power. Destructive power. Possibly enough to invite demons to jump from under my bed and into my mind, possessing me *Exorcist*-style. First I'd allow for a simple pentagram, and before I knew it I'd succumb to levitation, 360-degree head-spinning, and projectile vomiting of pea soup.

Shade, too, jumped back as though a bomb had exploded.

"Whoa," my voice yelled of its own accord. My hands rose between us, a trembling barrier. "No pentagram."

"Are you the *Christian*?!" he accused, spitting out the term with disgust. "Someone said there was a *Christian* here!" His hands flew up, too, a fighting stance.

I'd like to say I paused here and considered the question before answering, but I didn't. "I'm not a Christian," I retorted, meaning: *I'm not the kind of Christian you're thinking about.*

Everyone looked on, their collective energy gridlocked. I'd ruined their ritual, and half of them thought I was a Christian trespassing in their sacred space. I dropped my hands and started to cry. "I'm so sorry," I sniffled. "I didn't mean to offend anyone. I just can't…"

January jumped between us, palms facing both of us. "Shade, I'll handle this." She lifted my chin and said gently, "It's okay. It's really okay. I can give you a blessing without the pentagram." She placed a hand on my forehead. "Everything lost is found again; everything hurt is healed again. Despair turns to hope; sorrow to joy; want to abundance."

Her voice calmed me, and I felt the group relax. January smiled encouragingly, whispering, "Are you okay?"

I nodded and glanced at Shade. His features had also relaxed and he even smiled a little in encouragement: "Go on now."

"May you never hunger; may you never thirst," January intoned, handing me cookies and juice. "Blessed Be."

Solemnly, I ate and drank, reflecting on her words: *Everything hurt is healed again.*

29

Naked

The following weekend, shooting pain ripped me from a peaceful slumber. A vague dream lingered behind my eyes, making me wonder if I was awake—until my chest constricted again and sent fire down my left arm. *Yes, definitely awake.* Breathing heavily, I rolled to my back, shifting Oxley in the process. I looked at the time, then at Trent. It was 2:34 a.m. Should I wake him? Pain seized my chest several times in quick succession, wiping out any question. I cried out.

"What's wrong?" he muttered.

"I realize this sounds completely crazy and entirely improbable," I answered, "but I feel like I'm having a heart attack."

Having learned our lesson on Christmas Eve, we drove straight to the Emergency Room. Trent dropped me at the entrance, and I stumbled to the registration desk.

"Chest pain." I wheezed, gripping my left arm.

The clerk, a hefty grandmother-type with thick reading glasses, barely looked up from her erotica novel. "Driver's license and insurance card," she demanded in a voice befitting a cop writing a ticket.

As she entered my information, I noticed a strange silence. I looked around: dying fluorescent lights flickered over a completely empty waiting room. With nary a person in sight and no sounds except an infomercial playing on a distant TV, the situation felt eerie—like the opening of a horror film where you beg the heroine to run the other way. *Can't you see you're having a heart attack in the Twilight Zone of emergency rooms? Escape now, before it's too late!*

"Berta!" the clerk barked into an intercom, startling me. "Twenty-nine-year-old female with chest pain."

Like a magic trick, two nurses materialized out of nowhere. They grabbed my arms and pulled me through double doors into a long, dark hallway. I almost expected fun-house mirrors and a guy swallowing a sword. I imagined a creepy doctor wielding bloody scissors. "Step right up! The afterlife is right this way!"

Pulsating pain brought me back to the moment. "It...hurts..." I panted as the nurses situated me in an exam room. Nurse #1 thrust a half-gown in my arms. "Naked from the waist up, ties in the back," she instructed. "We'll give you a minute." Undressing, I noticed that my feet looked like I'd gone dumpster diving in the Goodwill donation bin: one slipper, one bootie, and two different socks.

"Breathe," Nurse #1 instructed when she came back to take my vitals. I endeavored to breathe as calmly as possible while Nurse #2 covered my body with electrodes and wires—which is to say, I breathed as calmly as a drowning snorkeler.

"Normal temp and regular heartbeat. Blood pressure only slightly elevated," pronounced Nurse #1. "But we expect that in the ER. How's your pain?"

"Better," I reported, even though I was confused by its abatement. "My chest still feels constricted, but the pain isn't bad anymore." I glanced at the clock: 3:40 a.m. "The worst of it must have lasted about forty-five minutes."

Nurse #2 studied the test results as they printed out. "Good news," she said. "Your EKG looks normal."

"We'll send the doctor in," Nurse #1 said, patting my shoulder. "Try to relax."

Relax. I told myself. *It's just a regular night in the hospital with a possible heart attack. No biggie.* I looked up and sighed, wondering how many more dropped-tile ceilings I'd have to face for the Sickness. Though I lacked proof that the chest pain was directly related to my other symptoms, it felt like an acute version of the muscle cramps and spasms I dealt with daily.

Shortly, I heard the doctor's cursory staccato knock. Luckily, he didn't resemble a horror movie doctor. A young, short black man, he walked with the jaunty confidence of a guy four times his size. He reminded me of a tiny, African American Mr. Clean who made up in facial hair what he lacked on his head. A thick beard jutted straight out from his face, as if a porcupine had escaped from the forest and attached to his chin.

"I'm Dr. Haziz," he said, taking a partial seat on the stool facing me. We chatted for a few minutes about my symptoms. Dr. Haziz smiled broadly, and the porcupine's quills puffed out. "I'd bet my house you aren't having a heart attack," he enthused, adding a large, double-armed gesture for emphasis. "In fact, I'd bet my house there's nothing wrong with you except a little indigestion and a lot of anxiety."

Indigestion and anxiety in my ARM? I shot flaming arrows at him with my eyes, but he failed to notice, possibly because he was too busy admiring his reflection in the paper towel dispenser.

"Is there any other medical history I should know about?" he asked.

I opened my mouth to tell him about the Sickness and promptly shut it.

"Nothing that would change your diagnosis of anxiety," I sighed, knowing years of weird symptoms would only make him surer of his opinion. "If this is all in my mind, when can I go home?"

"Do you have to work in the morning?"

"I have to go to church."

"I can write an excuse note for God."

"It's kind of important. I have a deadline to meet." As soon as the words were out of my mouth I regretted them. Now I'd have to explain.

"A deadline for God?"

Grimacing, I gave him the briefest possible outline of Thirty by Thirty. It was a sorry summary intended to discourage questions, but his face lit up like a casino slot machine. Oh no.

"Thirty religions?" I could see his internal gears shuffle, and he adjusted his posture to resemble the Thinker statue—if the Thinker was hunkering down for a nice, lengthy heart-to-heart. I remembered the empty waiting room. Clearly, he was bored.

"Religion and history—that's all I ever read." He petted the porcupine. "Tell me, do you believe in God?"

I wanted to fire back with, "Sir, with all due respect, it's four o'clock in the morning in the weirdest ER in America. I am mostly naked in a room approximately the temperature of an ice cube tray. Twenty-seven sticky electrodes are attached to my body; you have just become the 252nd medical professional to tell me my symptoms are mental, and you want to know if I believe in God?"

Nodding with exhaustion, I made a simple declaration that wasn't simple at all. "Yes, I believe."

The doctor still wasn't finished. "But what religion did you choose?" he pressed.

I mustered all the grace I'd collected throughout the year. Sometimes grace descends directly from the heavens in the form of a dove, but most of the time it manifests more modestly, like returning a gentle word instead of a well-deserved strangulation.

"I picked all of them and none of them. I chose something much bigger than religion: Love."

"Do you think all religions are equal?"

"Equally essential. Each adds something to our collective understanding of the Godiverse. Every service and ceremony and ritual and tradition is like a wedding, a representation of a love so big and mysterious that we want to cleave to it—Something Bigger. Someone Bigger. The Divine. God. Light. Whatever you want to call It. Now I can walk into any service anywhere and see through the trappings to the celebration."

The doctor adjusted his thinking posture as he reflected on this, and before he could ask another question I sputtered, "Can I please get dressed now?"

"Oh, yes," He blinked. "You're finished here."

"I'm naked in church!" I shrieked from our home office. "Trent, I look like Stripper Barbie, and I'm banging my head against a stained-glass window—help!"

I yelled this in my "technology-is-Godzilla" voice, perfected through years of marriage filled with broken electronics and drowned cell phones. Since Trent once created an antenna that received digital cable and three movie channels out of only an olive can, tin foil, and a wire hanger*, it goes without saying that my husband could and should save me from this Virtual Church embarrassment—the church being virtual, the embarrassment very real. The Godzilla tone implied that Trent should run, not calmly walk, to my rescue. So I bopped him on the head when he appeared a full five minutes later.

"What?" he rubbed his head. "I was eating."

"You want me to be naked in church!"

"I plead the fifth." He pointed to the screen. "Look: everyone else is naked, so either this virtual church is also a virtual nudist colony or our graphics card is having trouble with the Second Life program. I think I can fix it."

As Trent clicked away, I watched the computerized mini-Reba thump her small head against the virtual wall. "I suppose it had to end like this," I observed. "Reba Riley, naked and banging her head on the church wall like a mental patient. Better that it's the mini-me in a virtual church than the real me in the psych ward. It really could have gone either way, especially after the ER last night."

"How are you feeling?" he asked.

---

* Some women are golddiggers. I am a geekdigger.

I sighed. "Broken in body but mighty in spirit. The good news is I only lost most of the skin under the electrodes." I showed him the raw, red circles.

"Ouch," he grimaced as partial clothing appeared on the screen. "Ah! There it goes."

We considered mini-Reba, who was covered in rags. "Now I look like *Les Mis* Barbie!" I yelped, putting my head in my hands. "I'm finally crossing the Thirty by Thirty finish line, and I'm not even dressed for the occasion!"

"Actually, *Les Mis* Barbie is crossing it for you," he corrected. The screen's graphics cleared to reveal not only my clothes, but the interior of a striking Anglican church.

"Wow, pretty," I breathed, taking in mini-me's surroundings. With Gothic Revival architecture including vaulted ceilings, stone columns, and stained glass, the virtual church was everything you'd expect of a European cathedral, only digital. "One problem: mini-Reba's still stuck."

Trent deftly maneuvered her away from the wall before going back to his breakfast. Mini-Reba instantly got stuck standing backwards in the virtual pew.

"Psst!" A text bubble appeared over the head of a girl avatar to my virtual right. "Do you need help?"

"Is it that obvious :-) ?" I typed, a text bubble appearing over the mini-me.

"Just right-click on the pew to sit," she instructed, her blue-haired avatar walking to me.

Mini-Reba sat next to a kind stranger clothed like Mrs. Jetson. "I'm Cadie," said the blue-haired rescuer. "Are you new to Second Life?"

All 363 days of new spiritual experiences, and I *still* looked like a newbie. "Yep. I'm Reba," I typed, thankful Cadie had come to my aid.

"Well, welcome to the Anglican Cathedral on Epiphany Island! What do you think so far?"

"It's really lovely," I typed, wishing I knew how to make the mini-me smile. I settled for a ;) emoticon. "The rose window reminds me of Notre Dame."

"The service is about to begin, but we can talk after."

Though Cadie was behind her own screen, possibly thousands of miles away, I felt almost like she patted me on the shoulder. The pastor's avatar stood at a digital lectern at the front of the sanctuary. He welcomed everyone in a lovely English accent that I could hear through Trent's insulated headphones.

"Can everyone talk if they have a microphone?" I typed to Cadie.

"Right now only the minister and liturgist, but generally speaking—yes."

With dual-oversized monitors, sitting at Trent's desk was like attending church at NASA's mission control…except for my attire. Three words: flannel frog pajamas. I smiled; it seemed fitting that I should attend my final service wearing the pajamas that had accompanied me through the year.

As the pastor spoke, his words appeared over his head in tandem with his voice. When he summoned a liturgist to the lectern, my actual mouth dropped open at the virtual sight: The liturgist was a mermaid.

Though I had never imagined a finned creature wearing a pink seashell bra leading the Lord's Prayer, the scenario worked in Second Life. *Are Ariel and Snow White in the choir loft?* I wondered. No Disney princesses appeared, but there was a purple bear sitting near the back. The congregants joined the mermaid in the Lord's Prayer by typing the sacred words in time with her recitation. Collectively, we joined our hearts via our keyboards, and the stream of characters brought us together—a worldwide congregation, one in spirit.

The mermaid returned to her seat and the pastor took her place. "I am the Vine and you are the branches," he referenced John 15:5. "If you remain in me and I in you, you will bear much fruit."

The Amish lay minister had preached on this same passage, and the intersection of the two belief systems struck me. An ocean apart in practice but similar in core beliefs, they were probably closer on the Divine Disco Ball than either would realize. The Amish represented the faith of the past—the shunning of technology in exchange for a peaceful way of life. Second Life represented the faith of the future: pushing the bounds of technology in exchange for a global community. The Amish existed without technology; Second Life existed only because of it, and I existed somewhere between the two.

In a lilting accent, the pastor sermonized, expanding on the passage. "The two acts—loving God and loving each other—are connected by faith. If we love God, we will love each other. In our devotion to God, we should be devoted to each other."

"Let us pray for ourselves and the worlds in which we live," he concluded. I noted his use of "worlds," plural, remembering that while Second Life was only a world I was visiting, for many it is a full, actual-ish world. He read prayer requests from the box, and they were heartwrenching, probably more real than most "real life" services. I realized people could confess anything here with total impunity, but there was an attitude of reverence that reached past the computer screen and into my heart. Anonymous entreaties whipped quickly around the globe:

"I'm a disillusioned Catholic priest and want to leave the ministry."

"I am lost in a haze of depression and don't know where to turn."

"Terminally ill and fearing death."

The Second Life congregants typed prayers of support after each one, text bubbles echoing with support for the priest, care for the sad, and understanding for the afraid—virtual prayers that filled the digital church with real love. My own fingers flew across the keys writing words of comfort, and I hoped my intentions would cross the continents and transcend their digital form to reach the hurting.

"Let us close by giving thanks for our many blessings," said the pastor. Prayers of thanksgiving began to float above the congregation, many about mothers because it was Mother's Day.

I reflected on how truly thankful I was for my mother—her unfailing love, never-ending prayers, and her willingness to believe that God was big enough to meet her little girl even when she didn't understand how. I teared up as I typed, "Thank you for my mom, who is willing to accept my journey for what it is—mine."

Cadie turned to me after the service. "Would you like to join us for socializing in the courtyard?"

"Absolutely, if you can tell me how to stand up." She explained the mechanics of movement in virtual life, and we walked together through the church's open doors. The church was built on an island, so we were surrounded by glistening sea.

"I love the idea of being on an island without leaving home!" I exclaimed.

"The waves may be digital, but they can still be inspirational," she replied.

Congregants gathered in circles, talking and laughing together. Even if I hadn't been standing with Cadie, I would have felt at ease approaching one of those groups; the virtual world felt infinitely open.

She introduced me around.

"Where are you from in RL?" asked a blonde vampire wearing a ball gown. (It took me just a moment to figure out that RL stood for "real life.")

"Columbus, Ohio," I replied.

Cadie turned to me. "Really?" She threw up her virtual voice in an "O-H!", the universal Ohioan greeting.

"You're from Ohio, too? What are the chances?"

"Not just Ohio; I'm from Columbus!"

The rest of the folks were from around the world—England, Sweden, Boston, Wyoming, South Africa—but my new friend Cadie lived less than two miles from me.

"I'm having an interfaith ceremony on June 30. Would you be interested in coming?" I asked her.

"Yes! It's very rare that Second Life intersects with RL, but when it does it's pretty cool!"

A commotion broke out when the purple bear started scaling the front of the church. *Now there's something you don't see every day.*

"Bernard," said Melinda, a brunette with dangly silver cross earrings. "Stop horsing around!" She turned to me, "Bernard's always climbing everything—he's our class clown."

"One in every crowd," I replied, "even virtual crowds."

I briefly wondered if Bernard the Bear climbed in Second Life because he couldn't in real life. I'd read that physically challenged people live full lives in Second Life—the virtual world allowing them to do things their bodies couldn't. Or maybe he was just the class clown. Either way, I liked him.

"Hey, Bernard," I said after he jumped down to virtual earth. "I like your irreverent approach! I think we'd get along."

He threw me a ;) and I returned it.

"You guys have a really special community here," I said to the group, thinking that even if they couldn't deliver casseroles in person, it was obvious they loved each other. "Thank you for being so welcoming. I love your church and Epiphany Island."

As everyone said their goodbyes, I was aware that I was just moments from completing Project Thirty by Thirty. I turned to Cadie last. "I hope I'll see you in RL in June!"

"Wouldn't miss it ☺," she replied.

"Great!" I typed. "Okay, I'm signing off now. Bye!"

I clicked the program closed and stared at the screen for a moment with a sense of awe: Project Thirty by Thirty was officially complete. I'd brought my list into Trent's office, so I uncapped a marker and checked off my final visit. I bowed my head over the keyboard, a moment of silent thanksgiving between me and the Godiverse.

When I opened my eyes, a pop-up ad appeared on the screen.

"You've won!" read the text.

Under the sentence spun a glinting, winking disco ball, reflecting virtual light.

I could hardly believe this affirmation from the Godiverse. I kissed my fingers and extended them to the ceiling.

Then I powered down the computer and slowly emerged from Trent's office looking like a radiant victor. (Kidding. I looked like a sick girl in frog pajamas, but I *felt* victorious.)

"It's finished," I yelled to Trent and Oxley, who were lying on the couch in the living room. Trent walked in to hug me.

"You did it, babe!" He imitated a sportscaster after the Superbowl and stuck a TV remote out like a microphone. "What are you gonna do now?"

Fatigue rippled through my body. I felt like I'd crossed a marathon finish line after an all-out sprint the final mile. I was elated and exhausted, smiley yet shaky, and the Sickness held on just beneath my smile. "I'm going to go to sleep," I said, kissing his cheek. I called to Oxley with my daily refrain, "Naptime, Ox." He trotted with me to the bedroom, where I collapsed on the bed.

30

Victories

"Are you coming with me to Word Alive?" I asked Trent.

He squinted quizzically. "Wait, I thought you were finished with your project. Are you sure you want to sink *more* man-hours into that place?"

"Yes," I said, voice cheerful. "And I want you to sink man-hours into it, too. Maybe I've watched too many movies, but I feel like my project won't be complete without going back to where I started."

That's how Trent and I had arrived at my family's old pew on Pentecost Sunday. As we slid into our seats a few minutes into the opening worship, I felt giddy and loose as a yogi monk.

"I was so angry this time last year," I whispered to Trent.

The crowd sang, "There is freedom, freedom, freedom in the name of Jesus," forty-seven times in a row as I reflected on my project. Coming here for that first visit required the most teeth-gritting courage of the year; facing Word Alive was like rolling my entire spiritual trauma into a wasp's nest and then smacking it with a rod. I was bravest when I walked through these doors last year, my body and soul bruised, fully expecting a thousand wasp stings.

The "Freedom" song lasted for a long time, rising with emotional fervor. I floated along on the crest of the crowd's energy like I had at Hare Krishna when the words were unfamiliar. Privately, I strung my mantra along to the music and, to my surprise, it fit. The power of this group worship was the same power I'd felt everywhere; the lyrics were like the ribbons on the maypole, each person breathing in and out, weaving a melody that made us greater together. I was enjoying myself; Trent looked like he'd swallowed a long, squirmy worm.

I saw Flag Lady before Trent spotted her. She unfurled her sparkly Jesus banner near the stage, and loose glitter fluttered to the ground like fairy dust.

Flag Lady, who was old enough for grey curls, waved her flag boldly as if daring Satan to attack her whilst bearing the heavenly standard. Trent looked at her, then at me. His look translated, "If you ever drag me to something like this again I will boil your blankie and feed it to Oxley for dinner."

"No wonder you had Post-Traumatic Church Syndrome," he muttered. "This place is weird!"

Trent saw the same thing I had last year: a crazy lady waving a flag. But now I had a different perspective. I envisioned her at home on her knees, praying as she leaned over to sew gold sequins. I saw her whispering blessings over that flag as she prayed for her family and her church, a fabric altar. I assumed her spirit expanded with each movement like mine did when I chanted my mantra, and that waving it freed her from care. It was her sparkling, undulating bridge, spanning from this world to the next.

I looked around the sanctuary, wondering whose cars featured fundamentalist bumper stickers.

I still didn't agree with these people, but neither did I want to egg their windshields. I looked at them the same way I look at Oxley when he's digging in the sheet covers, searching for an invisible bone. It's a bit silly, but he's so earnest that it's hard to be critical. He's just doing what he knows to do, what he was bred to do; digging is his nature. And who knows? If circumstances were different, I might be the one whose car had a rear end full of Jesus fish. So I let the stickers go, not allowing them to adhere to my soul. *Love is bigger than everything.*

The music minister sang, and then Pastor Tom took the stage, his own hype man. "I got something to sing about! I got something to shout about!" he yelled. "I've got *God in me!*"

A chorus of "Amen!" resounded as the pastor prayed, "Give us enlightenment, Lord!" *Enlightenment,* I thought. *Isn't that what we're all here for? Isn't that what we're all* anywhere *for?*

He preached, and while I didn't agree with his message any more than I had the prior year, I gleaned the good from it. I found a connection when he spoke about Pentecost, when the Holy Spirit descended on Christ's disciples, appearing above their heads as tongues of fire. "When God comes down," he said, "It changes everything."

"Yes it does," I agreed quietly. Fire can destroy, or it can purify. Last year, the fire of my anger burned me up. This year, the fire of passion burned inside me.

"We can go now, if you want," I leaned over. "I've seen enough."

And I had—enough to know how much I'd changed. As we walked toward the exit I thought of the Reba with PTCS. She was someone I wanted to comfort.

As Trent opened the door to leave, Pastor Tom announced Testimony time.

I halted mid-step and grabbed Trent's arm. "I'm going up there," I said, drawn by a force beyond myself. "I have to testify!"

Trent gawked, detaching his arm. "You're going to what?"

"Testify! No time to explain." The seconds ticked; any minute I would lose my opportunity.

"Okay…I'll pull around the getaway car."

I was already halfway down the aisle. The force that pulled me wasn't God, and it wasn't the Energy. It was just me, following an instinct. I crossed the church as quickly as possible, but when I was a few paces from stage left, Pastor Tom boomed out a closing prayer.

Suddenly, the service was over.

I walked across the stage toward the pulpit; the sanctuary grew hazy with memories. *I'm behind Pastor Tom being baptized; my mother is playing the violin; I'm kneeling on the step asking God to "take my life and use me"; I'm standing to receive the prophecy and my calling.*

Last year, those memories were painful, but now they were so, so beautiful. I no longer saw a girl imprisoned by theology, heartbroken by rejection. In the reflection of the stained-glass dome where I used to look for angels, I saw the dancing light of a Divine Disco Ball.

I reached Pastor Tom, who had sweat beading on his face and body, nearly soaking his shirt. I tapped him on the shoulder and offered my maiden name and my parents' names by way of introduction. He nodded, but I could tell he didn't immediately remember me. He was winded from the service, so I didn't push.

Surveying the short man who had loomed so large in my childhood, I remembered how last year, everything from his casual blazer to his fiery speech made me angry. Given the opportunity, I might have spit in his single-serving communion cups.

Now, the bright lights surrounded him like a halo, and I saw him for what he was—a man tireless in his pursuit of his God and the care of his congregation. I saw exhaustion around his eyes and worry about keeping the church's lights on. I saw a warrior fighting a battle that I didn't share, against an enemy I did not believe in, to the sounds of heavenly trumpets I didn't hear.

But for the briefest of moments, I also saw myself. Aren't we all fighting our own battle, in our own way, using the tools in our possession?

I took a breath. "I came up here to testify."

He waited expectantly. Even though the congregation was dispersing and the service had ended, he was ready to hear my private testimony.

"I am free." I said, the force of the declaration expanding until my heart felt so large with thanks that there was room for everyone within it.

His look conveyed that he didn't understand, but I realized even as the words left my mouth that it wasn't the church I needed to tell, or Pastor Tom. The victory of this moment was only, ever mine.

"I've been working on this speech for ages, and I just can't get started," I agonized over my laptop several weeks later.

"Maybe you need to relax," answered Trent. "Why don't we take a walk?"

Outside the sun was bright; my mood was anything but. In three days all my family, friends, and representatives from seventeen of my thirty visits were convening at Stone Village Church for my interfaith Thirty by Thirty Rock Ceremony, and I had nothing but a blinking cursor.

"I can't get started because I feel too small for the message," I confessed as we walked.

"If there's one thing I've learned," Trent began, and my ears perked up, "it's that the Godiverse tends to come through for you."

I agreed, but with the begrudging sigh of a blocked writer. A quarter-mile down the road, we spied a box with a "Free Books!" sign sitting atop a bench.

"Free books always cheer you up," Trent said as we approached.

I peeked over the edge of the box. There was only one book left: a brown, oversized, aged volume. *The World's Great Religions.*

Trent and I looked at each other. If his expression read *I told you so*, mine said: *Oh my Godiverse!* I flipped open the glossy pages to the Introduction, penned by a Methodist minister in 1957:

"Every man should command respect in the moment when he bows before his god," I read aloud. "We may believe his conception of the Divine lacks valuable, even essential elements. His forms of worship may appear to us bizarre, sometimes repellent. But in that moment of prayer, every man is at his best; if we are as wise as we like to think ourselves, it is then we will try to understand him."*

After a minute of silence, Trent spoke. "I think you have your opening."

I imagined the day of my Rock Ceremony dawning bright and clear (cue chirping birds), the event coming off without a hitch (standing

---

* This is the book I'm holding in the picture on page 53.

ovation), my Sickness magically disappearing (wind chimes), and Trent and I and Oxley living happily ever after (amen).

Roll credits.

Unfortunately, my life is not a movie.

First, there was the hurricane-force gale that left half the city without power and the entire county in a state of emergency. The cancellations came pouring in—all but four interfaith representatives would not be coming—requiring a full rewrite of the program.

Then followed what amounted to every bride's Wedding Day Nightmare: My officiant, the Urban Monk, forgot what day it was, the bakery lost my order, my dress was somehow too tight, someone misplaced the candles, and the sound system wouldn't work.

And the bathroom was out of order.

Standing in the Stone Village Church balcony with Trent, I stared down at the fifty loved ones below, twisting my hastily scrawled notes for the new version of the ceremony.

"I have the uncomfortable feeling I'm supposed to be learning something today," I told him.

"Storms in life will come? Religious leaders will disappoint you? When you've found the bedrock of you faith, none of it matters?" His eyes glinted mischievously. "How about: Let go and let God?"

I groaned at the phrase, and he pulled me into a tight hug. "You're going to do great."

Together, we looked over the railing. My mom practiced her violin near the altar, warming up for her solo. A few book club girls chatted with Erin and Nick, who were holding hands tightly. I smiled, knowing it was only a matter of time until I'd be giving a toast at their wedding. My sisters talked with Becky, Pastor John, and my Muslim girlfriends. I'd recruited Andre and his new beau, Garrett, to help me with the ceremony; they sat front and center with the Urban Monk and Cadie from Second Life. My heart caught when my dad strode to the front with a video camera and tripod, looking every inch the proud father.

"Lesson number one," I said softly. "The people who love you will always show up."

Trent surveyed the crowd, thoughtful. "You've spent this whole year with religions, but I think you missed one. The religion of love—your family and friends. *That's* what today is about."

I teared up at his observation, both because it was true and because it came from such an unlikely source: my husband, Mr. Practical engineer/almost patent lawyer. Proof positive that I wasn't the only one whom Project Thirty by Thirty had changed.

"No tears," he said sternly. "You're on in five minutes." Squeezing my shaky hand, he gave me a kiss for courage, then disappeared down the stairs to corral everyone into their seats.

My eyes searched the altar until they landed on my bedrock. Its natural bowl, empty for the moment, would be filled stone by unique stone during the ceremony as I shared what each of the thirty visits had added to my faith, creating a physical reminder of my spiritual change.

Behind the bedrock, Chief Hoopwatcher's miniature disco ball glinted, flanked on both sides by peacock feathers. The image of my *Peacock Rising* flashed across the screen of my mind, its majestic plumage materializing out of flames. I realized the words of Pastor Judy, the Christian Spiritualist minister, had come true. "Transformation. Rebuilding," she'd told me. "These are the words for you. If you persevere, you'll be reborn."

The *Peacock Rising* was me.

As soft strains of Mark Schultz's song "I Am" echoed from my mom's violin, the crowd below quieted. The first bar of the song's chorus was my cue to descend, but I paused on the top landing to clutch the railing and check for anything that might trip me. (Flashing everyone I loved a second time was not on the agenda—even if I was wearing cute panties this time.)

Looking down the stairwell, I remembered the broken Reba of summer 2011 who had tumbled headlong into this year. I thanked her for being willing to slip and strong enough to get back up.

Sometimes you have to fall to find your footing, I thought. And then I descended with steps that were surprisingly sure and powerful.

After the ceremony, my family and friends gathered for my thirtieth birthday party in the upper room of a downtown restaurant. I couldn't help but think of Josh the Bartender when I saw the place. With leather seats, plush booths, and floor-to-ceiling windows, it was everything his hotel bar wasn't. I nearly laughed out loud when I received the message Josh had sent earlier with a picture of a Smurf birthday cake. *Sorry I can't be there! Have a Very Smurfy birthday!*

I shot out a quick thank you to the Godiverse for good bartenders everywhere.

"What'll it be for the birthday girl?" the cocktail waitress asked.

"Pinot Grigio," three friends and I answered in unison, and then laughed.

The toasts began as soon as the drinks arrived, and after two drinks everyone was chatting like old friends.

Daniel the Omnipresent Atheist tapped his glass. "Reba, on behalf of the Atheists; you made us think differently about people of faith."

"We have presents!" cheered my mother-in-law, coming forward with my boxes.

Presents? I didn't expect presents. "How exciting!" I said, feeling pleasantly like a ten-year-old princess as I unwrapped a fancy peacock-feather necklace from Becky and matching earrings from my sister Marcia, both of which I put on right away.

Mary, my artsy sister, gave me a "Religious Fanatic Barbie."

"She comes complete with a bunch of religious icons," Mary demonstrated, "Package wrapped in Bible-verse paper, icons from a bunch of faiths, and a few heads—you know, in case she needs to change her mind."

As Barbie earned a raucous laugh, the small crowd parted for my mother, who was carrying a larger gift. I gave her a questioning look. "This is from everyone," she said, putting the present on the table in front of me. Standing to untie the ribbon, I read the tag with its verse from the Gospel of Matthew: "Come to me, all of you who are weary and carry heavy burdens, and I will give you rest."

Rest. I thought. *Peace.*

"We're all so proud of you," Mom exclaimed on behalf of the crowd, before putting her arm around me and whispering:. "*I'm* so proud of you."

The room held its breath as I unwrapped a heavy hinged box. Inside, a diamond-shaped glass trophy lay nestled, a disco-ball prism floating in its center. I lifted it delicately and read the inscription: *30 by 30 - May 2012.* As I held it up, the sunlight from the window behind me threw innumerable rainbows around the room. I gasped.

It was *exactly* like something out of a movie.

Back at home after my party, I struggled under the covers in bed, the Sickness pulling at my body in harsh waves. I was aware this was how my twenty-ninth year had begun, and I hated that I was here again, stuck in bed on this day of victory.

But instead of resisting the pain and fatigue in anger, I thanked the Sickness for bringing me to this moment. The Sickness had revealed my brokenness, and in the revealing, showed me what needed to heal. It was like taking turpentine to a painted mirror; the smell was awful and the fumes almost knocked me over, but the harsh chemical uncovered the truth, reflecting the reality of my brokenness back to me.

Rolling to my side, I closed my eyes and considered what brokenness means.

Being broken is destruction—yes, it's pain and filth and ugliness and wondering how you'll ever breathe—or believe—again. But a break is also an opportunity, a crack opening worlds of possibility that don't exist when everything is intact. If a break can turn into something beautiful—and it can, because a breakthrough necessitates first a crack and then a chasm— isn't being broken, turned on the axis of perception, beautiful too?

I imagined myself during the Breaking, losing more of my faith with every tear. I thought of that broken girl, the girl I was no longer, and knew it was from her ashes that a new faith was able to arise, one stronger and more real than before. This faith was unshakable and unstoppable because it was mine alone.

Even though I was sleeping instead of celebrating, I knew this was a true victory—because life's real victories happen far from trophies. They happen in the space between heartbeats.

Life's real victories happen when we embrace forgiveness, when we set aside hate in favor of love, when we choose to look for God even if it hurts. They happen when we are lying in bed, crying our eyes out, and we choose to hold onto a bare sliver of hope that almost seems a delusion. They happen when illness pulls at the corners of our sneakers, knocking us down, and faith pulls us back up. And they happen on the floor of our closet, in the moment that looks and feels like broken defeat, when we are in pain and exhausted and seeking, hardly daring to believe.

It is in that moment that light surprises us by overtaking darkness, shining in its glory, showing us something more beautiful than we had dared to dream.

This is why being broken is so beautiful: being broken means you have cracks for love and light to shine through, gaps for the Godiverse to burrow and bloom, space to move from who you are to who you will become. Being broken means healing can find you and hope can gush forth like a geyser, flooding every part of you, until you can see why the Breaking was necessary in the first place: to give birth to you.

So I rested my healed spirit and broken body in this deep pool of hope, choosing to be thankful for both what I had and what I lacked. Because real victories?

Real victories happen in weakness, where strength is closer than our very next breath.

Epilogue

Six Months Later

"This is great news," the doctor chirped, her voice full of sunshine and rainbows. She clasped both my shoulders so hard I thought she might shake me in glee. "You are going to get better!"

I sighed. *Here we go again.*

I had dragged myself into Dr. Sandra Peters's waiting room resembling a zombified slug, and that's putting it charitably: my health had declined steadily after the Rock Ceremony.

After testing and a two-hour consultation, Dr. Peters had diagnosed me with celiac disease. "Gluten is your problem," she said. Not only did I not believe her "great news"; I wanted to throw something. Her windows were fortunate that I was too tired to use her cactus as a projectile.

"I already tried the 'no gluten' thing, and a million other diets. Nothing worked. My other doctor said it couldn't be celiac because I didn't have any digestive symptoms."

Dr. Peters looked alarmed. "Celiac disease is autoimmune; it can manifest in almost any system of the body. Fatigue, neurological symptoms, muscle spasms, joint pain—just because your stomach doesn't hurt does not mean you don't have celiac disease."

"How could hives, pain, spasms, killer fatigue, and imitation heart attacks come from *food*?" I asked. She gave a detailed medical explanation. "Okay…," I exhaled, still incredulous but too worn out to argue. "What do I have to do?"

"Your system is so damaged you can't eat any grains, period. Between that and my protocol, you'll start to feel better in…" she squinted in thought, as if peering into my future, "about ten days." Her eyes sparkled; mine looked like I'd been taking heavy sedatives.

"That's impossible. I gave up eating entirely for a month and existed solely on liquids and protein shakes, and I didn't get better."

She stared at me. "Thirty days? Don't you *ever* do that again!" But she had an instant answer for my skepticism. "My guess is your protein powder contained gluten."

"Ten days?" I asked doubtfully.

"Days," she affirmed, looking so upbeat that I guessed she was writing gleeful smiley faces in my chart. She presented two handouts with her diet and exercise protocol.

Slouching in defeat, I took them. "Fine." I yawned. "I'll try anything for ten days."

Four days later I woke up and felt…good. The next day, I felt even better. Seven days after my new diet began, my life turned Technicolor. After ten days I looked over the paperwork I had filled out for another specialist, and I screamed like the house was on fire. Trent and Oxley came running.

"I reported I was functioning at 60 percent most days, but it was more like 25 percent!" I yelled.

Over the next month, Trent learned he had married a maniac. I cleaned with utter glee. I practically skipped around doing errands, attacking mounds of paperwork, even exercising. I went to the grocery. I cooked. I talked on the phone. I worked. I wrote. *I did all of these things in the same day!*

Almost every day for two months, I cried with joy at 5 p.m. because I was so happy to be awake and pain-free. At night, though, I confessed my fear: "What if this is just a phase? What if it passes and I get sick again?"

"Then you'll get sick again," Trent would say into my hair, "and we'll make it work."

But I didn't get sick. I got radically, amazingly, joyfully better. "My own, personal miracle," I started telling friends and co-workers after three months, now that I was finally able to explain what had been going on for, oh, the past decade.

"To health!" Michelle toasted at book club.

To healing, I thought, lifting my glass.

Megan gave me a sidelong look, "It seems like you're well just in time to write a book about your project."

"Yeah, right," I laughed, saying: "I could never write a book…" just as the woman I would become whispered:

The impossible is far more possible than you know.

Author's Note

It is a great privilege to tell my story, but forming life's chaos into a readable memoir often requires condensing, reordering, or compositing events. I also changed some names, locations, and identifying characteristics of people and places to protect privacy. All the most remarkable "coincidences" occurred exactly as described...courtesy of the Godiverse.

IF YOU LOVED THIS BOOK...

Share your favorite *Post-Traumatic Church Syndrome* quote, story, or insight on social media with #PTCS #Godiverse or #SpiritualHealing and tag @RebaRiley

Connect with Reba on Facebook.com/RebaRileyAuthor, Twitter @RebaRiley, and on her Post-Traumatic Church Syndrome blog at Patheos.com. She wants to hear from you!

Visit www.RebaRiley.com for book extras including: interviews with Reba's family and friends, recipes—including the Amish peanut butter!—, a meditation for finding your spirit animal, photos, deleted chapters, and more.

Suggest PTCS for your next book club or group study selection. (It's no secret Reba LOVES book clubs, so she put together a bunch of book club goodies on her website, including: field trip ideas, suggested menu and decorations...along with photos of the very first PTCS book club hosted by her mother-in-law, Becky.)

Acknowledgments

Jana Riess: You said I wasn't allowed to give you an entire thank you page, so here is a line:

THANK YOU, JANA!

Jana Riess is the Sacagawea of memoir. My editor, coach, hand-holder, and friend, Jana guided me through the rocky, terrifying terrain of telling my story. Without her, PTCS would have been full of twirling little girls and red-headed cats. **Brad Lyons** at **Chalice Press** loved my work before it deserved it (and helped me string disco balls onto curtain rods). Marketing man, soothsayer, and fellow dreamer **Steve Knight** rescued me in the rain at midnight and never once laughed at my Really Audacious Goals. **Tess Clark** changed the ending, literally. **Iva Nasar**, my spiritual coach, eagle-eyed reader and friend, really does have a bat phone to the (God)iverse. **Helena Brantley of Red Pencil Publicity + Marketing** is simply extraordinary and continually amazes me. **Mick Silva** fought through to the Bitter Editing End; **Brigid Pearson** designed the perfect cover; **The Salt Project** made my film and disco ball dreams come true; **Gail Stobaugh and K.J. Reynolds** kept me on track and even used my peacock duct tape. **Hollie Woodruff** holds everything else together. **Tony Burkhart of Blacklite Productions** produced my awesome audiobook and made me many cups of (Earl Grey) tea. **Go Team Peacock!** (We are so very Pavonine.)

Sue Goodwin kept me from quitting the project and helped with the launch. **Samuel Autman** lent me his expertise in early drafts. **Susan Eaton** let me "turn in" my shitty first drafts. **Andrew Bowen** talked me off my first author ledge. **Elizabeth Wood**, my first, cherished reader, you had me at "Anne Lamott." Thank you to readers: **Amy Clark, Amy Sanders, Saumya Arya Haas, Iggy and Suzanne Garcia, Gary Herron,** who each gave invaluable feedback. **The Doepke family (Dan, Treva, Jordan, Stephanie)** swooped in just in time to make me cry with joy at what this book had become. To my **Book Club,** especially **Megan, Nadine, and Michelle**—I love you girls! To the **No Name Bookclub** in Centerville, Ohio: your meeting was one of the best parts of this project so far. To my friends, teachers, and pastors from **Ridgeville, Dayton Christian, Grove City College,** the **Focus on the Family Institute,** and the **Furnace:** Thank you for being part of my life.

Eric **Marrapodi** at CNN.com printed the first mention of PTCS on the Internet. I heart **Deborah Arca, Patheos.com, and all my fellow bloggers. Frank Schaeffer:** you were the first author to come alongside me, and you made my Dad believe my writing might be more than a hobby. **Brian McLaren** encouraged me when I needed it. **Mark Sandlin** and **Roger Wolsey** helped the PTCS is real article go viral. The **PTCS Facebook group** is great because of **awesome moderators** who keep it a safe, loving place and **awesome members** who share their stories and wisdom. Coach **Shelly Bamberger,** neighbor **Daniel Nash,** Pastor **Peter Edward Matthews** and **Eden United Methodist** helped me prepare for public speaking.

In addition to those already mentioned, I owe a debt of gratitude to: **Anne Lamott** (On 11/12/13, I gave Anne Chief Hoopwatcher's disco ball at a book signing in Cincinnati, because *Bird by Bird* kept me going); **Elizabeth Gilbert** (whose endorsement proves that Big Dreams come true); **William Paul Young** (I love that guy); **Drew Marshall** (who never fails to help me); **Jessica Buchanan, Sarah Thebarge, Teresa Pasquale, Frank Schaefer, Kristen Vincent, Nimue Brown; Jim Palmer,** I won't give up if you don't; **Christian Piatt,** who has shown me much more than I can share here; **A.J. Jacobs,** who let me email stalk him; **Martha Beck,** who said, "That's a great title… you're going to sell a gazillion copies"; **Julia Cameron** of *The Artist's Way,* for helping me recover creatively; **Rhoda Janzen,** I really, really hope you read this book because *Mennonite in a Little Black Dress* is my favorite; **Rob Bell,** your books made me believe there might be a Christianity I could believe in; **Marianne Williamson, Gabrielle Bernstein, Deborah Feldman, Cheryl Strayed, Ellen DeGeneres** (hey, can we dance badly under a disco ball together?), **Sara Miles, Malcolm Gladwell, Jen Lancaster, Tina Fey:** I adore your work. I would be amiss if I didn't also thank the departed: **Napoleon Hill, Erma Bombeck, Carolyn Keene, and Jean Kerr.**

Erin O'Brien Mickley: You are my sister and the world's best pep-talk giver. I wish I could hire you to sit beside me as I write. **Nick Mickley**: Your technical and design skills are only outweighed by your kindness. (Everyone: if you need a website, call **Green Gum Solutions!**) **Kelly Frere**: Only the three of us will ever know how fun that photo shoot was. (If you need an awesome photographer, call **Kelly St. James Photography!**) **Marquelle Garcia**: Thanks for the beautiful drumming photo. **Dr. Pinkham and Connie**: You saved my life. To the **Urban Monk**: You made a difference for me when no one else could. Bless you. **Josh**: XOXO, my Smurfy friend. **Pastor John and Stone Village Church**: Will always be home no matter how far away I am. **Chief Hoopwatcher** (aka Iggy Garcia) and the **Condor Eagle Chapter of Nemenhah** and **Bushi Yamato Damashii** of Daishan Buddhist Temple: Thank you for helping me go deeper spiritually and supporting this work. To **every person and congregation mentioned in these pages**, whether by name or pseudonym: This journey couldn't have happened without you. **Andre**: Best Neighbors Forever! **Becky**: MRM1 and the best mother-in-law ever, thank you for always sharing the magic with me. **Moyer family**: I'm so glad I married you. **Millers and Dallys**: Thank you for all the support! **Grammie**: Aside from Mom, you are my biggest fan (and critic) but mostly fan. **Mom and Dad**: Thank you for being brave, bold, and humble enough to allow me to share parts of your lives with the world. **Mom**: You are my light, my angel, my everything. **KC**: Thank you for the kind notes (and the Samantha doll). **Dad**: I'll always be your little girl…but please pass the Chardonnay because I'm ready to write our father/daughter memoir now. **Edie**: Your peacock gifts, prayers, and disco ball helmet helped me through. **Mary**: Thanks for Religious Fanatic Barbie and for avoiding haircuts in solidarity until I finished the book. **Marcia**: I love you more than life itself. **All of you**: I am more thankful than words can say.

Trent: I won the lottery of love when I married you. You believe in me even more than I believe in myself. Thank you for being the partner who—when I said I wanted to fly to the moon—asked, "Should I build the launch pad in the back yard or the driveway?"

Godiverse: Wow. Just, WOW.

About Reba Riley

As a voracious memoir-reader, I always want to know more about the author with whom I have just become imaginary BFFs. Just in case you feel the same way:

I sleep with a Blankey and believe it is my secret Power Object, like Samson's hair before Delilah had it chopped off. In addition to my Power Peacock, I also have a Power Insect (Ladybug), Power Mythical Creature (Dragon), and Power Nut (Acorn). My guilty pleasure is drinking cheap wine out of a mug while watching QVC's Diamonique midnight specials and *Star Trek Next Generation*. Once, I rode in a pig rodeo. Due in large part to my father's Sasquatch genes, I was hairy until age sixteen. This was a valuable, character-building experience I hope to never repeat.

Kelly St. James Photography

Reba Riley is an author, blogger, speaker and healer. She lives with Trent and Oxley in Cincinnati, Ohio, where she plans to write more books...once she recovers from Post-Traumatic Memoir Syndrome.

If I had three wishes, they would be: **#1 Fergie's song "Glamorous" to start playing when I enter a room**, like in the movies--except for real--because I would always look like a 1940s starlet. Unfortunately, I tend to look more like swamp-thing, so the chorus would have to be re-written to "F-r-o-g-p-a-n-t-s." **#2 Unlimited wishes** because I'm peeved when characters forget about this glorious option. Wishes for everyone! **#3: That *Post-Traumatic Church Syndrome* would spark a national conversation about the reality of spiritual injury and the many paths to healing**.

Speaking of this book, I wrote all seven (!) drafts in my frog pajamas and a fuzzy pink robe, with Blankey around my neck, Oxley at my feet, and a disco ball and metal peacock watching over me from the left corner of my desk.

It took four years, and I wanted to quit more times than I can count.

I am *so* glad I didn't.

Reba